JOURNEY THROUGH INDIA

MARK PROBERT

MGP PUBLISHING

First published in Great Britain in 2021 by MGP Publishing

ISBN 9781916305649

Disclaimer

This book depicts events in the author's life as truthfully as recollection permits, which he readily admits, becomes increasingly vague as the years go by. It also depicts events in the life of the author's best friend, Dr Nick Lindsay, to whom no blame should be attached for anything associated with this publication. This book is not intended to be an academic text; it aims to inform and entertain. Apart from descriptions and opinions provided by the author, this book includes information derived from many sources, including Internet research, with all the uncertainties that contains. Many more authoritative and academic sources exist; the author's comments on historic events or current affairs provide the briefest of overviews, with the intention of providing context to the events of the journey. The information represented is believed to be correct, but that is only valid if the source and its interpretation are also correct. The publisher apologises for any errors or omissions and would be grateful to be notified of any suggestions for correction to improve the quality of future reprints or editions of this book (please send comments via mgprobert.com). Occasionally, dialogue consistent with the character or nature of the person speaking has been supplemented. Some names, places, and identifying details have been changed to protect the privacy of individuals... and two camels.

'This is a brief life, but in its brevity, it offers us some splendid moments, some meaningful adventures.'

— Rudyard Kipling

CONTENTS

ILLUSTRATIONS

PREFACE: THE IDEA

Journey through India describes how two pensioners from Britain, allowed out on their own for five weeks, backpacked their way from coast to coast, in search of enlightenment and some exceptional curries. Exhilarated at being able to pick up their backpacks without falling over, they somehow managed a whistle-stop tour of many of India's most iconic landmarks.

Credit for the idea for the adventure goes to my friend of over forty years, Dr Nick Lindsay. He had visited India several times in recent years. When he spotted that I might have a bit of spare time on my hands in semi-retirement, the idea of a traverse across the subcontinent was born: a coast to coast journey across the northern part of the subcontinent. The details fell into place in the planning stage, inspired by regional Indian cuisine, the national team's cricketing schedule, and a few beers. I also had a personal reason to visit India that I will explain as the book unfolds. I believe the story of our adventure has a greater relevance, however, than being a mildly amusing record of two old guys fumbling their way across a big country. And that gives me the excuse to write this book.

The baby boomers, who were born in the 1950s and 1960s are all approaching, or have already arrived at retirement. When I think back to previous generations, I feel many were already old when they reached retirement. They became resigned to 'a quiet life.' That's what old people did, and for some people, that's still fine.

But I think today's sixty-somethings are more like the forty-year-olds of previous generations – you hear people say, 'sixty is the new forty' and there is something in that. Today's sixty-year-olds don't dress like previous generations. Nowadays, we still like our rock music, go to gigs to watch our favourite bands, drink slightly too much, and try to wear trendy clothes. The jury's still out on whether a hoodie is acceptable apparel for anyone over forty, by the way. You've got to draw the line somewhere – or have you? In Britain, despite our best efforts to eat and drink ourselves to early graves, the National Health Service is keeping us going for longer than ever. Life expectancy has gone up approximately ten years since the 1960s. Many of those now retired, and I know I'm generalising here, have sufficient disposable income to be 'comfortable,' and we have the chance to do things that previous generations of sixty-year-olds never had. I'm told some of us can even operate smartphones.

Part of my motivation for writing is to show people of a certain age that you really can get out there and do adventurous stuff. Many are already doing so, and I meet you on my travels. However, I fear others of my generation may need a bit of a nudge of encouragement to join in. I hope that in some small way, my trips can show what is possible with a bit of imagination and determination... for those blessed with reasonable health and finances. So, the road trip by motorbike you always wanted to do is possible... I did it and wrote about it in my book *Another Journey through Britain*. To begin with, I didn't have a motorbike or even a motorbike licence – but I did it. That bicycle ride to Paris? – you can do it. The five-week backpacking trip across India? – you're just about to read about it. When global pandemics allow, and if my health holds up, I still intend to 'do' Route 66 through the USA, and cycle across Europe.

I hope someone will read one of my books and say: 'If that old duffer can do that, so can I.'

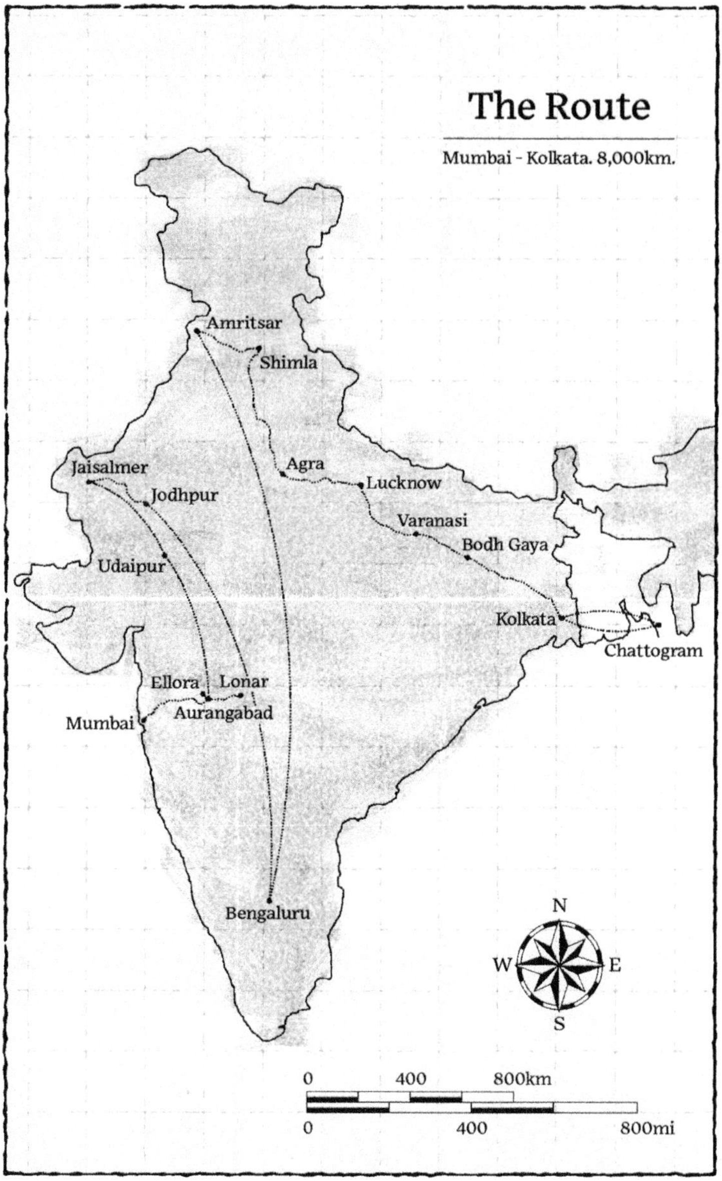

The Route
Mumbai - Kolkata. 8,000km.
Amritsar
Shimla
Agra
Lucknow
Varanasi
Bodh Gaya
Kolkata
Chattogram
Jaisalmer
Jodhpur
Udaipur
Ellora
Lonar
Aurangabad
Mumbai
Bengaluru
N
W
E
S
0
400
800km
0
400
800mi

BEFORE THE JOURNEY

The preamble to my life took place in India. At sixty-five years old, I'd almost left it too late, but I was at last going to see the country for the first time. I'd be a traveller, a visitor... perhaps even a pilgrim. Before that, I needed to do some research and planning.

In September 2019, I spent a pleasant working week in Moldova. In the world of development aid, in which I was employed before I retired, they refer to these trips as missions. My grown-up kids thought this was hilarious; it confirmed their long-held suspicion that I was a spy. How ridiculous!

I *was* a travel junkie, however, and it was hard to come off the drug after more than twenty years of visiting amazing places and working with wonderful people as part of my professional life. My Moldova mission interrupted a period of semi-retirement but gave me the chance to quiz a work colleague about her home country – India. Just three months later, I'd be setting off on a five-week adventure across the subcontinent with an old friend of mine. Meeting up with Naina in Chisinau provided a timely opportunity for research. We had worked together several times. She is a scarily intelligent millennial with great warmth, confidence, and common sense. Her family is from Delhi, and I knew she could answer any questions I might have about India. Before we met up in Moldova, Naina gave me some preliminary ideas by email and recommended the book *Midnight Furies* by Nisid Hajari.

I took my notebook and map along to dinner that first evening and prepared to jot down Naina's tips and recommendations. We met up at the hotel restaurant. To break the ice, I commented on how strange it was that the Siberian gulls flew south so early. She replied, 'The snows fall early in Moscow.' I still don't know what that was all about, but we ordered some drinks and got down to discussing the trip to India. I outlined the plan, which at that stage was quite simple; my pal Nick and I would fly to Mumbai and then head north and eastwards in a gentle arc, ending up in Kolkata. We'd take in as many interesting places as possible along the way. I downed another mouthful of overpriced but pleasantly cool Moldovan lager and eagerly awaited Naina's words of wisdom.

'Well, then,' she said: 'how crazy do you boys want to be... on a scale of one to ten?' With the disadvantage of half a pint's worth of misplaced confidence, I immediately replied, 'Well... ten, obviously.' My bravado instantly evaporated as I sensed a potential blunder. She paused momentarily but kept a straight face. Was she enjoying the moment or was she just unsure whether to say what came next? I tried to fill the gap by taking another mouthful of beer. The pause extended another moment, which seemed like an eternity, before she said, 'What about the ashram in Pune where they engage in sex and meditation as a route to spiritual awakening?'

There was a split-second of shocked silence before I choked violently on my beer. Grabbing my napkin, I dabbed the tablecloth to soak up half a mouthful of jettisoned Chisinau blonde, buying myself a couple of valuable seconds to recapture my composure. Suddenly feeling very conspicuous, I was desperately trying to think of a snappy reply that would simultaneously make me look cool and unflappable (too late), but not get me into anything dodgy. I would need considerably more than a couple of seconds, so I settled for a sheepish 'Uh, no, I don't think so Naina. Perhaps I mean more of a seven or eight on the craziness scale.'

It gave us a laugh, but Naina's response made me realise I hadn't put enough thought into my expectations for the trip and what I wanted to get out of the adventure. To be honest, I was just glad to be going to India at all. I had a special reason to go there, and I kept wondering why I hadn't done so years ago.

Since my sixtieth birthday a few years earlier, I had gradually been winding down my work, determined to fit more adventure into whatever time I had left. The transition into my sixties had been mentally and physically bruising. As they'd approached, my intention was to ignore the negativity of all those golden years metaphors. I wasn't ready for last orders in the last chance saloon. Let others board the last train leaving the station.

A senior railcard popping through the letterbox on my sixtieth birthday and the unwanted gift of a deep vein thrombosis (DVT) on the same day put paid to all that... maybe the last train had pulled in after all. It hit me hard. All milestone birthdays feel like big turning points in your life, but for me, stepping into the dark shadows of my sixties was unpleasant. I don't remember turning fifty as being dramatic, but maybe I was busy that day. But sixty... that was a big one. Or it was for me. On my sixtieth birthday, back in

2014, I began receiving a modest civil servant pension – I was officially a pensioner.

As a kid in the late 1950s and early 1960s, my image of a pensioner was a pale wrinkly person with no teeth, bent over double with a walking stick. Around the house, old women would wear a pinafore and curlers in their hair. If they could ever go out, they had a blue rinse hair-do, and if they let themselves go, they might sip a Babycham or play bingo. Who knows, there might even have been a few crazy ones who did both. Men were bald or had thin white hair. They smoked a pipe, drank stout, and played dominoes. Their trouser waistlines were always way too far up their bodies. Both men and women had stubbly hair coming out of their chins and ears. As I grew up, I knew this fate was lying in wait for me one day, when I became 'a pensioner.'

I decided against putting my feet up and tending the allotment. Both are reasonable retirement options, although it was unlikely to be a fruitful one for me as I didn't have an allotment. So, in between working my way through my wife's list of jobs around the house, I set out on a few adventures – the ones I hadn't had time to do until then, because I was too busy working. I cycled through Europe and across the Pyrenees with my two sons, and to Paris from Southampton with my daughter. The following summer, I rode a motorbike from Land's End to John O'Groats. With the odd adventure and regular visits to Scotland with my wife, I settled into the semi-retired life… and it was good. Then in 2018, my old mate of forty-plus years, Nick, suggested we should go to India. 'How long were you thinking of going for Nick?' I said. 'Oh, about four to five weeks,' he replied. 'OK, I'm in!' I responded.

And that's how the *Journey through India* adventure came about. It wasn't quite that simple, of course. I discussed the idea with my wife, Jan, and she was fantastic about it, as she had been so many times before... 'It's something you've always wanted to do, Mark, so go, and enjoy it.' What an absolute darling! My right to wander isn't something I take for granted. I am very fortunate compared to so many other husbands... was what she kept telling me. I expect with my reduction in work, she began to realise what it would be like if I was around the house more – she wanted to get back to the peace and quiet she had enjoyed while I was away. I can remember the moment I asked Jan about the possibility of a trip to India, and she gave me the all-clear to go. The authorisation came complete with the standard caveat that accompanies all such permissions: 'Just remember not to go off anywhere doing anything silly.' Her caution comes from many years of experience, and I'm glad to say, from love and concern for my welfare.

My mapping and land administration work allowed me to work on five continents for over twenty years. It involved recording land and property boundaries on maps and was nearly always in developing countries. Those are invariably the most interesting ones... the ones with deserts, tropical rain forests, flowing mountain streams, and 'colourful characters.'

Maybe Jan's concerns stem from occasional flashbacks to some of my previous adventures while working... for example, the time my 4x4 vehicle broke down miles from civilisation 'somewhere' over the Russian border in the depths of a Latvian winter. Perhaps she recalls that little misunderstanding when I said I'd come across gorillas in the Rwandan jungle, or maybe she thinks about the time I met a shaman in an Ulan Bator high-rise apartment. Anyway, you can probably now understand why it is that I frequently have the cautionary words '... and don't go off doing silly things' regularly popping into my head when I'm travelling abroad without the life-support system that is my wife.

Nick and I discussed our *Journey through India* over several months of meticulous planning, many curries, and even more beers. We eventually came up with a cunning plan, the semblance of a route, a timetable, and a spreadsheet. We set about organising the visas and vaccinations and continued to research as much as possible.

Nick had been to India three times in recent years as part of a project to survey the Scottish cemetery in Kolkata, so he had previous experience. I had a lifelong fascination with the country, and after a long wait, I was about to go there.

Bear with me just a few more paragraphs of seemingly interminable preamble, and we'll get going. First, I'll briefly mention my travelling partner and then give you a taster about India. I'll round things off with the route planning and a bit about logistics.

I first met Dr Nick Lindsay over forty-five years ago, when he was plain old Nick Lindsay, a wet behind the ears seventeen-year-old Welsh lad. He had just left his home in Cardiff (June 1974) to join Ordnance Survey in Southampton as a land surveyor. We found ourselves sat next to each other on the same nine-month training course. Our instant friendship was based upon a shared sense of humour and mutual tastes in music, travel, football, cricket, and beer. We regularly combined those mutual tastes in hazily remembered adventures at home and abroad, and regular unproductive pursuits of female company. Maybe we focussed too much on the football and beer. Over the years we went our different ways. I stayed in the world of mapping while he became a geologist, shopkeeper, and then local government worker. We kept in touch regularly, and we still get together whenever global pandemics allow.

It's hard to avoid India; it's the seventh-largest country in the world. With a population of over 1.4 billion, roughly a sixth of the people on our planet live there. The population is forecast to become the largest in the world by the end of this decade. It is the world's largest democracy. I don't think anyone should need any encouragement to visit the place, and especially anyone from Britain, with which (for obvious reasons) it shares many ties. Brits shouldn't be worried about finding someone to speak to in India – there are approximately twice as many English speakers there than we have in Britain.

Being in India provides a sensory saturation that I've not experienced anywhere else; it's full of contrasts and contradictions that will leave you shaking your head in disbelief. It has produced one of the world's most influential civilisations, been the birthplace of four of its major religions, and still manufactures the Royal Enfield 500cc Bullet. Then there's the cricket and the curries. Any of those should be more than enough reason to visit. Space industries, Bollywood movies, and hi-tech billionaires can be found side by side with poverty, slums, and pollution. In the coming decades, the Indian economy is forecast to overtake those of the US and China. Some say that the 21st century will become known as the Indian century, just as the 20th century was the American century and the British Empire dominated the 19th century.

Based on Nick's previous experience on the subcontinent, we decided that January/February was probably the best time to visit. Our plan was to traverse India from west to east, from Mumbai to Kolkata. Overall, we could expect the temperature to be in the mid-twenties so the weather would resemble a good summer back in Shropshire (where I lived at the time) or a heatwave in the Highlands of Scotland (where Nick lives).

Nick and I were determined to get to know the country, the people, the culture, the history, and its menus. By observing, mixing, and learning along the way, we intended to be travellers, not just tourists. We planned to go beyond the standard tourist sites. It sounds noble, and that was our intention – we'd try our best. We were expecting a stream of whacky incidents, countless kormas, and lots of cows.

What did we both want out of the trip? Nick and I discussed this at length. Apart from the essential daily intake of excellent curries and Indian beer, and a one-day international cricket match, the rest was up for grabs. To be serious for a moment, this is something anyone travelling to India, especially for the first time, needs to consider. You're going to see things you've probably never seen before. You'll be subject to emotional and moral strains that you have never previously confronted... it's as well to be ready for that. If the trip is to be more than a voyeuristic set of selfie opportunities, what do you want to get out of it? What do you want to learn? If you have these things in mind, it will help you interact with the local people, to ask the right questions, and to listen. Going with an open mind, ready to enjoy the experience, is a good starting point. The philosopher Alain de Botton wrote, 'The pleasure we derive from journeys is perhaps dependent more on the mindset with which we travel than on the destination we travel to'... although we definitely still wanted the curries.

My meeting in Moldova with Naina had been incredibly helpful. She provided information on a long list of tourist sites that were thankfully much further down the craziness spectrum than the ashram in Pune. I picked up some useful tips on mundane yet important things, like which low-cost airlines are most likely to fly on time, and which of them might even deliver your luggage to the same destination as you – useful stuff like that.

I was keen to look at the spiritual aspect of things. Despite being officially secular, India *is* a religious country, and it's something that appears from the outside to dominate the daily life of many people. As well as being the birthplace of Hinduism, Buddhism, Jainism and Sikhism, India has the world's third largest Muslim population and has at least four other recognised religions. The juxtaposition of the new mega-wealthy Indians and those still in abject poverty was also an intriguing aspect of the country that I was anticipating with mixed feelings. I was hoping our visit would help us to understand the issues better. Nick and I read up on some other topical issues – things like the new-tech' economy, corruption, healthcare, and the role/treatment of women. Nick wasn't so psyched about the spiritual side of things, but he *is* a lifelong geology fanatic, and our pre-trip research uncovered a couple of spectacular sights we had to visit. One was a sixty-metre-high basalt monolith in Mumbai (like the Devil's Tower from *Close Encounters of the Third Kind*), and the other was an asteroid impact crater – one of only four known hypervelocity, impact craters in the world. We looked at the guidebooks and plotted a selection of 'must-see' locations on a route that meandered from Mumbai to Kolkata. They included the Thar desert, the Golden Temple in Amritsar, Lucknow, Varanasi, and Bodh Gaya, where the Buddha attained enlightenment. It was impossible to see everywhere in five weeks, of course, but it was possible to plot a route that joined up a good number of well-known highlights. We knew we risked making our journey a tick-list dash. Still, by travelling on public transport and staying in a variety of accommodation types, including homestays, we thought we'd get to meet the people of India and see a bit of life beyond the standard tourist spots.

We booked our flights, outbound during the first week of January 2020 and returning five weeks later in February. With no input from our wives, we showed uncharacteristic common sense by booking a couple of nights in Mumbai to get over the flight and to acclimatise before setting off on our meandering traverse across the country. We booked up accommodation for two, sometimes three nights in advance, to give us some security, but also flexibility. Booking all of our accommodation online, through one of the leading hotel booking websites worked out well over the entire trip. We planned our route in fine detail. Nick is somewhere on the obsessive-compulsive disorder (OCD) spectrum with spreadsheets, so recording the day-to-day travelling and sightseeing itinerary was right up his street. He could then cross-reference our itinerary with the relevant transport timetables and budget worksheets. We used a shared spreadsheet that still drifts to this day somewhere out there in the cloud. One of these days, we should get round to totting up who owes who what. We knew very well that unexpected things would disrupt our carefully planned schedule. We were going to India for goodness sake! A missed train, a dose of Delhi belly, or wanting to spend more time somewhere were all possibilities: who knew what might happen? We were quite relaxed about chopping and changing our timetable if we needed to. We had a spreadsheet and we weren't afraid to use it.

Our departure day came around remarkably quickly after the 2019 Christmas and New Year celebrations. If I could have done so, I probably would have put departure off longer, but in hindsight, I'm so happy I didn't have the chance to. A pandemic spread around the world soon after we returned home. Travel was off everyone's agenda for well over a year.

We wanted to travel light. You do when you're going to be carrying everything you need on your back for five weeks and you're in your mid-sixties. Not that we'd really thought that one through... the last backpacking trip we took together was for three weeks in Greece in 1976. Could travelling with all our worldly belongings on our backs for five weeks be that difficult forty-odd years later? We'd find out.

Attempting to travel light

We chose forty litre rucksacks because it provided a limit to our loads. Larger bags would have given us the opportunity to carry too much. I packed the bare minimum I thought I'd need, and then tried the bag on my shoulders. I could hardly pick it up. I took everything out, put it on the bed and analysed it to see what was essential and what I could remove. My mind flew back to the Greek adventure. Nick and I had backpacks twice as big as our 2020 versions. We carried full camping equipment, several bottles of beer, and a football – a proper standard size and weight leather ball. Our definition of essential and our physical constraints had inevitably changed.

My mum-in-law kindly put together a traveller's emergency medical kit for me (including plenty of hand sanitising gels before they became an essential part of daily life). That survival pack had to go with me, as did my map, phone, and camera. Everything else was negotiable. I took just one pair of trousers (that was a mistake) and cut down my original quota of shirts and underwear (that was a good idea – those items are cheap and easy to replace in India). At the end of the trip, it was obvious what I should have taken and what was superfluous. I'll return to the subject later, but in the first week of January 2020, I stood staring at that pile of things to pack and had to decide. I made my final choices and got confirmation from Jan. That was it then. I was all set for my *Journey through India.*

GETTING THERE

When he's not on holiday in India, Nick lives in a tiny coastal hamlet in the northeast corner of Scotland. Apart from his Highland estate, the small settlement contains just a few scattered houses, a couple of crofts, and a distillery. The nearest sizeable village has a population of less than 2,000. Imagine the culture shock for him when he used to visit my previous home in Oswestry, in Shropshire, with its population of around 20,000. I could sometimes catch him staring in awe at big town luxuries like a pedestrian crossing, a bookshop, or a set of traffic lights.

Our *Journey through India* began with a minor culture shock. Having flown a quarter of the way round the world from London, Nick and I arrived in its seventh most populous city – Mumbai. It has a metropolitan population of over twenty million. That's slightly bigger than my hometown and over 7,000 kilometres away from Nick's comfort zone.

It was just after midday Indian time but still felt like 5:00 am to us. Our adventure on the subcontinent was underway. For a nine-hour flight, it hadn't been a terrible experience, even though my body was wondering why it felt like the middle of the night when everyone else was pretending it was afternoon. I'd survived the journey on about four hours of sleep, two meals, and *Fifty First Dates* (the 2004 romantic comedy film starring Adam Sandler and Drew Barrymore – not my initial attempt at eating a few kilos of the sweet and fibrous fruits of the palm tree).

Nick and I shuffled towards the exit door of the plane with the other semi-asleep passengers. It was a bit like the march of the zombies, but our walking dead had cabin baggage. The prospect of reaching the door and getting our first sight of Mumbai was enough of an adrenalin shot to arouse the two of us to something approaching wakefulness. We emerged from the plane doorway with our eyes open wide. We were expectant and excited.

Our gateway to India, which literally brought us down to earth, was an aerial walkway that funnelled everyone along a metal tube to the immigration desks. Swept along in the throng of new arrivals, we were soon approaching our much anticipated first encounter with Indian bureaucracy. It was about then we realised that it would have been good if we had a couple of those immigration forms that weren't available on the plane. We looked around in confusion, wondering what to do next, while zombies with completed immigration forms shuffled past.

Help arrived in the reassuring shape of Debbie, a middle-aged hippy from Kent who had sat next to me all the way from Heathrow. She came up behind us and swept past confidently, seemingly awake, in a blur of rainbow tie-dye linen, beads, and teeth. She beamed a huge friendly smile and handed us an immigration form each as she bustled her way confidently past us. 'I was just randomly given three immigration forms by some guy back there – welcome to India! This is what I was telling you Mark – this crazy shit just happens here!'

And so, the weird stuff – the random, strange, and often

fortuitous events, known affectionately by Debbie as 'crazy shit' began. It was to continue to varying degrees for the next five weeks. It ranged from the slightly odd and mildly amusing, via the head-scratchingly improbable, to the plain bonkers. Every time something inexplicable like this happened on our trip, which was often, Nick, and I would just give each other a puzzled look, hands upturned, and with an over emphasised sigh we'd say, '*This is the Subcontinent.*' It didn't take long for us to truncate our newly invented go-to phrase to its acronym form which, for grown men, we found more amusing than we should have done. But I'm already getting ahead of myself... I should really begin the story back home and fill in the gap between leaving the quiet country calm of Shropshire and landing in the Mumbai metropolitan mayhem.

Nick and I had set off from our respective homes at about the same time; me from rural Shropshire, and Nick from his estate in Sutherland. My journey began with a train ride to London via Birmingham. His involved a drive down to Inverness and then a flight south to Heathrow. For reasons known only to the gods of flight ticket pricing, his combined flight from Inverness to Mumbai was cheaper than my direct flight from London. The plan was for us to converge at Heathrow and catch the same plane to Mumbai later that evening. And that's pretty much how it played out, with no great dramas. We met up as planned at Heathrow Airport around 6:30 pm, feeling every bit the intrepid adventurers. Security formalities dealt with, glasses were soon raised at the first convenient bar, and before we knew it, we were boarding our flight and on our way to India.

Many friends who had already visited India had warned me of potential diet related health risks. I'll admit that the possibility of spending five weeks with a semi-permanent dose of the trots had crossed my mind, but my mother-in-law had stockpiled a good percentage of the world's supply of Imodium for me by the time I set off, and I tried to put any negative thoughts of the bowel department out of mind. The idea briefly re-entered my mind before being instantly dismissed again, when I faced the culinary highlight of our relatively uneventful flight out to Mumbai. It came in the form of an unexpectedly splendid vegetable curry, complete with lime pickle, and mint yoghurt. But I'm one of those weirdos who, most of the time at least, quite likes airline meals.

In the high-stakes DNA poker game of life that we enter without choice at birth, my hand included a mild protein S deficiency. This means there is a tendency for my blood to clot more quickly than it should. On long-haul flights, I take suitable precautions, which include avoiding alcohol, and regular leg stretching. Even at 30,000 feet, every cloud has a silver lining, and the positive side of my minor physiological inconvenience was that Nick had a two-person ration of beer and wine with his meal, which only left him about one bottle of wine down on his usual nightly intake.

After seven hours of flight, there was a brief outburst of drama as the cabin crew put out an appeal for a doctor. Despite spending the last twenty years travelling around the world by plane for my work, it was the first time I'd ever witnessed the classic 'Is there a doctor in the house?' announcement. Dr Nick Lindsay remained calmly rooted to his seat. He was in sight of the incident and correctly diagnosed that the unfortunate woman lying flat out on the aisle floor required an expert in diabetes rather than a discussion about igneous intrusions. If expertise had been needed on 'Contrasts in Caledonian Tectonics of the Northern and Central Highlands of Scotland,' I've no doubt that Nick would have rocked up, and his geological expertise would have saved the day.

After the meal, we had several hours of darkness during which a fortunate few slept. The cabin crew turned the lights on when we were within an hour and a half of landing to make sure everyone was awake. They served us curry for breakfast, and even in my sleep-deprived state, I could spot a developing food theme. I speculated that in five weeks, I'd either be sick of the sight of the stuff or a complete spice junky unable to function without a daily fix of aromatic flavours and heat.

I looked across from my aisle seat to the window, hoping to catch my first sight of somewhere eastern and exotic. Instead, blocking the view, was a woman wrestling herself free from several layers of a blanket. When her head finally emerged, I asked her if she'd got much sleep. She introduced herself as Debbie from Kent, and told me she'd 'slept like a lamb' for most of the journey. She put it down to the sleeping tablets she'd picked up in a little village pharmacy on her last visit to India. She told me she was afraid of flying and being knocked out by the tablets stopped her from thinking about it. I tried to reassure her by telling her how tiny an aircraft is when compared to the enormous volume of airspace surrounding the world; the chances of collision are miniscule. I didn't think it was appropriate to add that those long odds are drastically reduced by funnelling aircraft more closely together down narrow flight corridors. Those air traffic controllers have to make a living somehow, like the rest of us.

Debbie from Kent turned out to be a charming fellow passenger, and she spent what was left of the flight telling me tales of the strange and improbable happenings that she'd experienced in India over a lifetime of regular visits. According to Debbie, something magical but inexplicable happens to people when they visit India. She was on her way to Kerala for a month of yoga, vegetarian cooking, and wellness therapy. Debbie told me about some great places to visit in India and gave me an insight into each of its regions. I had to get my map and notebook out at one point so I could make the most of her encyclopaedic knowledge. She made it sound amazing, and by the time the aircraft began its descent, I was close to cancelling my adventure with Nick and re-rerouting to Kerala.

The small amount of sleep I had during the flight wasn't the ideal preparation for five weeks of madness in India, but I was feeling excited when we finally arrived. As we prepared to disembark, Nick, and I set about gathering our things and trying to convince our senses that it was daytime. As we discussed the flight, Nick told me how he'd been following our flight path on the moving map and spotted an unexpected change of route at one point. He had, of course, been monitoring our track as we sped across Europe, into the Middle East, and across Asia. Not much gets past Nick when it comes to flight times and routing. He'd probably knocked out a temporary flight schedule spreadsheet on the way. The flight attendant overheard our conversation, and as we extracted our bags from the overhead lockers, he casually told us that our flight had indeed been re-routed. Apparently, it was to avoid getting too close to Iranian airspace. It turned out that a US airbase in Iraq had come under missile attack at about the same time as we passed through the area. Well spotted Nick! Nothing to worry about there then, I thought, as my wife's words 'And don't go off doing silly things' briefly flashed up on a screen inside my head.

Our spirits lifted by the unexpected good fortune of obtaining the all-important immigration forms, thanks to Debbie. Nick, and I sailed through the formalities with none of the delay and difficulties we'd been fearing. Our run of good luck continued when we discovered that our luggage had also arrived in Mumbai. We rode this crazy wave of fortune as long as we could by trying our chances at getting some cash and an Indian SIM card each. Both went without a hitch and so, formalities completed, we set about procuring the services of a taxi to find our hotel.

Hang on, something didn't feel quite right. Although I'd never been to India before, I had read many reports and thought I knew what to expect. But instead of seething crowds and chaos, everything was eerily quiet.

Large colourful signs hanging from the ceiling pointed new arrivals towards the airport exits and a long line of taxi booking desks. It was still strangely quiet. Nick and I tried one taxi desk, and they offered us, 'Very good price, Sir, for a very nice car, air-conditioned taxi, Sir'. We worked our way down the line of desks, just in case the first company wasn't offering the best price. The guys at the next few desks were far too occupied with their smartphones to have time for customers, so we kept moving down the line and found a nice lady, without a phone, who quoted us half the price offered at the first desk. We'd hit lucky and were directed to a lovely woman driver called Preet, who spoke excellent English, had a nice cool cab, and drove along serenely. Preet was a middle-aged lady who was immaculately dressed and very polite. It turned out that everyone employed in that company was a woman. No wonder it had all gone so smoothly.

This all seemed too good to be true. We'd just sailed through a hushed airport, got some money and a SIM card each, and then just stumbled upon the best ever taxi driver – an amiable lady who was driving carefully in her air-conditioned cab. We didn't realise just how rare it was to stumble across such a careful driver in India. Or to find any careful driver in India... Or even any driver prepared to stick to the rules of the road... Or any driver prepared to stick to the road. Statistically, Preet must have been in a small subset of approximately one. This was too good to miss, so before we were halfway into our hour-long ride to the hotel, we negotiated a city tour with her for the following day.

Our introduction to Mumbai was going well. The arrival went incredibly smoothly, and we were on our way to our hotel without a hitch. It was a delightful twenty-five degrees centigrade, which felt fantastic after leaving behind a grey and cold Britain. Up above, the sky was a milky haze, and that was how it stayed for most of our five-week stay – a daily reminder of our abuse of the planet in the form of a high-altitude cocktail of smoke, dust, and urban pollution.

Our trip to the hotel took us through the suburbs and right into the heart of Mumbai, with our progress gradually slowing as we joined more and more traffic. We saw bits of urban everything – business areas, industrial areas, open markets, shops, residential areas, and slums. Welcome to Mumbai! My overall initial impression was of the colour and noise, and the sheer magnitude of people going places. It was like looking through a non-symmetrical kaleidoscope – lots of different shapes and colours tumbling around in all directions at once. Everyone seemed to be on the move by every means of road transport imaginable. This impression of vast volumes of people, all on the move, lasted with me throughout our stay in India. What was everyone doing, and where were they all going?

We were gradually making less and less progress in ever denser traffic. Every now and again, the traffic completely ground to a halt. Endless queues of noisy cars, lorries, and motorcycles jostled for position, forever trying to inch that bit further in front of everyone else, forever changing lanes, and speeds. If there was a car-sized gap anywhere on the road, several other cars, trucks, or motorbikes felt it was their duty to fill it. By whatever means it takes – you must be in front of that next vehicle. And with that horn going all the time. Really guys, does it make any difference? No, because everyone else is doing the same bloody thing!! Calm down Mark, you've got another five weeks of this.

The most headway seemed possible on two wheels, and I swooned at my first sight of a Royal Enfield in its home environment. However, motorbikes often had manoeuvrability issues because of the need to carry three or more riders, assorted shopping bags, and the occasional farm animal. The slowest progress was being made by the odd horse and cart we came across, or pedestrians with improbably large loads on their heads. The one thing they all had in common was that they were all in a hurry to go somewhere.

It didn't take long to encounter the poverty, the beggars, and the squalor. By that stage of the taxi ride, everywhere seemed grimy, and covered in rubbish. The colours were more muted. We saw innumerable poor folk picking through bins and piles of debris for remnants that might have the slightest monetary or nutritional value. The ragged scraps of clothes worn by little kids squatting in the piles of garbage made it difficult to distinguish between what they were wearing and the surrounding rubbish. Packs of feral dogs fought over scraps – leftover food, rotting garbage, and leftover packaging. There was plenty to go at. The tidiest pavement we saw on the way to our hotel was a small stretch that had been swept clean to spread out some grass for a cow.

We drove through mile after mile of dense Mumbai traffic before eventually arriving at our hotel in the Fort area. By then, we were enveloped in a seething mass of vehicles, noise, and traffic law infringement. Maybe we'd spoken too soon about our subdued arrival in Mumbai; the traffic had done its best to counterbalance our quiet introduction to the city at the airport. It felt like Preet had given us the full Mumbai traffic experience.

A four-legged Mumbai resident being given her lunch

The Fort area of Mumbai is mainly a business district that boasts many classic Victorian style buildings from the days of the British Empire. The name derives from the old Fort George, built by the British East India Company but demolished back in 1862. Nick and I chose the Fort area because it seemed reasonably central and an excellent base from which to explore the city during our brief time there. The Fort area has been described as South Kensington by the sea, and it's easy to see why when you look at the many examples of Victorian – Gothic style architecture. By far the highlight for me was the enormous Chhatrapati Shivaji Terminus Railway Station, built in 1887, and inspired by London's St Pancras station. The Bombay High Court, Rajabai Clock Tower, and Elphinstone College are all similar architectural jewels close to the station, and they make a convenient walking tour.

Talking of which, due partly to our ongoing flow of good fortune, but even more to brilliant planning, that walk was right on our hotel's doorstep. We checked in, stashed our bags in a comfortable but fairly spartan bedroom, and prepared to explore.

First things first, though. When an Indian hotel porter asks, with a knowing look, if there's anything you need, it seems they mean *anything*. Our experience during our five-week trip showed us that most things are available. We didn't test that theory to the extreme. The porter's brother or cousin is the usual source for obtaining whatever you might want, and there seems to be an infinite supply of alternative relatives if required. The hotel porters' questions often assumed a need for alcohol, which many hotels aren't licenced to sell. And if you were interested, it was 'No problem, Sir.'

If it wasn't the room porter, there was usually at least one other member of staff who could adopt the fixer role. Beers, wines, and spirits of varying quality could, of course, be purchased from them, in which case they would pop round to the nearest 'English wine shop' or what in Britain we call an off-licence. If the Indian licensing laws appear complicated to the outsider, it's because they are. As well as individual establishments needing a licence, different rules apply from state to state and on different days of the week. The state of Bihar is completely dry on any day of the week, as Nick was to find to his horror later in the trip. Some restaurants and hotels get around the licensing laws by serving you an alcoholic drink and then describing it on the bill as 'special cold/iced coffee.' The first time I saw this, the wording threw me as I didn't remember having that, but this little work-around seems to be practised widely. Nick was wise to these subtle cultural protocols from previous visits and immediately ordered four bottles of premium strength Kingfisher beer for later.

Known as Bombay till 1995, Mumbai is now the financial and entertainment capital of India. It was once a series of seven swampy, malaria-ridden islands that were not much use to anyone. Back in the 16th century, the local Sultan sealed a deal that ceded the area to the Portuguese, who passed it on to the British in 1661 as part of a marriage dowry to King Charles II. It's crazy how cities and countries just got swapped around in those days with no say from the locals. Power does what power wants to do... no change there then. The British East India Company rented the area from the Crown on a relatively cheap lease and made good use of their asset. As always in life – it's not always what you know... With swamps drained and facilities constructed, Mumbai gradually developed into a major commercial and naval port, becoming Britain's gateway to India in the 19th century. Today it is home to billionaires, tech industries, high-rise skyscrapers, slum-dwellers, and the Bollywood film industry. For two nights, it was also going to be home for a pair of intrepid British adventurers.

Nick and I strode confidently out of the hotel that first evening, looking like a couple of strapping Indiana Jones explorers with our lightweight trousers and technical safari shirts. To everyone else on the streets of Mumbai, I'm sure we looked like a pair of pale British pensioners, slightly out of our comfort zone. On the inside, we were like a couple of excitable boys on a school trip, and we couldn't wait to start exploring somewhere new.

We headed for the ocean via a stop at the magnificent Chhatrapati Shivaji Terminus. The station, built from sandstone and limestone in 1888, is a classic example of Victorian Italianate Gothic Revival architecture. It was the first of many UNESCO World Heritage sites we were going to see on our travels across India and was a glorious sight – the epitome of grand, with an extravagant flourish of turrets, towers and pointed arches.

The architecture of the Fort area is very photogenic, and to our great surprise, Nick and I discovered we were as well. Or that's what we kidded ourselves. We kept being stopped by Indian people who wanted a selfie with us. We couldn't go a hundred yards, it seemed, before someone else would stop us, start chatting, and then ask for a photo. Some (although a minority) would skip the small talk, put up their hand to stop us and whip their phone or camera out. However, most people wanted to talk – and talk a lot. It seems that a couple of old white duffers are a bit of a novelty in India. I'm not sure whether it was our age, being very white, our sartorial elegance, or stunning Western good looks that were the attraction. Maybe it was just having one head of thinning silver hair between the two of us.

Nick's navigation skills came to the fore and we headed, like a proper couple of tourists, for the iconic Gateway of India monument down by the seashore. It was a zig-zag walk of about thirty minutes down the pavement, dodging pedestrians, and hundreds of street vendors along the way. Many of them placed their wares on a rug across the pavement, making it difficult to avoid a detour or a purchase. We homed in on the monument like a laser, a meandering, lazy laser, along with hundreds of other, mostly Indian tourists who had the same idea of being there by sunset.

The Gateway of India is an imposing twenty-six-metre-high triumphal arch, completed in 1924, and built of yellow basalt stone and concrete. Think of a 16th-century Islamic style Arc de Triomphe with Hindu decorations, and you'll get the picture.

Gateway of India (right) and Taj Mahal Hotel (left)

It stood imperious on the waterfront, looking out over the Arabian Sea with the setting sun as a backdrop. Enthusiasts of pre-cast reinforced concrete are likely to make a beeline for the monument, as its foundations contain India's first example of the construction material. Across the road inland was the equally impressive Taj Mahal Hotel, the scene of a horrific terrorist attack in 2008.

As one of the 'must-see' spots in Mumbai, the Gateway of India is a magnet for visitors. It was designed to be the triumphal entrance to India for the first British monarch to visit the country in 1911. Unfortunately, the arch hadn't been finished by the time King George V and Queen Mary arrived. In Blue Peter style, they erected a cardboard cut-out version and didn't complete the monument properly for another thirteen years. Although that all-important royal arrival date was narrowly missed, the archway became a symbolic ceremonial doorway to British India for the high and mighty arriving from the old country. The imposing structure shouted out to the locals, 'Look at us! This is what you can do when you rule an empire. We're powerful and important.'

Indians are more likely to see it as a symbol of the British leaving. It was from the Gateway of India that the last regiment of British soldiers, the First Battalion of the Somerset Light Infantry, left on the 28th February 1948. One hundred and ninety years after establishing their rule over India, the Brits had left the building.

Nick and I circumnavigated the monument, took a few photos, posed for several more selfies, and stared meaningfully for several minutes at the Arabian Sea. As the sun dipped below the horizon, streaking the sea with silver and orange, those profound deliberations naturally turned to thoughts of food and beer. Fortunately, Nick was one jump ahead, having already done some research to identify a recommended restaurant nearby. The Leopold Café is one of Mumbai's most iconic and goes back to 1871. Our meals were excellent. Amongst the background chatter of satisfied customers enjoying their meals and quenching their thirst, we toasted our good fortune. It had been a brilliant start to our adventure, and we'd only been in the country a matter of hours.

First impressions? It was pleasantly warm in Mumbai, but we hadn't travelled all that way just to escape the British winter. The sheer size and complexity of the city was almost overpowering and came with all those aspects that every foreigner notices – the visual stimulation of colours and movement, the sounds, and the smells (both aromatic and not so). And everyone in a hurry. Everyone says how India is unique and overwhelms your senses and it's difficult to capture in words just how astonishing it is. For two old pensioners used to the quietness of rural Britain, it was – *different.*

MUMBAI

By evening, Nick and I were ready to sleep. We'd only had a few hours in Mumbai, but the sleep lost during our flight east was catching up with us. It's just as well we were so tired. The downside of being so close to the action in the Fort area was – well, we were so close to the action. The road next to our hotel was one of the main routes in and out of the city centre, and a new metro line was being constructed right underneath it. As if the regular traffic cacophony wasn't enough, the Mumbai city centre car horn orchestra was supplemented that night with the percussion section from a major national infrastructure project. A rattling air conditioning unit completed the perfect sleep deprivation storm. The combined effect of the previous night's flight, the adrenalin rush of our arrival and four bottles of premium beer seemed to help, however, and Nick and I both had a good night's sleep.

Sunrise brought us our first full day in India, and we attacked it with gusto, or with as much gusto as a couple of sixty-somethings can muster first thing in the morning. We left the hotel at 8:00 am armed with a tip-off from one of the hotel staff for a good place for breakfast. We set off for the Marine Drive and the Arabian Sea coast.

India is a nation of cricket fanatics, so Nick and I felt quite at home there. In Mumbai, there are two magnificent grounds, and both the Wankhede and Brabourne stadiums were on our hotel's doorstep. As we were passing the Brabourne, we popped in to see if we could catch a look inside. By chance (this is how it happens, isn't it, Debbie?) we met Samit, the captain of the local Mumbai District team, and he invited us inside the ground. We posed for a few pictures, talked enthusiastically about the current India v Australia one-day international (ODI) series, and then continued our quest for breakfast.

Our new friend, Preet, the taxi driver, picked us up after our meal, and we launched into our day's sightseeing. Apart from wanting to visit Gilbert Hill, a geological site in the city's north, we were in Preet's hands for the rest of our day's sightseeing. We left her to decide where we should go. I'm sure we could have used our five weeks in India just for sightseeing in Mumbai, and as with the rest of our trip, we knew that we were hardly scratching the surface in the time we had available. Our visit was more of a brief stopover to recover from the flight before we moved on, so like the rest of the adventure there was a hint of tick-box tourism about it, which we were all too aware of, and it made us feel uncomfortable.

We set off for Gilbert Hill, our only 'must-do' stop for the day, and our taxi ride took us over the famous Rajiv Gandhi Sea Link bridge, which seems to be known by just about everyone we met as the Bandra Worli Sea Link bridge. The cable-stayed suspension bridge with pre-stressed concrete-steel viaducts on either side is an engineering marvel, but most people simply appreciate its graceful lines that just ooze beautiful design... it is very stylish. The bridge is 128 metres high at its highest point and was completed in 2010. It sweeps five and a half kilometres across the bay on the west side of the Mumbai peninsular. That's an impressive stat attack, but if you find the right Internet sources, you can discover even more. For example, the length of the cables used to support the bridge, if placed end to end, would stretch all the way around the world. Even more impressive – the bridge is equal in weight to 56,000 African elephants (there are people out there working this stuff out and posting it on the Internet).

We continued northwards in search of Gilbert Hill, which was about twenty kilometres from our hotel. That's a long way in Mumbai traffic. According to our research, the hill is one of only three basalt features of its type in the world. One is the Devils Tower in Wyoming (used in *Close Encounters of the Third Kind*), the second is the Devil's Post-pile in California, and the third, lesser known one, is Gilbert Hill, in Mumbai. The sixty-five-million-year-old monolith is sixty metres high, but it's almost lost amongst the enveloping suburbs. Imagine the Devils Tower from the film *Close Encounters* almost surrounded by sixteen-storey residential apartment blocks. For spine chilling cinematic drama, I can see why they chose the Wyoming version.

Preet told us that the seemingly random road junction where she was dropping us off was a ten-minute walk from the entrance to the site, but that was as close as she could get in the car. For the first nine and a half minutes of that journey, we had to shuffle our way through dense pedestrian traffic in a street market area. Nick, and I followed the directions Preet had given us, past the crowded traders to the fenced compound that surrounds the hill, and the Gaondevi Temple, which sits on top of the basalt stack.

A smartly dressed security guard emerged from his guardhouse to greet us. We couldn't tell what he was saying, but he was pointing to the concrete steps that led up the hill. He was shaking his head and waving his arms a lot. It was difficult to establish precisely what was happening because he didn't speak any English, and we didn't speak any Hindi. We tried our best to ask him if we could just have a quick look at the steps to see if we could climb them, but he didn't seem enthusiastic. We weren't getting anywhere, and we didn't get any further with a group of builders who were on site. They came across to act as go-betweens, but none of us could understand each other. There was a communication impasse, so Nick and I walked hesitatingly towards the steps to see if they were passable or not.

Gilbert Hill, Mumbai

We set off up the stairway, with some trepidation, and sure enough, the path completely disappeared about halfway up. There was a chasm of about ten metres in which there were no steps – just the bare earth and rocks of the steep-sided hill. That was that then. So that's why the builders were at the base of the hill. There are apparently fantastic views to be had from the top of Gilbert Hill in all directions. Black kites are said to hover on the wind as it whistles around the Gaondevi Temple, but we would have to see them another time. When we returned to the base, the guard muttered something in Hindi and once again shook his head a lot. Nick and I nodded politely and headed for the exit gates – where we discovered that we'd been locked in.

It was our first full day on the subcontinent, and within a few hours, Nick, and I were in a spot of bother. Somewhere in the dusty, sprawling suburbs of northern Mumbai, we'd got ourselves locked into a securely fenced compound by an angry Public Works security guard. Standing about as close as he could to our collective personal space, the guard delivered an animated lecture in Hindi (probably) accompanied by more waving of arms. He kept pointing at the path. I had a job to take it all in. The man seemed upset, but he didn't somehow come across as threatening. I actually felt sorry for him; it was like he was pleading to be understood, and he was frustrated that we weren't listening. We were. But the language barrier was definitely a problem.

As we tried to reassure the security man, the half a dozen semi-clad building labourers came over and joined in the discussion again, trying to translate the guard's pronouncements and explain our predicament. From what we could make out, it wasn't good. Our exit from the compound was blocked by a ten-foot-high fence and locked gates, so we couldn't leave. In the chaos of the moment, I drew on my inner Kipling to select an inspirational quote. If we could keep our wits about us while all others were losing theirs…

I scanned the fence and gate, and amidst the commotion, spotted our most likely escape route. Well, the *only* option as far as I could see. The fright part of my brain was saying 'This is just ridiculous. It can't be happening,' but it was being over-ruled by the flight part that was saying 'You're in a spot of bother here. You'd better find a way out, quick.'

It looked impossible to get over or through the fence on either side of the gates, but I reckoned it might be possible to shimmy up the side of the gates, using the gateposts. When we discussed the drama later, I discovered Nick had also identified the same exit option at precisely the same moment. We must have both been simultaneously calculating the right time to attempt our dash for freedom. Look at us – a couple of sixty-somethings – having to bust our way out of a Mumbai Public Works compound. We were just over halfway through our first full day in India. Five more weeks to go. It was about then that a little voice popped back into my head '… and don't go off doing silly things.'

As luck would have it, an alternative escape route presented itself, as if delivered by a benevolent elephant headed deity, in time to save us from any further embarrassment. At least we wouldn't have to add falling off a ten-foot fence to our catalogue of awkward moments on day one.

Settling disputes wasn't the main reason the semi-clad building labourers were on site. Their primary function was to re-build the broken path that takes visitors up to the Gaondevi Temple. Being nearly lunchtime, they'd knocked off for a break. At that moment, their wives, dutiful, and beautiful, had turned up at the compound to deliver lunch. Little did they realise their arrival was also timed perfectly to avoid an international incident. The builders' wives were carrying, in their arms and upon their heads, pots and platters of the most excellent looking home cooking, and drinks. Even for such a relatively mundane task, the wives all seemed to be turned out in beautiful and colourful saris. The meal looked more like a feast for a special occasion than something to fill a gap. Seeing the ladies approaching, and keen to look after the workers who were under his temporary supervision, the security guard undid the padlocks to the compound and let the ladies enter with their lunchtime spread. They did so serenely and gracefully. I'm not sure if the guard was also letting Nick and me out at that point – possibly – but we didn't wait for clarification. We shot out like rats from a drain. Programmed by sixty-plus years of British manners, we simultaneously attempted to shout out our apologies, and our sincere thanks and acknowledgements to the security guard and the builders – and their wives. What an utter shambles.

Still not really sure what had just happened, we discretely upped our walking pace to almost jogging speed and melted into the crowd of people in the street market – and out of sight. As politely as we could, we elbowed our way back down the same busy market street that we'd gone up when we left Preet earlier. It was a sea of pedestrians dressed predominantly in black; with a handful of rattling tuk-tuks weaving their way through the crowd, horns bleating pathetically, as if anyone took any notice.

In case anyone doesn't know what a tuk-tuk is, I should explain – they are the underpowered three-wheel vehicles that form the go-to means of transport for most people in urban India. They look like they're made of tin, are often yellow or black, and can be ornately decorated. Most are borderline unroadworthy and held together with bits of string but can still transport up to a dozen people and their livestock in no comfort at all. They would probably be outpaced by a ride-on mower.

A few motorcycles wobbled their way through the crowd, each with a minimum of three passengers carrying bulging shopping bags. Our nostrils were bombarded as we fought our way through the bodies and past countless market stalls of meat, spices, and vegetables. We saw a goat's head on a wooden block, and a sheep's bloody intestines and testicles, hung up like a disturbing modern art installation. I could just see that on a white marble plinth in the Tate Modern surrounded by appreciative connoisseurs: 'I think this one really encapsulates the artist's repudiation of the post-modern paradigm, enigmatic in its conceptualisation of the new millennium condition but a clear repudiation of neo-liberalism's stranglehold on societal values – the brutally confrontational interface with the viewer shows an emotional honesty and strength of moral purpose that few contemporary artists could conceive, let alone deliver – I wish I had the guts to do that... or the balls.'

Nick and I continued to shuffle our way through the crowd. We went past a stall with several blue plastic containers, the size of oil drums, containing what looked like dead fish and lots of flies – another potential exhibit. Eventually, with the ten-minute walk reduced to five minutes, we got back to the main road and, thankfully, found our driver, Preet, and the safe sanctuary of her cool white taxi. Well, that went well.

Apart from Gilbert Hill, Preet gave us her standard tour and one by one we rattled off the tourist spots of Mumbai... Nariman Point, Wankhede Stadium, the Bandra Worli Sea Link bridge (again), Juhu Beach, Mount Mary Church, the slums, and back to Nariman Point for sunset.

Mount Mary Church, or to give it its more formal name, The Basilica of Our Lady of the Mount, is a Roman Catholic church that looks out over the Arabian Seas from a small hill in the Bandra district, just north of the Bandra Worli Sea Link bridge. Although the current church building only goes back a hundred years or so, the history of the site goes back to the 16th century, when Jesuit priests from Portugal brought a holy statue to the spot and constructed a chapel. Preet dropped Nick and me outside the church and left us to look around. With a densely packed schedule of the world's major religions awaiting us over the coming weeks, it was prudent to get our eye in on day one. Roman Catholicism would be as good a place to start as any.

Once inside the Mount Mary Church, I felt an instant calmness. Apart from the quiet and solemnity of the building there was a re-assuring familiarity in the design and proportions of its semi-Gothic style architecture. Perhaps I was feeling the comfort of surroundings that felt like home. It felt like we'd walked into a church back in Britain. Whether or not you're a believer, there is undoubtedly something calming about being in a church. I find that very satisfying but feel slightly guilty that I'm taking advantage of all those soothing vibes without signing up for the religion that's responsible for the church being there. I'm also always fascinated to watch peoples' devotion in action. In Mount Mary Church, some worshippers seemed to be going through the motions on auto-worship. They were just doing what they'd been brought up to do. Others were more devout, with a serious intensity etched into their expressions. Some were very relaxed. Others appeared completely in the zone, in another world altogether. It made me ponder on the human relationship with faith, belonging, tribalism, security, and hope. I would return to those thoughts in Amritsar, Varanasi, and Bodh Gaya.

Nick and I looked around the interior of the church, admiring the dignified statue of the Mother and Child for which it is famous. We then spent some time walking up and down the street outside. The road was lined with rickety market stalls selling religious souvenirs. This was the place to come to for your fridge magnets, rosaries, baby Jesus models, key fobs, and beeswax body parts. Wait a minute – beeswax body parts? What was all that about? Many of the stalls had rows of legs, arms, heads, and just about anything else in the form of model body parts ranging from about six to twelve inches long. We had to ask.

'Very nice leg Sir, for curing problem,' was the obvious answer from the smiling face of the friendly stallholder. Oh well, that's OK then. We were told that the body parts were made from beeswax, and Catholic devotees used them for seeking religious favours. When I looked it up later, I discovered this was a legacy of the colonial days and linked to the Shrine of Fatima in Portugal, where a miracle is said to have taken place. The body parts are known as 'wax promises'... not to be confused with the dubious guarantees given by ear syringing specialists. If a person burns the wax promise body part, in the same way candles are lit in church, and the person has faith, then it is said that the relevant body part (theirs or that of their family or friend) will be cured/restored. Resisting the temptation to seek a beeswax version of my dodgy left knee (they were available), or a whole leg to take home for Jan as a stocking filler, we headed back to the taxi.

As she drove her two foreign guests around town that day, Preet somehow displayed a competence for multitasking I could barely comprehend (being a man). It seemed effortless to her and must have resulted from years of experience. Nick mentioned to her at one point that we were trying to get to Aurangabad the next day by train, but at the station the previous evening, we'd had no luck getting tickets because they'd all been sold.

Pah, why did we think that was a problem? Preet had a suitably connected family member, or friend of a family member who was a travel agent in Aurangabad. At one point on our grand Mumbai tour, Preet was negotiating the price for two train tickets for Mumbai to Aurangabad on one of her phones, while simultaneously setting up a WhatsApp connection with Nick's phone and photographing images from our passports on another one. Oh, and did I mention the traffic? The multitasking was all going on while playing dodgems with millions of other Mumbai drivers. In the unlikely event that anyone ever gets to read this, I just made all that up. I wouldn't want anyone getting into trouble for not paying attention while driving. If it had happened, however, it would have been pure genius to witness.

After Preet had dropped us off at the seafront, perfectly timed for the sunset, Nick and I finished our day with another walk around the crowded and noisy streets that surrounded our hotel. The range, quantity, and price of goods on sale, late into the night in the shops and along the pavements astonished us. From one ten-metre-strip of pavement sellers, I was very tempted to buy a toaster, some thick bed blankets, and a hessian shopping bag. I settled instead for an affordable wristwatch, called Kevin, for 150 rupees, or the equivalent of about £1.50. That's not the name I gave it. Kevin was already emblazoned across the face of the watch. I would have opted for something sexier, like 'Rolex Submariner' but they weren't available in the same budget range. The best retail deal of the night was offered by a very loud Indian Del-Boy who drew an enormous crowd by offering four polo shirts for the equivalent of a pound. It's incredible to think he must have been making a profit on that.

The last part of the walk back to our beds for the night took us along a popular traffic-free road opposite the hotel that we christened 'piss-alley,' for obvious reasons. No one seemed shy about it. We celebrated emerging unscathed from our first full day, just about, with another five-star curry, and another couple of beers. The pattern had been set.

It was only our first day. The sensory overload everyone talks about in India, that I will no doubt mention several times, was real, and already the sights, the people, and the food had been extraordinary. Somehow, we hadn't been arrested. Apart from the unaccustomed battering our senses had experienced, Mumbai had been a pleasant surprise and a relatively gentle introduction to India. Perhaps we were lucky with Preet's choice of sights. It was certainly a city of contrasts and although we had only dipped our toes in the water, we had seen a good cross-section of what it had to offer. Parts were uncomfortably raw while others had great charm. We saw, from a guilty tourist distance, the sizeable mass of one slum area, while the well-maintained colonial buildings in the area around our hotel held a hint of more chic Kensington and Chelsea. The weather was warm and comfortable, as was our reception with everyone we met. We were selfie stars for a while, but I couldn't see that lasting when we got back to home soil. Nick and I discussed the day and the plan for the morning. We were already excited to see what lay in wait for us beyond Mumbai.

AURANGABAD

Visit a new country, see some unusual sights, and have an adventure. That was the plan. Well, seven hours sitting in third class accommodation on Indian railways is quite an adventure and involves quite a few unusual sights... and smells.

It took our train most of the day to travel the 385 kilometres from the coast at Mumbai, inland through Maharashtra State to Aurangabad. There was never any danger of us breaking any speed records. We averaged less than 35 miles per hour. I wouldn't usually spend much time describing a train journey, but if you've not been to India, or even if you have, and want a little nostalgic reminder, the next few paragraphs will hopefully be of interest.

After two days in the metropolis, Nick and I headed northeast on the first leg of our journey across India, and we couldn't wait for our first experience of Indian railways. The train ride would take us over the mainly flat Deccan plateau, through endless rice, wheat, and oilseed fields, to our second major city of the trip. Our base in Aurangabad would be the kick-off point for a dash to the meteorite crater at Lonar and the UNESCO World Heritage caves at Ellora.

Indian trains have so much to offer, including travel

We were only going to be there for two nights of our whistle-stop adventure, before moving further north to Udaipur.

It is hard to avoid the legacy of the British on the subcontinent, and the great Indian railways are part of that and an integral feature of modern life in India. When I think about the British impact on India, my brain springs into Monty Python mode, and I want to convert their 'What have the Romans done for us?' sketch into an Indian version. So OK, apart from national unity, a common language, democracy, the legal system, a national railway network, an education system, civil service, bureaucracy, sweet milky tea and cricket, what did the Brits ever do for India? Except the reality is not at all funny. As I've grown up and travelled extensively, I've understood that the version of history I learnt at school was a very one-sided interpretation. The reality leaves me feeling considerably more shame than pride. In his book *Inglorious Empire*, Shashi Tharoor claims that 'The British left a society with 16 per cent literacy, a life expectancy of 27, no domestic industry, and over 90 per cent living below what today we would call the poverty line.'

More of the British Raj later, but on the subject of railways, I'll just change the points and pull over to a siding for a moment to discuss the background. It's true – the Brits brought the railways to India, starting in 1853, when 400 passengers took the thirty-three-kilometre journey from Mumbai (Bombay at the time) to Thane. Over the following 50 years, some 40,000 kilometres of railway line were constructed, using British management and know-how and Indian labour and taxpayer's money. This was very much an investment made for the benefit of Britain. The railways united the various parts of the subcontinent in more ways than one. From a political point of view, the railways allowed the British bureaucrats, officials, and military to move around. From an economic point of view, it allowed the transport of vast quantities of raw materials, such as coal, cotton, silk, spices, and iron ore, to be exported back to Britain. Transportation of Indian people seems to have been a by-product. It was all about the Brits.

You need a lot of trains to make the most of that amount of railway line. In less than a hundred years after that first journey, India imported over 17,000 locomotives, the vast majority from Britain. Local workshops kept the trains rolling, and by the early 20th century, Indian mechanics were designing and building their own engines. That was no good for British companies and exports, of course, so a law was passed in 1912 to prevent it, and the imports from Britain continued. It was a similar story for shipbuilding. Since Indian independence in 1947, the railway network has continued to flourish. Indian Railways, under the Ministry of Railways, now runs over 20,000 passenger trains daily, from 7,349 stations, on a network that stretches over 66,000 kilometres (the UK network is about a quarter of that).

When we did our planning, Nick and I decided we'd like to make several long-distance trips on the Indian railways – it was a 'must-do' part of our travel experience, although we weren't entirely sure what to expect. As inexperienced newbies, we had a few unanswered questions. We weren't sure, for example, who we'd be sharing our carriage with, whether there would be any toilet facilities on board, anything to drink, or what our chances were of arriving on time, or in the right city. With images in our minds of passengers hanging out of train windows and falling off crowded carriage roofs, Nick and I approached our first train ride with some apprehension. The experience of travelling from Mumbai to Aurangabad turned out to be a delightful one, and we soon became big fans of the Indian railway system.

Our taxi driver, Preet, collected us from our hotel at 8:30 am and drove us northwards through quiet streets to Mumbai's Karla terminus train station. It seems the standard bumper to bumper Mumbai traffic doesn't kick off until after 9:00 am. Perhaps everyone stays up so long into the night that the following day doesn't begin until relatively late, which is the opposite of what I'd expected. I thought everyone would be up early to beat the heat of the sun – the one that was up there somewhere behind that high-level haze. By the way, if I omit to give a daily report on the weather on our *Journey through India,* it's because, first, it would get boring, and second, except for a few days in Shimla, the weather was the same every day. It was invariably pleasantly warm, bordering on hot, with a high haze blocking out direct sunlight.

We'd got two train tickets to Aurangabad after all, via Preet's cousin, but there was a small caveat. We had to depart from one of the out-of-town district train stations instead of being able to use the impressive St Pancras lookalike just down the road from our hotel. On our drive out to the terminus, about half an hour from the hotel, we stopped off at a café near to Preet's house, which was in a slum area. You would probably put Preet in the 'middle-class' pigeonhole if you saw her, so I was surprised when, with some pride, she pointed out her house in the middle of what looked like the definitive shantytown. There was clearly no stigma attached to living there, and she reeled off a list of neighbours and their jobs with obvious pride. I think half a day more in Mumbai, and we would have been invited round for a meal, and we'd have jumped at the chance.

In Preet's part of town, well away from the tourist trail, there seemed to be little English spoken, so once in the café, she talked us through the breakfast menu. Spoilt for choice, Nick and I both opted for a simple cheese and tomato omelette, although even that wasn't simple. It came packed with subtle and delicious spices. With fresh orange juice, toast, and as much chai as we could drink, our morning feast was again delicious. The simple pleasure our breakfast gave us, in friendly company, was many orders of magnitude more than we could rightly expect for its modest cost. It's difficult to put a price on such simple pleasures.

Preet dropped us at the station and packed us off with the fond farewell you'd normally reserve for relatives and dear friends. She made us promise to text her when we were safely inside the train and sat in our seats. She wouldn't drive away from the station until she knew we were safe, just in case we needed back-up. This touching act of kindness turned out to be the first of many we experienced in India. On several occasions, Nick and I met people, who after knowing us for all of ten minutes, insisted on leaving their phone number, just in case we got into trouble.

Twice shy from previous travel experiences, I was wary when I first arrived on the subcontinent. I treated everyone with caution, in case first appearances were deceptive and the friendly stranger was just out to rip us off. I hated feeling like that; I'd much prefer to see the good in people, but a lifetime of travel experiences had taught me to be cautious, and then perhaps relax a bit later. I was quite noncommittal towards the first few people who came up to chat with Nick and me on our travels. After a while, though, after many such encounters, I felt guilty. Everyone just seemed so lovely, and just wanted to ask about our families and our trip, and what we thought of India. Oh, and they usually wanted a selfie.

The only place where this generality broke down was in the tourist hotspots, and our itinerary took in quite a few of those. In those places, we had to be on our guard; there were one or two shady chancers around and even some of the innocent locals found it easy to treat a couple of white Western pensioners like slow-moving ATMs. That's understandable given the relative levels of income; you've got to see it from their point of view. Imagine being in their sandals as a local without two rupees to rub together, when a couple of impeccably dressed handsome foreigners come waltzing in (or Nick and me), with their fancy smartphones and cameras, buying whatever they want.

The woman in the station ticket office told us confidently, 'Train will be on platform four… or maybe five.' Nick and I lugged our rucksacks in the direction to which she was pointing and found our way to what we thought was the right platform. We did so with some uneasiness – with visions coming back of trains packed like sardine tins and people fighting for space. However, like our arrival at Mumbai airport, everything went incredibly smoothly. I'm sure it helped that we arrived over an hour early. It's always good to build in a bit of contingency time, and we used ours to good effect by purchasing some water and snacks, and repeatedly asking people if we were on the right platform.

Impressively, the Tadoba Express turned up bang on time, and the waiting passengers stirred. The platform had filled up since we first arrived. With the appearance of the train, there was now what seemed like the population of a small village on the move. Many of the waiting passengers were in little encampments of what looked like extended families. Half of them were still asleep, and they spread out across the platform on blankets, with all their possessions, in a patchwork of colourful family circles, in groups of half a dozen or more. Individuals with bulging bags and rolled up rugs busied themselves up and down the platform, weaving in out of the encamped families. There appeared to be just as many going one way as the other. There were a few body-shaped piles of rugs that remained motionless, underneath which were presumably poor souls who'd wandered in off the street for somewhere safe to sleep.

As the train rolled in, the platform – full of recumbent and slumbering bodies – came to life. The men of the families looked grumpy and disinterested. Many of them registered their annoyance at having their slumber disturbed by clearing their throats with a loud and substantial spit. Males of all ages wandered lazily to the edge of the platform to engage in an unspoken spitting competition. The younger lads performed with more competitive edge; it was all about distance and extravagant performance. The older gents were more concerned with efficiency and conserving effort. The irritated disdain with which they effortlessly dragged phlegm from the darkest depths showed years of experience. Little children ran around excitedly, women carefully gathered up their saris, and the younger family members helped ageing grandparents to their feet. Nick and I had to fend for ourselves.

A behemoth of a diesel engine rumbled past us loudly, all testosterone, grease, rust and flaking paint. It temporarily cloaked everything and everyone on the platform in a blanket of grey smoke and fumes as it grumbled and belched its way through. It took an age for all its carriages to clank their way past and slowly shudder to a halt. Illuminated signs hung down from the roof of the platform to show passengers the number of the carriage due to stop at that point. Nick and I stood in the appropriate place, according to our tickets, and the system seemed to work. We were soon aboard and in our seats – two window seats in a compartment built to house eight passengers. We sent a message to Preet to let her know we were OK, stashed our luggage, and sat back contentedly and relieved. All was good. We each had comfortable six-foot-long seats on which we could lie down if we so desired. There was air conditioning, a fan, window blinds, and electrical sockets. It looked as though the compartment had seen better days, but everything was perfectly acceptable and relatively clean. Remarkably, to begin with, we were on our own. After a few minutes, the guard walla came round with some fresh blankets, pillows, and sheets for us, reminding us of how long our journey was going to be.

Just as we concluded that we might have the place to ourselves, a pleasant young Indian couple joined us, settled into their seats, said hello, and asked for a selfie. That was it though, no one else – just us cosy four in a compartment for eight. We had loads of room and could even settle down for a sleep, if we wanted to. The train left exactly on time. It pulled forwards hesitantly for about 100 metres, stumbled, and screeched to a halt again. After a brief pause, we lurched forwards again, and with some loud metallic banging of carriage couplings, we were off. Just another seven hours to go then.

Our train trundled its way lazily through the suburbs of Mumbai, clanking and screeching its way across the junctions and points as we made our way north-eastwards towards the Indian interior. Those scenes, as the train snaked its way slowly through kilometres of dusty rubbish covering just about everything in sight, have stuck vividly in my mind ever since. It wasn't pretty. One moment that felt especially poignant was when I was checking emails on my phone and looked up to see groups of kids on the adjacent set of railway tracks picking through piles of old newspapers and packaging. Litter seemed to be everywhere for hundreds of metres. That was their world, separated from mine by a thin sheet of glass and a few thousand kilometres of contrasting opportunities. The poor ragged youngsters were scavenging for whatever they could find that might have the slightest value. I sat there in a bit of a daze, contemplating our relative lifestyles, and feeling guilty. How lucky Nick and I were, in the crazy game of chance we call life, to be born where and when we were.

Poverty is one of several things you need to consider before you go to India. People tell you what to expect, but you need to think about how you will deal with it mentally when you're there. It can be numbingly upsetting, something that's amplified when those involved are kids and/or disabled. You wonder what sort of lives those people are living and the future they can expect. India is such an enigma; such a land of contrasts, but those extremes are part of the fascination and partly why we visit such places. With the fastest rising economy in the world (pre-COVID), India leapfrogged into the world's top five. It has become a big-league player in industries such as technology, communications, biotech, films, and space. It is also home to a quarter of the world's poor, and almost half the population still has to defecate in the open.

The main reasons for poverty have been around for centuries – illiteracy, unemployment, unequal wealth distribution, overpopulation, corruption, and discrimination. Some of these issues have been handled better than others in recent times. By whatever means used to measure poverty, and there are many, India has made good progress (statistically) in recent years. Although the poverty rate has reportedly halved, with 271 million people moved out of poverty in the decade up to 2015, that still leaves hundreds of millions remaining in poverty in the 21st century. And these are not just statistics; each number is an actual person with their own story. Visiting India isn't theme park entertainment. These issues are tragically real. The victims appear in front of your eyes, and for anyone with a conscience, it will be troubling. You will be left wondering how to respond, and it's as well to be prepared for that before you arrive.

Eventually, the litter-strewn suburbs of Mumbai thinned out, and the train rolled into the agricultural and wooded countryside of the Deccan plateau. The young couple sharing our compartment settled down to get some rest, so Nick and I left them in peace. Instead, we went off to explore the surrounding carriages, venturing out on our scouting trips one at a time to keep our bags safe. The rest of the train was nothing like as tranquil as our compartment. It was almost full. The carriages with children in them were a hubbub of high-pitched noise, and often music. The older folk dozed, and the millennials stared at their phones, simultaneously engaged and disengaged with the real world. Everywhere was colourful, and in some compartments, there was a heady mixture of aromatic food and body odour. It was like someone had spilled a packet of Bombay mix in the gym changing room. Nick and I seemed to have missed the message that said you have to bring as many relatives and lifelong possessions with you on the train as possible.

The train comprised fifteen carriages, and we were in B2, one of three in third class, somewhere near the middle. Just beyond our compartment were the doors for getting on and off the train. Leaving those open for air conditioning seemed to be standard practice, and it was a great place to stand and watch the world go by at 35 miles per hour, clackety-clack, clackety-clack... in a non-risk taking, not going off doing silly things sort of way.

It was a clackety-clack sort of journey. The Indian countryside drifted past in slow motion, the hours passing by to a slow metronomic clicking rhythm played on steel rails. Clackety-clack, clackety-clack. The steady hypnotic rhythm was regularly supplemented by the piercing refrains of the vendors who shuffled their way through the carriages. Their regular cries echoed through the corridor as they passed up and down. 'Pani, pani, pani'(water) or 'chai, chai, chai' (tea) bellowed out from the next carriage to herald their arrival and give you time to get your money ready. There were plenty of other things on offer – sweets, biscuits, chapatis, fruit, or phone chargers. Just as one of these guys disappeared, the next one seemed to follow up close behind. They were all men, and I noticed a common characteristic in their loud voices. They were all very penetrating, and resonant – like the street newspaper vendors of old, if anyone is old enough to remember them ('Read all about it'). I'm sure these chaps could stand at one end of the train and easily be heard at the other end. I pondered whether it was the job that made their voices evolve to such a piercing pitch, or whether they had that voice in the first place, and it naturally selected them for the job? Someone softly spoken would be at a competitive disadvantage and would soon lose their job – it was evolutionary survival by voice pitch.

As the kilometres ticked by, and the rhythmic noise of the train carriage lulled me into a spot of daydreaming, I developed a theory that I will call Aptitudinal Determinism, in which someone's innate DNA characteristics sets them on a pre-determined career path. I think it is instinctive for human beings to want to explore unknown places... we are predisposed to travel. Maybe it was that, linked to a graphical way of viewing the world, an aptitude for spatial awareness and a borderline OCD tendency to be neat that funnelled both Nick and me into careers as mapmakers. I'll throw that one out there as a gift for someone who knows what they're talking about. I'll let them bring the Aptitudinal Determinism label into the mainstream via a PhD thesis, a number of peer-reviewed papers, a series on Netflix, and a best-selling book.

Every time we neared a station, the train slowed down, and the clackety-clack from the metronome slowed its beat. The number of chai vendors suddenly increased. They would appear randomly on the trackside a few hundred metres before we got to the station. They'd run alongside the train as it slowed down and jump on, to sell whatever they could. Sales clinched, they'd get off at the station. These canny entrepreneurs were getting the passengers' money before the train got to the station and before anyone had the chance to get off and buy things at the platform kiosks. It was an excellent example of applied economics, or survival of the most competitive, in action. The funniest example was when one quite elderly chi walla got over-run with demand and suddenly realised the train was moving *out* of the station. He made a mad dash through the carriage, as fast as the poor old fella could manage a mad dash with his huge flask and armful of cups. He then had to leap athletically out of the train as it gathered speed, just before the end of the platform. I was expecting to hear a loud crashing sound as an elderly body and tea related products smashed into stone paving slabs. Defying the years, however, he completed his performance with ease, softly alighting on the last inch of the platform, Bolshoi style. It wasn't the first time he'd pulled that stunt.

Time for a meal on Indian Railways

About an hour into the journey, our tickets were inspected and then the dinner walla came round to take our meal orders. We ordered something although I wasn't sure what. About an hour later it appeared: tarka dal, vegetable curry, rice and chapatis with lime pickle –

fantastic! I'm not sure ordering something unknown in Britain would have resulted in such a good outcome. Nor could anyone complain about the quality or quantity of the Indian Railways' catering. It had the usual subtle aromas and flavours, generous portions, and all for less than £1.

We had eight stops along our route and at each one Nick and I waited with bated breath to see if the other seats in our compartment would get snaffled up. However, most of the way we remained undisturbed. While I watched the world go by, dreaming up new socio-behavioural theories, Nick monitored our progress on Google maps and provided a regular update on where we were and the principal economic, touristic, and geological features of the area. That's the sort of travelling companion you need.

There were hordes of people waiting on the platform at the holy Hindu city of Nashik, which was about halfway to Aurangabad. They all seemed to jump onto our train when it stopped. It looked like our cosy train ride might be over... but fortunately, it wasn't. A long stream of hyperactive passengers filed straight past us, some glancing and giggling at the spectacle as they did so, as they moved down the corridor and further into the train. Our journey continued, and encouraged by the soporific sound of the rails, I took advantage of our relative solitude to have a short kip. Nick kept track of our progress and especially the changing topography through which we were passing.

I woke to see the sun appear briefly through the haze, an enormous, blurred orange ball perched on the horizon. I was just in time to watch it go slowly down at 6:00 pm and an hour later we arrived in Aurangabad, only twenty minutes late on a seven-hour trip. With no real justification, we suspected that might be an above-average effort by Indian Railways. Our trip had gone quickly and was very comfortable. The meal was great, the toilets were serviceable, and the vendor entertainment an unexpected bonus.

I'm ashamed to say I'd never heard of Aurangabad before I came across it during the route planning stage before our adventure. I don't know why but I had imagined a small rural town with nothing of note, but an excellent base for our visits to the meteorite crater at Lonar and the caves at Ellora.

Just like the chai wallas, who jumped onto the train before it arrived at the station, there were one or two taxi drivers on the platform at Aurangabad. They were cleverly finding passengers before anyone got as far as the taxi ranks outside the station. Nick negotiated a deal. We didn't know if it was good or not, but at least the guy knew our hotel – or at least he said he did.

As our taxi driver weaved through the dense rush hour traffic the short distance from the station to our hotel, he explained the city had a population of two million and was expanding fast. Historically, it had grown through cotton and silk but was now a thriving industrial centre. In recent years, it had established massive business parks that were home to some major motor, financial and pharmaceutical companies, including ŠKODA, Audi, Goodyear, Siemens, Colgate-Palmolive and Johnson & Johnson.

Our relatively inexpensive hotel turned out to be of the five stars variety. Nick said he couldn't remember staying anywhere better. We checked in, put our bags in the room and immediately got the paperwork out to check that we were in the right place and how much we'd paid.

One of my most vivid emotional memories of the entire trip goes back to that evening. Nick and I freshened up after our epic transit of the Deccan plateau and wandered down to the hotel restaurant. It had already been a great day, and we'd ticked off the all-day Indian train journey experience.

A four-piece band played traditional Indian music. The chef had come out to discuss his personal recommendations with us. When our order arrived, we enjoyed the most fantastic meal of fish curry, chicken biryani, chapatis and Kingfisher Premium beers. After hearing about our love of cricket, the restaurant manager had placed Nick and me at a table in front of which was an enormous TV screen. We could watch India thrash Sri Lanka in a T20 cricket match live from Pune (India won by seventy-eight runs). For once, I stopped to take in the moment and realise where I was and what I was doing. Maybe it had taken that long after arriving in India for it to sink in that we really were on a five-week adventure in such an amazing country. Many will wonder what the hell I'm talking about, but that moment with my best pal will stay with me. When I sat back and took it all in, that slight lump in my throat was nothing to do with my meal – what a soft lad.

LONAR / ELLORA

Throughout this book, you will find a few travellers' tips. Two of them are well illustrated in the next few paragraphs. The first one is about leaving sufficient time to see the sights on your itinerary. Seasoned travellers, no names mentioned, already know this, but sometimes they get it wrong. The second tip relates to the horrors of road travel in India, but I'll explain more below.

The day's schedule seemed so simple when we planned it back home. First, we'd visit a meteorite crater at Lonar, about 150 kilometres to the east of Aurangabad. Then we'd come back to the city and go about 36 kilometres in the other direction to visit the world-famous caves and temples of Ellora. We completely misjudged the time needed to cover the distances involved. Nick and I discussed our proposed schedule with our taxi driver on the way from the train station to the hotel, when we first arrived in Aurangabad. His immediate reaction was to shake his head with exaggerated drama before saying with great seriousness, 'This is not possible. This will take two days, my friends, maybe three.' He reconsidered, however, when we explained that we would be heading north after two nights on our pre-booked flights. Realising there was a day's driving money at stake, he made a financially enforced backtrack and considered it might be possible after all. So, we made the arrangements, he phoned his mate to subcontract the job, and we paid our deposit.

To fit both tourist sights into one day, our driver Rahul came to pick us up at 5:00 am. It was going to be a three-hour drive to Lonar and the meteorite crater. A look around the crater with a guide would take two hours, and then we'd have a four-hour drive back through Aurangabad and out to the Ellora caves, before heading back, once again, to our five-star hotel in the city. It was going to be a long day.

Now then, talking about driving in India... where shall I start?

First the good news; they drive on the left in India. Readers who have seen Indian driving at first hand are already in fits of laughter. Driving on the left is a good start, because it's the proper side of the road to drive on. The trouble is, they also travel quite a lot on the right. Driving on the left seems to be optional, with the law presumably being for guidance only. Speeding, where possible, appears to be obligatory. Overtaking on bends and blind brows is standard practice. This often involves meeting slow moving and/or overloaded trucks or buses taking up most of their carriageway, coming in the opposite direction. I guess the blind bend overtaking trick is part of Indian driver training module one, with negotiating the unlit truck at night in a more advanced lesson. Not to take on these manoeuvres, although marginally improving your chances of completing your journey, and your life, will put you at a disadvantage compared to all the other road users. Rule number one seems to be that you must get in front of everyone going in your direction. In all urban areas, there appear to be local byelaws obliging all vehicle drivers to use their horns. Some horns are presumably hard-wired in the on position to save wrist fatigue. A full set of lights on your vehicle at night doesn't appear to be obligatory and marks you out as a show-off.

These observations are, of course, tongue in cheek, but road traffic accidents are a serious issue that cause thousands of deaths and injuries each year. In India, you will find 1 per cent of the world's vehicles, but according to the World Health Organisation, those vehicles account for 6 per cent of the world's road traffic accidents. There are around 400 deaths per day on Indian roads. Most of the accidents involve young drivers, with speeding and driving on the wrong side of the road being amongst the leading causes. Driving at night is another contributory factor. I came across these unfortunate statistics just before setting out at night on a long taxi ride with our young driver.

Right on cue, at 5:00 am, our taxi driver came to pick us up from our Aurangabad hotel in his little white hatchback car. When we got outside, it was so cold that Nick dashed back to our room to get more clothes. We set off in the dark and freezing cold of the morning. Nick took up the co-pilot seat while I sprawled across the back seat. We seemed to fall into this configuration for all our drives in India. I guess it reflects Nick's more gregarious character and my need to spread out my old bones. Our driver, Rahul, turned out to be a bubbly and chatty companion, which was a good sign – it provided ongoing reassurance that he was awake. He set off as if his life depended on breaking the Aurangabad to Lonar road speed record. As we made the jump to light speed, he gave us a running commentary on places we couldn't see as we whistled past them in the dark. He could answer any question we could think of, except the one about why his car heater wasn't working on such a chilly morning. An icy draught forced its way from the boot into a sizeable gap between the rear seat and the backrest, to which, ideally, it should have been attached. After ten minutes, I gave up looking for something to fill the gap or trying to re-position the seat. I wasn't keen on the thought of having to perch on the front edge of my seat for six hours travelling, so I sat back and joined in with the lively conversation coming from the front of the car. This was a distraction strategy that I hoped would keep my mind off the temperature until either the sun rose, or I succumbed giggling and carefree into the inevitable icy numbness of hypothermia.

Unlike his car, Rahul was a warm and likeable guy. He loved to talk about his family, his country, and anything else he could think of. Our driver was 31 years old with a wife and three young girls. He told us how his mother had chosen his wife for him, following Indian tradition. According to Rahul, around 70 per cent of marriages in India are still arranged. He reckoned it was the 30 per cent of 'love marriages' that were the ones most likely to fail. He summed it up with a simple statement, 'You know, Mums will arrange, and Mums know best.' Well, it's difficult to argue with that.

Nick and I reeled from a barrage of comic anecdotes, political outpourings, and non-essential tourist trivia. Rahul was relentless and very funny. If I hadn't been scared speechless by his driving, I'm sure I would have remembered more of his prodigious output. One snippet that stuck in my mind, however, was the story about his favourite meal. It was cow biryani. This anecdote was clearly a well-rehearsed favourite of his, and he could hardly contain himself as he approached the punchline. He just about got himself composed enough to say... 'You see – this is alright in India because I am Muslim.' At this point he threw his head back and burst into uncontrolled laughter, thumping the steering wheel several times. I filed that one away for later recollection. As I began to slur my words with the temperature dropping further, I left Nick to cope with the small talk; a task for which he has a natural aptitude.

After we'd been on the road for about an hour, with still no sign of sunrise, Rahul suggested we could stop for some chai, which seemed a great idea. I'm not sure why his car heater wasn't working, or why the back of his car was so draughty, but for whatever reason, I would have slowly faded away without that chai stop. We pulled over to a roadside café beside a large gravel lay-by, somewhere in the middle of nowhere, and still in the dark. Also parked there was a row of huge and very colourful Indian long-haul lorries. The drivers were presumably catching some sleep.

My use of the word café might be generous; there was a pot of chai bubbling away on a long wooden bench, under a flimsy white gazebo. Two grubby white plastic chairs awaited potential customers, and the chai maker had clipped a light bulb to one leg of the gazebo so he could see what he was doing. The wire for the light led down to a car battery, to which it was tethered by a couple of bulldog clips. A small, enclosed metal fire pit half full of charcoal sat on the wooden bench, keeping a pot of boiling chai up to temperature. Down on the ground, in the gravel at the roadside end of the wooden bench, was a small log fire. We all made a beeline for it. Nick and I were treated like royalty. By that I mean we were given the two grubby white plastic chairs and a special chai brew that didn't contain sugar. The 'classic' standard chai is heavily sweetened.

Now and again the café owner would blow hard into the charcoal pit with some bellows and send a spectacular firework display of sparks high up into the sky. There was quite a lot of laughter and banter between Rahul and the chai maker. I expect it was mostly at the expense of the pale male foreign visitors, but it was all good fun and we felt warmed by both the fire and the welcome. It was an impressive scene, and not one you're likely to come across in an M6 service station.

A lorry driver came over, out of the darkness, to join us round the fire. His name was Sandeep, and he squatted down almost in the fire in his attempt to get warm, dressed only in a flimsy tee shirt, shorts, and flip-flops. He was a mere slip of a lad; I couldn't imagine him being able to see over the steering wheel of a lorry.

Early morning tea at a roadside service station

Rahul explained we were on a trunk road and the lay-by was a popular spot for lorry drivers trucking backwards and forwards across India. Sandeep was on a two-day trip hauling bricks on a 500-mile journey from Mumbai. You'd think there would be brick factories at closer intervals than 500 miles apart, but it didn't seem the right time to discuss it. Sandeep seemed quiet and distant, not really in the mood to debate the economics of building material distribution.

He was possibly lost in thought, pondering why the hell he had to drive 500 miles with a load of bricks when surely there must be brickworks nearer to his destination. I felt a Proclaimers moment coming on and considered a quick burst of '...and I would drive 500 miles...', but I thought it would be lost on Sandeep, and with Nick having disappeared into the darkness for a wee, the moment passed. Body re-heated, Sandeep eventually drifted back to his lorry, but his place was soon taken up by another trucker looking for a bit of warmth.

When we were back in the car, Rahul told us that when they stop overnight somewhere, it's not unknown for some lorry drivers to pass the time by getting off their faces on weed. I'm paraphrasing his explanation slightly, but that was the gist of it.

We got underway again, with the novel experience of once again being able to feel all body extremities. Before long, the first warming rays of morning sunshine spilled out across shimmering fields of golden wheat. As the sun rose, so did my spirits. As well as bringing much needed warmth to the new day, we could now see where we were going. I no longer had to worry about thumping headlong into unlit and unseen vehicles coming the other way when Rahul performed his overtaking manoeuvres. To compensate for that, I now had the nagging worry that some lorries thundering past us in the opposite direction might be driven by guys as high as kites.

In my limited experience, someone who comes across Indian driving for the first time goes through three stages of reaction. Stage one is an initial speechless terror, closely followed by a thought or comment like, 'Surely this can't be happening?' The next stage involves semi-delirious, nervous laughter, which comes with the realisation that it *is* happening, and everyone is doing it... and mostly they're getting away with it. In the ultimate stage, the newcomer becomes enveloped in emotional numbness as conscious reactions shut down. A fatalistic resignation takes over. It's happening and there's nothing that can be done about it. I reached stage three by around 8:00 am, just as we reached Lonar.

Rahul took us to the tourist office where he introduced us to a man called Vaibhav, who was to be our official guide for the visit to the meteorite crater. Nick and I didn't know we were getting a guide, but as things turned out, it was a good idea to have one. Rahul drove the three of us a couple of kilometres to the edge of the crater and then drove off, leaving us to begin our descent.

When I was doing my research before the trip, I read up about the meteorite crater on a well-known travel website and discovered 'Only those with a keen sense of visiting offbeat places, appear to be visiting this place.' Lonar meteor crater won't be on everyone's list of sights to see in India, but it's a fascinating place and well worth a visit if you like unspoilt nature and rare geological features. When I say unspoilt, perhaps the violent impact of a high velocity meteorite arriving from outer space around 50,000 years ago would be enough to spoil anyone's day.

The entire spectacle of the meteorite crater is laid out in front of you as you stand on the rim and wonder at the view. The crater is 1.8 kilometres in diameter and 4.0 kilometres in circumference. It was quite a sight, with a rim that rises 20 m above the surrounding land surface and 60 m of cliffs that lead down to the base which contains an extremely saline lake.

The day had taken a while to warm up, but the sun was making up for lost time as we made our way down the sides of the crater. We followed a footpath that weaved a lazy path through verdant woodland on the steep inner face of the rim. Our excellent guide, Vaibhav, reeled off a list of facts and the story behind the crater. It was one of only three such craters in the world and was formed by a meteorite that impacted with a force equivalent to sixty times the Hiroshima nuclear bomb. The meteorite is still down there under the lake somewhere, and the subject of regular scientific probes. Moderately lush, wooded slopes gradually morphed into dense jungle, from which came a steady soundtrack of exotic bird and animal noises. It felt like we were entering our own Jurassic Park. Continuing down, we passed several of the fourteen semi-ruined, stone-built temples that lie within the crater. They just lie there, abandoned, and unprotected, for anyone to walk in and explore. I thought for a second that I was going to have an Indiana Jones moment. Nick tried his best to rise to the occasion by swinging Tarzan style, impressively for his age, on some tree creepers. Fortunately, no harm came to Nick or the environment. Vaibhav stepped away as if he wasn't really with us. I think Nick only did it for the photo opportunity, but that's what happens when you take an excitable pensioner out of the Highlands for more than a week.

By the time we got to the base of the crater, the vegetation had disappeared, and a flat circular floor opened out. We walked towards the lake over hard and cracked grey mud, and Vaibhav turned the conversation to the wildlife that lived down there. We caught sight of some peacocks, flamingos, and golden ducks. Although we didn't see any in the flesh, we saw the tracks of some wild boar and a leopard – the former being the meal of choice for the latter. As we admired the lake shimmering in the morning sun, a flamboyance of pink flamingos disturbed the mirror-flat calm of the surface, rising lazily and silently into the air in slow motion. We'd walked into a David Attenborough documentary.

We thought we had the crater to ourselves, but nine very

excitable teenage lads approached us and disturbed the calm of the morning. They seemed to think it was an absolute hoot to come across a couple of old white duffers. They were extremely friendly, however, and just wanted to say hello and get a photo with us... well, who wouldn't? The boys were army cadets based in the village of Lonar, and they were undergoing training before becoming professionals. The cadets had been down in the crater for their morning run and were trying to cover 1,500 metres in six minutes because that was the standard they had to reach before they could sign up (I think those were the numbers). Nick informed them we were fellow athletes and could easily do that sort of distance in the time. That slight exaggeration seemed to reduce the lads to fits of uncontrollable laughter, and then they wanted more selfies.

Nick and I took photos of the lake and then set off for the top of the crater again, aware of the short time we had. Making myself heard over a chorus of fruit bats, I made the mistake of asking our guide about snakes. 'Yes, of course, there are lots of snakes' he said, as if the question didn't need asking. Just what I wanted to hear (I'm not a big fan) ... but thankfully we didn't see any.

People coming the other way and wanting to be photographed with us were regular interruptions as we meandered our way back to the top. At least it gave Nick and me the excuse to catch our breath without looking like we needed to stop. We knew by then, of course, that this was more than just our fifteen minutes of fame. In India we were selfie superstars. Nick was provided with rich entertainment when I realised that I'd left a jumper at one of the stone temples. I had to re-trace my steps and do most of the descent and ascent again while he relaxed and chatted with Vaibhav.

When we reached the road at the crater rim, Nick, and I

met up with our driver, Rahul, again. We gave our thanks and said farewells to Vaibhav. We had to get back to Aurangabad, and then out to Ellora, so there was no time to hang around. It was a dilemma; we had little time to spare, but if I mentioned it to Rahul, he'd drive even more recklessly than usual. I needn't have worried; Rahul knew what he had to do. We sped back to Aurangabad at Mach one, even venturing onto the left side of the road occasionally if we needed to. I can't recall much of the journey back to Aurangabad, but I might have had my eyes shut.

We headed out towards the town of Ellora, which is only about 36 kilometres north-west from Aurangabad, for part two of our day's sightseeing. Halfway there, Rahul found us a little café where we had yet another excellent meal before continuing to Ellora to meet up with another guide.

Sahil was a 36-year-old locally born guy who had been showing people around the Ellora caves for most of his working life. I liked him immediately; he was an amiable chap, intelligent and with an obvious passion for his work. We only had about two hours until the closing time at 6:00 pm, so Sahil gave us a quick overview, asked us what we wanted to see and worked out how we could best use our limited time. Clinical efficiency – I liked his style.

The Ellora caves, which date back over 2,000 years, are one of India's thirty-eight UNESCO World Heritage locations. They are one of India's most popular tourist sights, with up to 20,000 visitors per day in the peak season, which is November to March. One cave contains the largest single monolithic rock excavation in the world, the Kailasanatha Temple, dedicated to Lord Shiva. The breathtaking sight has been described as one of the most remarkable cave temples in the world and the climax of the rock-cut phase of Indian architecture. I'll explain more when we get to cave number sixteen.

Ellora has been on an important trading route for thousands of years. For centuries, caravans travelled through the area between the west coast ports and the prosperous cities in the north of India. The topography and geology of the area were key to its development; the landscape and the rock were just about perfect for making caves and temples. At Ellora, there was a long stretch of 30-metre-high cliff face made of smooth-grained dark basalt. The rock was soft enough to shape but hard enough to endure. I couldn't help but think the location would have been a handy distribution point for bricks had someone thought about it, saving many a drug-crazed 500-mile overnight road trip.

A hundred caves and thirty-four temples are carved into an escarpment that sweeps round in a long semicircle, stretching for almost two kilometres. As the cliff face progresses, it forms a topographic timeline displaying the different styles of cave and temple building by different religious groups. The Buddhists were the first to build caves at Ellora and when they left, for whatever reason, the Hindus moved into the next available section of cliff and built a new set of caves and temples. When they vacated, the Jains moved in and occupied the rest of the escarpment. I'm generalising a complex process that took place over centuries, and it probably wasn't so conveniently time sliced as that, but that's the gist of it.

Sahil began our Ellora tour at the southern end of the escarpment, furthest away from the entrance to the complex, at the twelve oldest caves. Buddhists had excavated and occupied this group between the 7th and 8th centuries. Caves thirteen to twenty-nine are the Hindu caves. Although you could tell it was hurting his professional pride to do so, Sahil skipped many of the caves and picked out some of the more spectacular ones. I felt we were insulting both Sahil and his beloved heritage site by treating the visit so flippantly.

What must leave every visitor incredulous is how those fabulously complex and elaborate temples were carved out of solid basalt cliffs by hand. My fumbling description can't do it justice – the carvings and intricate artwork were just breathtakingly beautiful. The most famous of the caves and top visitor attraction is the magnificent Kailasanatha Temple, which, as already mentioned – is the world's largest monolith, and oldest single rock carving. Sahil steered us past this one, and we headed to caves thirty to thirty-four, which are the Jain caves. Again, the intricate carvings were beautiful, and it hurt to keep moving without giving them more attention. Sahil knew what he was doing, though, and had timed our visit to perfection. We arrived back at the Kailasanatha Temple at precisely 5:55 pm. Nick and I felt unreasonably privileged as the security staff ushered the last remaining tourists, apart from us, out of the area. Sahil was clearly a friend of theirs. Apart from a group of a dozen maroon clad monks, we had the place to ourselves, and it was a jaw-dropping spectacle.

The Kailasanatha Temple is one of the most impressive sights we saw in India, and we really should have spent longer there to do it justice – I should just cut that sentence out now and paste it into the description of everywhere we went. When it was built, the temple was intended to depict Mount Kailasa, which is in Western Tibet, and the sacred home of Lord Shiva, the Destroyer, and third deity in the Hindu holy trinity (with Brahma and Vishnu). The temple stands boldly and magnificently, all turrets, arches and obelisks, surrounded on three sides by the 30-metre-high rock cliffs from which it was carved.

Kailasanatha Temple

Let me confuse you with a few dimensions – the temple complex is approximately 84 metres long and 47 metres wide. It is 30 metres high. To get some idea of what that looks like, imagine a dark grey temple about the size of the Parthenon in Athens, made up of a series of interconnected rooms, halls, and shrines decorated with ornate pillars, domes, and sculptured panels. But here's the killer fact – instead of being built from the ground up, they carved the temple from solid rock, from the top down. That involved the sculptors working their way through about 85,000 cubic metres of rock – if that means anything to anyone. If my back of a fag-packet calculation is right, that's enough to fill approximately thirty-four Olympic sized swimming pools – which of course makes a lot more sense. Sahil took us around the temple and eked out every second he thought he could get away with as the security chaps waited patiently. Again, we felt so guilty that we were dashing around; it didn't seem respectful enough for such incredible examples of human engineering, art, and devotion. When we couldn't stay any longer, Sahil took us back to the town, and we said our goodbyes.

Nick and I looked around the many gift shops in the town of Ellora. He was in seventh heaven when he found a shop selling rocks, gemstones and crystals. The geologist owner and Nick immediately hit it off. If we hadn't got our *Journey through India* to complete, they would still be chatting now. It almost goes without saying that having a travelling partner with a doctorate in geology is an immense privilege and advantage. Apart from knowing a monolithic basalt column or a hypervelocity meteorite crater when he sees one, Nick could spot a genuine crystal or rare gemstone at ten paces. The jewellery in the gemstone shop looked beautiful, at least to my uneducated eye, but at least I had an expert with me. You can probably see where this is going.

Buying my wife's presents so early on the trip wasn't my best decision. I knew I'd have to carry them around India on my back for another four weeks, but then again, I might not see such gemstones again, or get such a bargain. Which ones should I go for? Torn between the tiger eye, garnet and green jade necklaces, I went completely crazy and splashed out on all three. I wasn't sure who to give the garnet beauty to, but I thought our daughter Sarah would love the golden and red-brown colours of the tiger eye gemstones. My wife, Jan, would appreciate the delicate colouring of the jade... also known as the stone of fortune. Those beautiful greens mainly come from traces of chromium and vanadium or iron, and I had the comfort of knowing that even if Jan didn't like them, she would at least appreciate the gemstone's reputation for bringing wealth and success to its owner.

Let's fast forward several weeks... 'Oh Jan, that's a beautiful necklace you've been wearing all evening, but it seems to have left a light green stain around your neck.' A thorough wash under a hot tap and all colour soon disappeared from the necklace. Jan and I watched in disbelief as her chances of wealth and success drained down the plughole and out of sight. Jan's elegant jewellery had morphed into a string of dull, slightly stained, white stones. More jaded than jade. On this occasion, the fortune associated with the gemstone was confined to its first owner. I wasn't sure what the shop's returns policy was, but I don't think it would have been cost effective to go back and seek compensation. We had a laugh and put it down to experience. Instead, I thought I needed a chat with my old mate, and renowned geology expert, Nick.

Back to India – we left Ellora at dusk and rattled back to our hotel in Aurangabad by tuk-tuk. Another curry, another beer, another very short sleep, and we were up early the next morning to move on to Udaipur. As with so many of our stopovers, it had passed in a flash.

UDAIPUR

It was different by the end of our five-week adventure, for me at least, but on day six our energy levels were still high, and we were still very much raring to go. Nick and I were straight into another day of travelling, and more sightseeing. The plan involved getting to Aurangabad airport early in the morning to fly up to Udaipur. Arriving in time for breakfast, we'd have most of the day and the whole of the following day to look around the City of Lakes. In theory, at least, having the best part of two days in one place would give us the chance to catch our breath after a hectic start to our trip. Nick had been to Udaipur before, so we had a reasonable idea of where to go and how long it would take. As it turned out, we still tried to do too much in the time available, of course.

Our taxi driver picked us up at 5:00 am again, as arranged, to take us to the airport. He decided it would be fair enough to charge us the equivalent of £5 for the two-kilometre drive to Aurangabad airport after charging us £1.50 the previous night to drive us three times that distance from the train station to our hotel. If we'd done our home-work and checked where the airport was, we'd have realised it was within walking distance of the hotel. When we queried the charge, our driver gave us a rambling and incomprehensible justification for his pricing policy – something to do with unsociable hours and fluctuations in the diurnal transport demand coefficient. He didn't really say that: his English wasn't that good, but I think that was the gist of his explanation. We let it go. The poor old UK pensioner argument wouldn't wash in India, and rightly so, and really... is there any point in arguing the toss at that price, and at that time of morning? No, Nick, let it go.

We had our bags security checked in a big scanner as soon as we were through the main doors at the airport. It was our first internal flight in India, so we weren't sure what to expect. Going through the security check at the same time were two young cabin crew from the Indian airline 'Spice Jet.' Both girls were super friendly and smiley, in fact, ridiculously so for that time of day. They must have been running on high energy caffeine drinks. Somehow, the Spice Girls showed sufficient self-restraint to resist asking us for a selfie. We almost felt offended. I had a quick flashback to my Aptitudinal Determinism theory, prompted by the Indian Railways chai walla on the Aurangabad express... were these girls smiley and warm because they had to be like that to survive in their job, or was it their naturally sunny disposition that got them the job? Either way, their charm and energy spiced up an otherwise routine morning in the airport.

We checked in without further incident and went through to a second security scan. I went straight through, but Nick had to go through three times. Each time the security guard took more items out of Nick's hand luggage, presumably, in case he'd picked up a couple of duty-free AK-47's in the tax-free shopping area after going through the first scanner. The serious-looking army chap on security duty seemed concerned about Nick's potentially unstable combination of AAA batteries and Bombay mix. I guess that's a mixture that could do a lot of damage in the wrong hands. He didn't seem so happy with Nick's pocketknife either.

We had an uneventful flight, the sort I prefer, and arrived at Udaipur airport at 8:45 am, just over one hour after leaving Aurangabad. We were in Rajasthan, a name with a grand and imperial ring to it. It conjures up images of maharajas' palaces, forts, deserts, tigers, and elephants. We didn't see any of those at the airport.

Now then, talking of volatile combinations... I've had to deliberate how to write this next paragraph, and even whether I should write it at all. The squeamish, and those not comfortable with discussions of bodily functions, should look away now. Do yourselves a favour and fast forward to the next paragraph. Udaipur airport, and more precisely the gents' toilets, will always remain special to Dr Nick. Eight curries and three breakfasts after arriving in India, he finally dispatched his first 'number twos' on the subcontinent. There was much rejoicing on the streets of Udaipur that day... not so much amongst the workers in the Public Works water treatment facility. For travellers concerned about the effects of sudden changes in diet, this may or may not be reassuring, but it gives me a cheap joke at Nick's expense. Let's quickly move on.

Acting on a tip-off from a passenger that Nick met on the flight, we downloaded the Uber taxi app onto our phones. Although Nick and I are both reasonably technology literate, we are also country bumpkins, so neither of us had any experience of Uber. I fired up the app and typed in the hotel's name we'd booked and waited to see what would happen. Almost immediately, I got a message back to say a car was on its way. We walked out of the arrivals terminal just in time to see the car pull up. Very impressive. We popped our bags in the boot. Nick took up his customary position in the front passenger seat of the car while I spread myself out across the rear seats. The driver spoke excellent English and was very efficient. Until that is, Nick and I made the mistake of trying to put our seat belts on. What were we thinking? The driver said, 'Please Sir, there is no point putting those on, there is no tension.' For the time of day, I felt quite smug with my riposte of 'Sorry pal, but from what I've seen of Indian driving, I beg to differ.' It was lost on the driver, but I think I detected a quiet appreciative chuckle from my pal.

We checked into our hotel, which was near to the city centre, and the owner invited us up to the rooftop terrace for some breakfast. Everything about the hotel was superb. It was clean and beautifully decorated with hand-painted murals of flowers and exotic Indian scenes. My favourite was a mural of a giant blue elephant. I'm going to skip a potential chapter's worth of text on elephant symbology in Hindu art, but let's just leave it for now as representing good luck, wealth, and prosperity.

I can't move on entirely, however, without mentioning the revered and much-loved Hindu god Ganesha, because he soon became a welcome companion on our adventure. Nick and I first came across Ganesha in the market stalls of Mumbai. He's the Hindu deity with an enormous elephant's head and a potbellied human body. Ganesha is the son of Shiva (Lord of destruction) and Parvati (Goddess of fertility, love, beauty, marriage, children, and devotion). I can explain the elephant's head, which might at first seem odd. The full story is complex and more nuanced than my simplified version, but the following few lines are how I've interpreted various explanations. Ganesha had been with Parvati in her bathroom, and for a while, Shiva had not been allowed in.

Shiva had never seen his son Ganesha until that moment. When he eventually got into the bathroom, he cut his son's head off in a fit of bad temper. Realising what he had done, Shiva was full of remorse. He asked Lord Brahma (creator of the Universe) to bring back the head of the first creature he encountered. Brahma returned with the head of an elephant, so Shiva placed it onto Ganesha's body and brought him back to life.

Nick and I discovered that Ganesha's job description, while complicated, has two main strands. He is the remover of obstacles, and deity of choice for bringing good luck to new beginnings. Both seemed very appropriate for setting out on an adventure across the subcontinent, so we thought of him being with us for the next five weeks. We'd pay our respects whenever we saw a Ganesha Temple, and in return, hopefully, but without our presuming, he might bring good luck to our venture. We had enjoyed such a smooth introduction to India at the airport and then meeting Preet, that we felt Ganesha might even have been with us from the start.

Udaipur is a lovely place, and perhaps more Western friendly than many other places in India. I quickly need to explain that, and I'll try to do so without making things worse. Some aspects of India are harrowing and not for the faint-hearted. My wife would love to visit India but was so worried about how she would react to the poverty and squalor that she chose not to go. I understand that, and those aspects are extremely challenging. I'm sure Udaipur has its fair share of those things but in my brief experience, the areas we visited, hotels we saw, the restaurants, and tourist sites we went to, were of a standard that Westerners would find less of a culture shock than many other places in India.

Udaipur is variously known as the City of Lakes, the

Land of the Dawn, the Venice of the East, and the City of Romance. Along with Jaipur, it is the third most visited tourist location in India, after Delhi and Agra. It certainly has a romantic setting.

Udaipur

Not wanting to do things by halves, the city has two palaces: the magnificent City Palace, which overlooks Lake Pichola and dominates the city, and the Lake Palace Hotel, on an island in the lake. The City Palace has been described as one of the architectural wonders of Rajasthan. It has been developed over four centuries by successive generations of the Mewar dynasty and now stands over Udaipur as a vast fortress-like architectural statement, tall and impressive and overlooking the tranquil Lake Pichola. Large parts of the palace are a subtle yellow; others look like the ornately iced tiers of a white wedding cake. The Aravalli mountain range provides a photogenic backdrop.

The Lake Palace Hotel, which occupies the larger of two

islands on the lake, is one of *the* iconic images of India, and is undoubtedly one of the most photographed buildings in the country. From the mid-18th century, the Palace on the island was the summer residence of the Maharanas of Udaipur. In 1963 it became a hotel, and in 1983 it became famous worldwide as the lair of the James Bond villain Octopussy (oh, *that* palace on an island – now you know where I mean).

From the hotel's rooftop restaurant, where Nick and I had breakfast, the City Palace seemed a near neighbour, although it was about a kilometre away. On other rooftops around us, the people of Udaipur worked and played, bathed in mid-morning sunshine. An old woman in a green sari hung out the washing, two children giggled excitedly as they ran around chasing each other, and a teenage girl soaked up the sun in a deck chair with headphones on and eyes shut – lost in her music. It was a beautiful, warm day. The view was stunning, and the breakfast delightful. After a couple of very busy days, I suddenly felt relaxed. Ganesha must have been with us. Nick and I took our time and had another coffee.

I got the guidebook out and spread the map of Udaipur over the breakfast table. 'City Palace, Nick?' I suggested, thinking it was an obvious starting point for our tour. Nick thought for a second and then came back with, 'Home win.' 'Very good Nick – very sharp' I said, 'for your age.' For the record, the English Premier League game between Manchester City and Crystal Palace was played five days later at the Etihad Stadium, Manchester, and was a 2-2 draw.

We reviewed and fine-tuned a comprehensive sight-seeing plan for the day ahead, assessing numerous alternatives and considering each on its merit. We decided to look around the City Palace and take it from there. On our leisurely walk to our sightseeing starting point, we stopped off at a hotel where Nick and his wife Ellen had stayed three years earlier. Showing typical Indian hospitality, the owner treated Nick like a long-lost family member, and we were treated to morning tea and a long friendly chat. The owner recommended an Indian cultural dance show that was taking place in the city that evening. It had been sold out long ago, but of course, that was no problem. The hotel's fixer set about using his contacts to get us tickets. I can't go into details, and I'm not even sure I know what happened anyway, but it happened.

The City Palace is a stunning piece of architecture comprising eleven adjoining palaces and covering an area of over two hectares, which is around three football pitches for people whose minds work like that. It dominates the city, and like many of the forts and palaces we saw, it was a display of power by the rulers to those they ruled. Work to build the palace began in 1553, and it evolved over the centuries. Seamlessly combining Rajasthani and Mughal styles, the building looks down imperiously from its hilltop position over the city on three sides and Lake Pichola on the other. Since its creation, the City Palace has been the home to successive maharanas from the Mewar dynasty. The titles 'maharana' and 'maharaja' are a bit confusing, or they were for me, so before I describe how Nick and I shuffled our way slowly round the City Palace, maybe I should attempt to explain those exotic sounding titles. I'll keep it simple and hope it doesn't add to anyone's confusion.

The administrative areas known as Indian states, sometimes called kingdoms, or princely states, go back centuries, way before the Brits arrived. There was once a patchwork of hundreds of states, varying in size, status, religion, culture, and wealth. There were various titles for the rulers, including raja, maharaja, maharana, and in the case of the Muslim states – nawab. The title 'maharana' is associated with the rulers of the Udaipur, or Mewar state. By the time India became a British colony in 1858, with some exceptions, the name maharaja had become accepted as a generic title for rulers of all states. The British let the maharajas keep their kingdoms and some administrative power. They could maintain order, continue their involvement with cultural traditions, raise taxes, and allocate taxed monies. That was it though. They were still subject to colonial rule like everyone else, and they were to be known as princes instead of kings. The British 'divide and rule' policy rewarded those maharajas who recognised and complied with British rule and cracked down on those who didn't. British tutors educated the more favoured maharajas in Europe or India. Many of the new princes adopted Western dress – suits instead of traditional Indian attire – and they embraced fashionable pursuits such as driving posh cars, playing polo, hunting foxes, and flying aircraft.

The role of the maharaja survived after independence in 1947, but they disbanded the states under the newly unified country of India. The Indian government provided an annual 'privy purse' allowance, but in 1971, Prime Minister Indira Gandhi took that away as well. Several former rulers still had palaces and forts to maintain, and over the years, they have had to diversify and find alternative incomes. Some have converted their properties into hotels or museums, or both. The Mewar royal family of Udaipur still owns the City Palace and has separated part of it into a tourist attraction, maintained by various trusts, and part into hotels (The Fateh Prakash and Shiv Niwas Palaces).

Nick and I looked around the part of the City Palace that's open to visitors. We hired a guide and set off. Back in the parallel universe of Manchester, the City Palace game drew a crowd of 54,439 in January 2020, and there seemed to be the same number of people following Nick and me from room to room in Udaipur's principal tourist attraction. Had we realised the number of fellow tourists who would visit at the same time as us, we might have dressed more appropriately – as sardines, perhaps. For the first time on our trip, we found ourselves surrounded by masses of tourists, and looking back at the end of our journey, the City Palace was the most crowded place we visited in India, even more so than the Taj Mahal.

Our guide was polite and helpful, but he was clearly getting us around and out as quickly as possible. It was a contrast to our friend Sahil from the Ellora caves – who gave us the best possible experience and was generous with his time and knowledge. In the City Palace, Nick and I felt we were just the latest in a long line of visitors who had to be processed, which we were, and we had no grounds for complaint: we were adding to the crowds ourselves!

The masses of fellow tourists didn't detract from the utter awesomeness of the palace. Far better writers than me will struggle to describe it in a way that does it justice. It's hard for non-royals to get their heads around the sheer opulence and extravagance on display when looking around any palace, but Indian palaces seem to take excess to new levels and the City Palace is as sumptuous, glittery, and jewel-encrusted as they come. The former occupants must have had more money than they could find things to spend it on. They bought the best of the best, and lots of it.

Even the cut down version of the City Palace, without the hotel part, felt enormous. Nick and I wandered, open-mouthed, between rooms that ranged from elegant, full of fine silks and tapestries, to completely over the top, with jewellery and gold and mirrors covering every surface. The tour takes you through spectacular archways into cool courtyards and back into sumptuously decorated chambers. Some rooms were an overdose of exotic colour. Between ornate marble columns, works of art hung on walls that were a riot of pure gold, silks, mirrors, and coloured glass. Most of the rooms were decorated with great taste and style but from time to time I thought 'Wait a minute: this is pushing the blingometer off the scale.' The palace was adorned with countless towers, balconies, and cupolas, and as we shuffled our way around with the other tourists, we regularly emerged onto yet another veranda, with breath-taking views over the city, the lake, and the island.

Everything about the Palace was opulent and extreme. I'll never look at the magnolia walls of our hall and living room back home the same way again. It was exceptional, but to see the extraordinary and the different is one of the reasons why we travel.

Nearly all the other tourists on the City Palace tour appeared to be Indian. There was a wide age range and many families. I'm generalising as usual, but they had a thing about taking photographs... hundreds of them. The sad part about it, looking from the outside, was that so many visitors spent all their time looking for the next photo opportunity: they probably didn't notice where they'd just been or what they'd seen. The reassuring approval of a friend, in the form of a Facebook 'like,' was presumably more important than soaking up the significance of the place and its history in real time. The go-to poses adopted by most young women were cute and pouting, or beaming with wide eyes and hair tossed back. I guess some Bolly-wood celebrities have set the trend. The lads were just as bad. The millennial boys liked to strike up a mean and moody pose – arms folded and staring meaningfully into the distance through cool shades. Despite their preoccupation with the search for the perfect photo, hundreds of them still found time to ask Nick and me for a selfie.

At the end of the tour, we found ourselves deposited in a

courtyard where former rulers used to park their elephants. It's a residential feature you don't come across much back home. It was also, by some bizarre coincidence, next to the souvenir shop. Their little marketing ploy wasn't very subtle, but it worked; I came away with a magnificent linen shirt to add more weight to my backpack. We felt mentally and physically battered after a couple of hours of intense sight-seeing... well, it was a lot of stairs for a couple of sixty-year-olds. Our senses had been assaulted from the palace experience and our nerves worn thin from the overwhelming number of tourists. It was time to chill out with a boat ride.

We calmed down with ice creams in the shade of a lake-side palm tree and then joined twenty other tourists for a trip around Lake Pichola and its two islands. It was rather sedate and relaxing. Our captain took us around the Lake Palace Hotel (the Octopussy lair) on Jag Niwas and then dropped us off on the smaller Jag Mandir island for a quiet walk around. I loved the boat ride; it was so nice to calm down in some wide-open space after the City Palace visit. The gentle pace of the boat and the quiet ripple of the water were very soothing. The views of the city and the islands, as we serenely motored along, were stunning. Under clear skies, the water appeared bright blue, and the sun sparkled on the tiny wavelets to give a perfect foreground to our photos of the city and the islands. The only slightly odd thing about the experience was having to wear lifejackets labelled 'Trident IX Monrovia.' When I looked it up later, I found out it was an oil rig service ship. Well, that's OK then.

We returned to our hotel to get changed and left for our night out. We flagged down a passing tuk-tuk to take us to the cultural dance show just as the evening was becoming dark. Our journey to the venue took us via narrow streets packed with souvenir shops, and alongside some lakeside ghats, busy with people enjoying the warm evening. When we arrived, we asked to see the person whose name they had given us at the hotel. It seemed a bit cloak and dagger... back to Octopussy. They waved us in and took us past the long queue of other visitors to our seats. As simple as that... don't ask how or why, but thank you!

The one-hour performance took place in front of an intimately packed audience of about 300 people. I looked around and saw no other grey heads apart from mine; all the others there were jet black or belonged to Nick. Maybe that's why we kept getting asked for selfies – we were a couple of freaks. The performance was mainly a series of dances in the Rajasthan tradition, with a bit of puppetry and singing thrown in. Taking photos was not permitted unless you bought a licence for the occasion – an interesting little extra revenue-earner. Once the show was in full swing, some of the audience reached for their phones as an automatic reaction. I don't think it was a conscious decision: a hand just pulled out a phone and took a picture without its owner realising what had happened. They couldn't help themselves. The show was very entertaining, and the artists looked like they were having as much fun as the audience. The highlight was a very energetic dance featuring a woman with a cooking pot on her head. As the music gathered pace, someone added another pot. There was a gasp from the audience every time another pot was added, until there were twelve perched precariously on her head as she gyrated across the stage. She looked mightily relieved when the music came to its climax, and they rapidly removed the twelve pots, one by one, still intact.

After the show, we headed into the darkness of night and found a fantastic restaurant with a rooftop dining area. This was one that Nick had researched, and the boy had done good. The restaurant was right next to Fateh Sagar Lake, and the scene in front of us was quite breathtaking.

You could see why they used the location for a Bond film. Our view took in a wide sweep of the lake including the opposite side. The lights on the waterside buildings shimmered and sparkled in the inky black water. One hotel opposite had some spectacular cauldrons of fire, with flames leaping high into the air. Strains of Indian music drifted across the water. It was the sort of romantic setting that was wasted on a couple of old duffers. We clinked a couple of Kingfisher bottles and drank to absent wives.

As we left the restaurant and made our way back to our hotel, we ran the gauntlet of shop owners trying to sell us clothes, rugs, paintings, and trinkets. Nick remembered a shop that he'd been to on his previous visit, and we made the mistake of going in. We got chatting to the owner, who remembered Nick, of course (he said), and we narrowly avoided buying a £75 Kashmir pashmina, which of course '... would cost £400 in the UK, maybe more.' We made our excuses and left – it would have been too heavy to carry around for the rest of the trip. My first day in the City of Lakes had left a huge impression on me.

Our second day in Udaipur was going to be one of leisurely sightseeing. To enable this, we used the services of a tuk-tuk driver called Krishna, who Nick had met on his trip to the city three years previously. Nick keeps copious notes in his diary, so it was easy for him to look up his previous visit and retrieve Krishna's contact details.

Before Krishna picked us up at 10:30 am, Nick and I had the pleasure of breakfast with the owner of the hotel in which we were staying. He came over for a chat and then just stayed with us for the best part of an hour. He said he was married to a foreign woman, which gave Nick and I the chance to discuss Indian weddings once again. 'So, yours was a "love" marriage then,' asked Nick. 'Oh my god, that was my big mistake!' came the instant reply, as he threw his hands in the air and guffawed with laughter. After a brief pause for reflection, maybe trying to remember where he'd last seen his wife, he followed up with, 'Just joking, of course!' He then talked about the expectations of having an arranged marriage and all the family politics involved. It was an interesting supplement the conversation with our taxi driver in Aurangabad. Despite changing values and Western influences, there are still many parts of the country where the subject is very delicate, and there is enormous resistance to cultural change – to the point of extreme violence against people proposing any form of variation from the traditional approach. It's a serious subject. There are many problems with the way women are treated in some parts of India, as in other parts of the world, and this was our first real chance to discuss the matter.

On a lighter note, the owner gave us an entertaining account of when the American White House chief of staff visited the city and stayed in his hotel. He told us how the eight security guards were armed to the teeth, and each one could take on 500 people. I imagine that would necessitate a James Bond-like fight scene, where each ferocious baddie patiently waits in the wings to take on the hero one at a time. One American agent, who turned out to be the boss, was described as a slim, nicely dressed woman. Our host told us – 'She had at least five weapons on her, but you couldn't see a thing, and she was lightning fast... So quick thinking!' I thought about telling the hotel owner about my recent missions to Kosovo, Albania, and Colombia, but I was saved from inevitable embarrassment when our tuk-tuk turned up.

Our driver, Krishna, was quite a character. He was greying, possibly in his fifties, with an enormous smile, despite a few missing teeth, and not an ounce of fat on his wiry mahogany coloured frame. Krishna's ruggedly handsome looks could lead you to think he was Freddie Mercury's long-lost younger brother – the one who opted out of the sex, drugs, and rock-and-roll lifestyle and decided instead to drive a tuk-tuk around Udaipur. Perhaps he just wanted to break free. Before we got underway, the secret agent theme continued as Krishna told us about the time he appeared with his tuk-tuk in Octopussy. I couldn't wait to watch the film again to look out for him.

Krishna gave us a brief introductory lecture before we got underway, covering the basic history and geography of the Udaipur area. He described the four principal cities of the state of Rajasthan. Jaisalmer, where Nick and I were heading to the next day, is associated with camels, which represent romance (allegedly – they do little for me). Jodhpur, on our list for a few days later, is the Blue City. Jaipur is the Pink City and is associated with the elephant, which brings good luck. And lastly, Udaipur, the City of Lakes, is associated with the horse, which represents power. Fair enough.

The first stop on our day's tuk-tuk tour was the bustling Babu bazaar vegetable and basket-making market. Nick and I wandered around and tried to take in all the sights, sounds, and smells. A sea of countless colourful baskets, laid out on the ground like a giant artist's palette, seemed to contain every exotic spice, vegetable, and herb imaginable. The sellers all seemed friendly, and were happy to tell us about their produce, with free tastings if we were interested. One lovely lady insisted on giving us a cup of chai. It was sickly sweet, but we were hardly going to complain, and anyway, we were getting used to the taste by then. Nick rewarded her by buying a bag of peas that would act as an emergency snack for later in the day.

Walking around the market reminded me I needed to find an ATM for some cash, and luckily, Krishna had a spatial database in his head holding the location of every ATM in Udaipur. Finding one in working order was a different matter, however. On our eighth attempt, we struck lucky, and the three of us celebrated spontaneously and wildly with a handful of peas each.

The Ahar royal cenotaphs were next up on Krishna's itinerary for us, and this proved to be quite a moving experience. The site has been the burial place for the Mewar royal families of Rajasthan for over 400 years. It holds 372 separate cenotaphs, each one different but all built to traditional Rajasthan architectural design. Most took the form of a large white dome, like an ornate umbrella, standing on pillars atop a plinth, with steps. It is about two kilometres from the old city centre and Krishna did us a real favour by taking us to what seemed like a relatively unknown spot for tourists. The site was quiet and atmospheric; when we visited, we were the only people there.

Krishna drove us to the main lake, Fateh Sagar, and onto the Saheliyon Ki Bari gardens. These were lush, with attractive pools and fountains. Any lush place is a pleasant place to be in the Indian heat, of course, and the gardens had a cool and relaxed feel to them. The name means 'Garden of Maids.' Maharana Sangram Singh had the gardens built for his royal ladies in the 18th century. The story we heard was that forty-eight maids were needed to assist the Maharana's queen, and the gardens were presented to her majesty and her ladies as somewhere cool and relaxing to hang out and escape from the heat of royal duties. We also heard from several sources that all the fountains were naturally powered. We weren't sure what that meant, but by a strange coincidence, they stopped working at the very moment there was a power cut – spooky.

We ambled around the gardens and relaxed; there was no rush. Because he didn't need one, Nick displayed formidable negotiating skills with a guy trying to flog him a 64GB (SD) storage card. Walking away seemed to do the trick, but the salesperson was persistent, and he re-joined us several times on our walk around the park. He knew he was up against an experienced adversary in Nick. Just before we left the park, Nick decided he might need an SD card after all, and he struck a deal at about a quarter of the original asking price. He tells me he's never used it.

At some point on our tour, I mentioned to Krishna that I had seen several very elegant waistcoats on Indian gentlemen. Of course, Krishna's spatial database included every tradesperson in Udaipur, making it easy for him to stop off at a shop run by a collective of clothes-makers. To snip to size what is a very long story, I came out without a waistcoat, but with two shirts and two scarves. Nick came out of the shop with a splendid new waistcoat, which he hadn't gone in for, and a shirt. It hadn't worked out quite the way we'd planned it, but you can see by now how these things happen in India.

After lunch in a delightful little restaurant overlooking the pretty Fateh Sagar Lake, we requested the bill and checked it over. Here we had another example of the 'special cold coffee with ice cream' which of course was our beers. By now, we understood the code, and we felt part of the game. Our tuk-tuk spluttered on again on its tour of the city. We got Krishna to stop briefly while we took some photos of a group of roadside monkeys and it nearly resulted in Nick losing his wedding tackle. In search of the perfect angle, he must have got an inch too close for the monkey's liking. The monkey got its defence in first and made a lunge for Nick's groin. Nick wasn't known as 'the cat' in his goalkeeping prime for nothing. Forty years later, those lightning reactions were still good enough to save the day, and his prospects. No damage was done, but it was a close call and we decided to move on to our last stop of the day.

You're never far from your next temple visit in India, and right on cue, Krishna rattled his tuk-tuk up to the base of Machala Magra Hill. We caught the cable car, in this instance called a ropeway, to just short of the summit, and walked the rest of the way to visit the Karni Mata Temple. If I have my Hindu deity facts correct, Karni Mata was born in 1387 as the incarnation of Goddess Durga, the warrior form of Pavarti, wife of Shiva. Nick and I have to declare an interest in this one because the temple is in honour of our friend Ganesha's mum.

There were modest numbers of visitors/devotees visiting the temple, but everyone coming up on the cable car took the short walk to the summit of the hill to admire the spectacular views over Udaipur and beyond. Like Sahil yesterday, Krishna was extremely skilled at his job, and he timed our arrival at the summit perfectly to allow us to watch the sun dipping behind the mountains in the far distance. The hazy orange sunset provided a perfect backdrop to the city of Udaipur and Lake Pichola. It provided a wonderful final curtain to our day's tour.

While we waited in the cable car building for the last ride down, I ticked off another first – a fish pedicure. You would, wouldn't you? I wasn't sure what to expect. In my mind, I imagined a piranha-like experience where you dangle your feet in the water and five seconds later you pull them out to find your feet and legs stripped to the bone halfway up your calves. I told myself that was unlikely; they'd never get repeat custom, so I gave it a go. For the equivalent of about £1.20, I dangled my feet in a tank of cold water and scores of tiny fish set about nibbling them. They were at it for ten minutes. It was tickly; in fact, it was *very* tickly and borderline pleasant. Without all the cable car passengers watching me, I can imagine the watery foot massage would have been a relaxing experience. Anyway, my feet had never been so clean.

Nick got Krishna to stop off at an English wine shop on our bone-shaking ride back to the hotel, and we felt we'd well and truly done Udaipur. Not quite though – we still had another curry to enjoy that evening. This time we dined on a superb Rajasthani vegetarian thali (a collection of several dishes) for about £3 in a garden restaurant sited next door to a vintage car museum. Over a celebratory beer back at the hotel, Nick and I reflected on the day, with Udaipur now ticked off.

We were kidding ourselves. Of course, we both knew that there was so much more to do, and so much more time needed to do justice to even the handful of sights we had visited. Like so many other places we visited, that would have to wait for another time. The following day, we were heading for the desert!

JAISALMER

On day eight of our adventure across India, Nick and I journeyed further north into Rajasthan, to the Golden City of Jaisalmer. It was going to be another long day of travelling, but we were excited at the thought of experiencing the Thar desert.

From our hotel in Udaipur to the airport was just over twenty kilometres. That's a relatively long, cold, and bumpy ride in a tuk-tuk but our chauffeur, Krishna, had looked after us well during our brief stay, and it seemed rude to abandon him just for a warm and comfortable ride to the airport. Krishna cajoled his creaky tuk-tuk into action for another day and collected us from our Udaipur hotel at 8:00 am, by which time we had cajoled our creaky bodies into action for another day. It left us plenty of time to get to the airport for our flight via Ahmedabad to Jaisalmer. When we asked how much it was going to cost for our ride to the airport, Krishna said, 'we don't talk about money, my friends – let's go.' Nick and I flung our rucksacks in the back of the tuk-tuk, and off we went.

We rattled slowly out-of-town, in the freezing cold, half-light of morning. Krishna wrapped his scarf, which had seen better days, several times around his head. He was feeling the chill even more than us hardy Europeans. The temperature ventured little above zero until the sun appeared, about halfway to the airport, encouraging the subcontinent back to life for another day.

A tuk-tuk is the ideal transport option for urban India. Those three-wheeled glorified tin shacks, powered by lawn-mower engines, are the perfect mode of conveyance for scooting around town and nipping in and out of busy traffic. In that ideal operating environment, it doesn't matter that they are noisy, have no doors, have very little upholstery, and only get up to about 25 miles per hour. The traffic doesn't normally allow you to go that fast, anyway. They're not ideal, however, for the big fast roads going out to Udaipur airport. Still, it was another experience.

Krishna's pricing policy was fluid and was mainly based upon his customers' ability to pay and/or what he could get away with. This was applied market segmentation and differential pricing theory in action. At the end of the half-hour journey, we asked Krishna again how much we owed him, but he turned the question back on us and asked how much we wanted to pay him. Over breakfast, spreadsheet Nick had already looked up how much the same trip, with the same driver, had cost him last time he was in Udaipur, and so we were ready for the question. Krishna looked mildly offended at Nick's opening suggestion. He counter proposed 1,000 rupees (about a tenner). His figure was more than double what we'd paid for a nice, air-conditioned taxi (the Uber taxi with no tension in the seat belts) from the airport when we'd arrived two days earlier. Krishna was probably compensating for what he saw as his low earnings the previous day when he'd given us our tour of Udaipur city (£7.50 for an eight-hour tour of the city). Who can blame him? The fare to the airport of just £5 each for Nick and me meant a lot more to him than us, and when you're in the middle of these tense financial negotiations, it's as well to keep things in perspective. We should have paid him twice what he was asking. Nick paid up. We all shook hands, embraced with manly hugs, and recorded the occasion with the obligatory selfie.

We were returning to the scene of Nick's exceptional effort two days earlier, and I, for one, was expecting to see a plaque in honour of the achievement. The City Palace may be number one on our highlights list for Udaipur, but the airport gents' toilet must surely claim the number two spot.

Apart from the usual madness and chaos, there's little to report about the two flights that took us to Jaisalmer. That in itself is worthy of comment. In reality, there was a constant stream of 'crazy shit' happening, but by day eight of our trip, we had accepted most of that as normal. Our dog-leg trip took us 200 kilometres southwest of Udaipur for a two-hour stopover at Ahmedabad. We then flew 470 kilometres north-west to Jaisalmer. The brief halt in Ahmedabad was insufficient to check out its credentials as a UNESCO city of culture, but that would have been difficult from the transit lounge of the airport. As we waited there, gregarious strangers frequently interrupted us, wanting to know where we came from, where we were going, and what we thought of India. Everyone seemed incredibly friendly, and they were suitably impressed when we told them we were going to watch India v Australia the following Sunday... to support India.

Nick loved being in the spotlight, and to be honest, he does all that stuff really well... fielding the questions, chatting with the locals and showing off his 'I love India' bandana. I'm more of an introvert and while Nick was busy deflecting the attention, I used the time to good advantage to catch up with my diary.

Before we boarded our flight, we noticed that the two most prominent billboard signs in the airport were being used to advertise cement. This prompted a brief discussion on why that might be, and a round of concrete related puns. There was no set answer; there were probably many factors in the mix. Rumours that our discussion lasted so long that we missed our flight are without foundation. We had to stop it there; any more would have been hard to take. Seriously, though – it's difficult to imagine the most prominent billboards in Heathrow being used to advertise building materials. I tried to find out more on the Internet but couldn't get past websites such as 'Top ten best cement companies in India' and 'History of cement and concrete in India.' Like the statistics about the Bandra Worli Sea Link, it's amazing what gems are out there on the Internet waiting to be discovered, but you can only take so much of that stuff. My thoughts went back to the re-enforced concrete foundations of the Gateway of India. I'll just leave you with this thought – India is the second largest producer of cement in the world, and the industry provides employment to more than a million people. Mortar the point, that's the equivalent of the entire population of Birmingham, the UK's second city... all making cement.

The second leg of our flight took us further north and west into India, quite close to the border with Pakistan. Nick and I watched the landscape gradually changing below us, getting drier, less lush, and browner. Patches of sand appeared, and by the time we arrived in Jaisalmer, we were on the edge of the desert and in a place that qualifies, as well as anywhere, for the title 'in the middle of nowhere.'

Jaisalmer civilian airport is shared with the Indian Air Force, and as we taxied to the arrivals building, a couple of MiG-27 fighter aircraft roared down the runway. It was deafening. I don't think the relevant authorities would give permission for that sort of take-off racket at Gatwick airport. Nick and I were just hoping the MiGs were off for a bit of training or patrol work, rather than anything serious. It was a noisy reminder of the ongoing tensions with the neighbours to the west. After our mid-flight diversion around Iraq on our way out to India, we were a bit twitchy about international flash points.

Once our hearing had returned sufficiently for the task, it was time for more negotiating. Nick and I had to get a taxi into town and eventually we agreed on a price somewhere near half of what we were initially quoted. We were getting the hang of the procedure: the taxi driver or shop owner quotes about double what they'd ultimately settle for. If the customer is making the offer, it needs to be about half what you expect to pay. You gradually work your way to the middle ground, and everyone is happy. My mind drifted back to the negotiating module I did on the civil service marketing course. The average Indian taxi driver or shop owner would whip the pants off most negotiators I've come across – but they'd do it in a very likeable way, with a big toothy smile and a wobble of the head. I must admit, I left most of the haggling to Nick. I think it appealed to his Scottish thriftiness and he seemed to enjoy the sport.

The most striking thing you notice as you approach the City of Jaisalmer is that everything appears to be painted in a honey gold colour palette... think of a rich korma sauce. Dominating this compact city is the magnificent 12th-century fort, which sits impressively on an eighty-metre-high ridge of golden yellow sandstone. It is enormous, another UNESCO World Heritage site, and another Indian jaw-dropper. Housed inside the ten-metre-high fortified walls are a palace, temples, shops, and houses... and its 2,000 residents make it India's last living fort. Huddled around the base of the hill is a supporting cast of buildings, mostly built from the same golden sandstone. It's an impressive sight and sits right on the edge of the Thar desert.

The city developed in medieval times on caravan trading routes that connected the region to places like Africa and Persia. The people of Jaisalmer became rich, and they hired the finest artisans to build luxurious palaces and ornate temples. It's easy to imagine long winding caravans of camels, laden with spices, silver and cotton, slowly emerging from a shimmering desert mirage and resting overnight in the fort.

It was mid-afternoon by the time Nick and I checked into our hotel. We were eager to see our room, not really knowing what to expect. For the first few nights of our trip, we had used relatively expensive hotels, but for Jaisalmer we'd gone completely crazy the other way. We'd booked a twin-bedded room for three nights for £27. Our hotel was one of the traditional sandstone buildings at the base of the hill. It was old and relatively basic, but if you can live without external windows, the room was perfectly comfortable, and it even had an en-suite toilet and shower. The building had extremely thick sandstone walls, and the owner had decorated the place with traditional Rajasthan rugs, cushions, and artwork. There was definitely a medieval trading post feel to the place.

The friendly owner invited us up to the rooftop where we had a couple of beers and a few samosas with him and admired the fantastic views of the city, overshadowed by the impressive golden sandstone hill fort. The samosas were piping hot from the hotel's kitchen – little crispy pyramids stuffed with a delicious spicy potato mix. As luck would have it, we'd arrived on the day of the annual Hindu kite festival. From our experience over the five weeks, it seems the annual kite festival happens most days. We could see at least thirty kites dancing colourfully in the air around the hotel, and the surrounding rooftops rang out with the excited chatter and squeals of children cajoling their little squares of cloth high into the sky. Most attempts were successful, but there were a few casualties. One kite made a crash landing onto our roof, and we went about returning it to its rightful owners, dropping it down to the street below, trying to avoid a dense network of tangled electricity and phone lines on the way.

A tourist celebrates the annual kite festival

Our rooftop was soon echoing to excited childish chatter and squeals also, as Nick and I showed the locals how kite flying should be done. Like a couple of seasoned professional kite flyers, we eventually got our kites about ten metres up in the air (after about fifty attempts) before they crash-landed. We were doggedly persistent – mainly because we needed at least one successful flight recorded in the photo album. We concluded that the wind conditions on our rooftop weren't conducive to kite flying compared to the other rooftops, and anyway, the string wasn't of the right calibre and the design of the kite was rubbish.

We had a fantastic evening meal on the hotel's roof terrace. We dined under the stars, looking up at the illuminated walls of the city fort. It was an incredible sight and a romantic setting that was, once again, somewhat wasted on a couple of old geezers. The subtly spiced bhuna chicken and egg curry dishes, in that most modest of hotels, washed down with a couple of beers, cost just a few pounds but were out of this world in terms of taste and flavours – just exquisite. At the end of the trip, I looked back on that simple, inexpensive meal, as the best I had in India. Nick and I felt so lucky to have landed in that hotel. Ganesha was still with us, it seemed. We downed the last of our beers and looked forward, like a couple of excited schoolkids, to the camel safari we'd booked for the following day.

The highlight of the morning on day nine in India was a hot shower. It's funny how the day-to-day things you take for granted at home can seem so important in a trans-continent adventure situation. When we'd arrived at the hotel the previous afternoon, we were told there was no hot water in the hotel, but 'No problem, Sir – will be very nice working by 8:00 pm tonight.' It wasn't, but when it arrived in the morning, it was even more welcome. What do you expect for £9 a night?

Delight at having a nice hot shower turned to several hours of frustration for me in an unfulfilled quest to book two tickets for a train. Although we'd only just arrived in Jaisalmer, we had to think about the next leg of our journey, and we needed to book train tickets to get to Jodhpur. I hesitate to relate the story; it's not exactly a thrill a minute, but it's a typical example of the realities of independent travel in India.

As part of our planning process back home, several months before flying out to Mumbai, I'd booked up some tickets for the narrow-gauge railway, known as the toy train, from Kalka to Shimla. It's another 'must-do' experience on the World Heritage list, and I had read that it's prudent to reserve tickets in advance. In the comfort of my study, back home in Shropshire, I'd successfully found my way around the complex maze of the Indian Railways online booking system. On day nine of our adventure, I was attempting another booking, but in a hotel room in Jaisalmer, on an iPad with a dodgy Wi-Fi connection. I failed. I tried several times but came up against some insurmountable problem each time. I shuffled up to the rooftop restaurant disconsolate, looking for, and finding, comfort in a honey waffle and coffee.

Vidur, the restaurant manager, was very hospitable and always keen to help his guests. He insisted on solving the booking problem for us, and at that moment, I lost my morning in Jaisalmer. While Nick went off for a relaxing walk around the town, Vidur and I sprawled, like a couple of old maharajas, across sofas that were covered in exotic rugs and cushions. He began the battle with Indian Railways online. He was operating three mobile phones simultaneously and bringing his bank manager and several cousins into the equation. To cut a long story short, two hours later, after I'd repeated countless times, 'It's OK Vidur. Thanks so much for trying but we'll go to a travel agent,' he conceded things weren't working. Phew, thank goodness, I could move on with my life. But my heart sank when he then he said, 'No problem, I'll try again this afternoon.'

Fortunately, Nick, and I had booked up our desert safari for that afternoon, so we could decline his kind offer. The railway ticket booking saga would just have to wait. We mentioned the ticket issue in passing to the owner of the hotel as we left for our safari. I think it was in response to the question 'Have you boys had a good morning or completely wasted several hours of your life?' He calmly promised to sort it out for us the next day – which he later did, in a matter of minutes. I felt sorry for Vidur when we told him. He looked a broken man. He had tried so hard to help us and he had shown such kindness and patience. Anyway, the lesson of the story is: beware! Sometimes these things aren't necessarily straightforward, and it's a good idea to build in a bit of contingency time for when things don't go to plan.

Enough of Indian public transport reservation tribulations... we had a safari to go on! We had been told that the safari would involve an afternoon Jeep ride into the rolling dunes of the Thar desert, a camel ride, an overnight camp, another camel ride in the morning and then a Jeep ride back to civilisation. Nick and I packed an overnight bag each, and we were off. Our driver and guide, Mahendra, showed us to the Jeep in which we'd be travelling, and after stopping off to get a big box of bottled water, we were soon driving off to the west... towards the Pakistan border.

We had a few hours traversing the baked earth and scrub of the semi-desert before we got to the big rolling dunes of the Thar. Mahendra had a few things lined up for us to see along the way. The first was a visit to the abandoned village of Kuldhara. It was challenging to get the story of the village out of Mahendra. All we were told was that the villages in the area were abandoned suddenly, overnight, a couple of hundred years ago. I'm not sure if he didn't know more or was reluctant to say. Mahendra stayed in the Jeep and left us to look around. Nick and I went our separate ways to explore the village and met up after half an hour. The streets and over 400 sandstone buildings remain intact, although the buildings are in various stages of decay. Everything in the khaki brown coloured village is crumbling and dusty, and none of the buildings have roofs. There is hardly a scrap of vegetation to be seen – just a few small, scattered shrubs, more dust than leaves, somehow clinging to life.

I met a couple of other visitors as I walked around the ruined buildings. One had heard a legend about a curse, and the other one thought the place was haunted. Ah, that's more like it. My later research unearthed several theories – the village was either abandoned because of dwindling water supplies or maybe it was the result of an earthquake. Then there's the mystery of the tax-collector and the village girl. Maybe one or none of the explanations is true.

Centuries ago, the village was one of many in the area that was home to families of Paliwal Brahmins. I'm going to divert briefly at this point to mention the caste system in India because it will provide context to the tax-collector story (although its relevance is debatable). As usual, my overview is simplified and will inevitably skim over many nuances. Serious scholars should find more authoritative reference sources. I'm still not sure what to believe about the caste system, in terms of how prevalent it still is. The constitution of India is intended to protect discriminated communities, but you still hear many examples of the caste system in Indian society today. A five-week dash around the nation's main tourist spots is probably not a sound base from which to make judgement. Anyway, if it does still exist, what is it?

The caste system goes back at least 3,000 years and divides society into classes based upon their actions (karma) and duty (dharma). The Manusmriti, which (in very general terms) is to Hinduism what the Bible is to Christianity and the Quran to Islam, states that the caste system is necessary as the 'basis of order and regularity of society.' Hindus believe that a supreme being called Brahma is the creator of the universe and all beings. You don't get any further up the scale than that. Brahma is highest in the triad of great Hindu gods which includes Vishnu, preserver of the universe, and Shiva, who destroys it so that he can re-create it again. I'll leave the deity count there, but there are many more (you will find references of up to 330 million).

Hindus see (caste) society divided into four main classes which are derived from different parts of the body of Brahma. They divide the four main castes into thousands of sub-castes that account for all occupations. Brahmins (teachers, administrators, and priests) are believed to come from the head of Brahma. The Muslim rulers of the Mughal Dynasty and the British Raj both employed Brahmins as advisers and government officials. Kshatriyas (warriors, rulers) come from Brahma's arms, Vaishyas (tradespeople and merchants) come from the thighs, and the Shudras, who come from the feet, do all the unskilled menial jobs. The Dalits, or untouchables, are the poor people who are born outside the caste system.

The tale of the dodgy tax-collector (the Diwan of Jaisalmer) cropped up several times in my research to find out why Kuldhara was abandoned all those years ago – not that repetition on multiple websites makes it more credible than the other theories about the abandoned village. It seems the lecherous money collector, well known for his debauchery and shady tax-gathering methods, took a shine to the beautiful daughter of the village chief. Unless she was surrendered to him, the story goes, he threatened to abduct her, increase taxes, or possibly both. I'm not convinced the issue of caste, as described in some accounts of the story, is really at the heart of the problem – the tax man was just a randy opportunist. Rather than surrender his daughter, the

Kuldhara village chief ordered everyone to leave the village (and eighty-four nearby villages), throwing a curse on the old settlement for good measure as he left. Hence the ghost stories. I'm sure the story could be pimped up a bit and made into a Bollywood epic... maybe it already has been.

The second stop on our journey to the desert was a village that is still inhabited. As soon as our Jeep came to a halt, two likeable eleven-year-old boys ran up to us. They were all smiles, and they led us around the village, including a visit to their house. I suspect it's a routine they do several times a day as another consignment of foreign tourists is delivered to their doorstep. They seemed genuine enough, but then Mum appeared on the scene. Initially, she was also all smiles, but she soon got down to business. She insisted we should give the boys a gift – in the form of money. That seemed fair enough, so Nick and I each dished out a generous handful of rupees. Mum wanted to find out how much more change Nick had in his pocket and insisted that he showed her. She turned away in disinterest when it was clear there wasn't much left. There was a distinct change of mood once the financial situation was clarified. It's easy to understand; rich foreigners are being delivered every few hours to gawp at the day-to-day life of those poor people.

Our third stop was at another village, where we met four wizened old gents who were also very welcoming. They looked like octogenarians, if they were a day, and they smiled warmly at us with their few remaining teeth. I was just thankful to come across someone older than me at last. Using seven metres of bright orange material for each of us, they dressed us both in very stylish turbans, much to everyone's amusement, and then we got back in the Jeep and drove off again.

Another hour and we finally arrived at the 'real' desert

of rolling sand dunes. We parked the Jeep and our camel master Samir appeared with two camels called Baloo and Mr Rama. Nick and I were asked to choose which one we wanted. I asked Samir which of the camels was the more docile and immediately pulled age rank on Nick, selecting the more pensioner-friendly Mr Rama. I felt guilty diving in like that, but it was just my old special services training coming out (Southampton Sea Cadets, aged 13) – he who hesitates, etc.

Our ships of the desert laid passively on the ground as Nick and I saddled up with confidence, like the experienced men of the desert we are. Our beasts then lurched clumsily upwards and forwards, with terrifying jerks, to full standing height. I'm sure our camels had a view on who the terrifying jerks were. Anyway, somehow, we looked the part, and we rode off majestically for an appointment with the sunset. Somewhere out of sight, behind a nearby sand dune, the London Philharmonic Orchestra burst into the *Lawrence of Arabia* theme tune. It was just like a scene from the movie, if you're extremely flexible with the location and the dashing good looks of the participants and turn a blind eye to the lack of white flowing robes... or guns. OK, it was nothing like *Lawrence of Arabia*.

My mount was a gentle old thing, but we were told he was a previous race winner, so he had a bit of form. Nick's camel was feistier, and as I was on the camel in front, they gave me a stick to tap Baloo on the nose and keep the young rascal in check when he caught up with me and tried to take a nibble. We rode for an hour in spectacular rolling dunes. The wind had shaped the long golden waves into dramatic sculptures, with their sharp ridges constantly renewing as the breeze blew away the tops in long fine wisps of dust. We rolled and lurched, occasionally in unison with our beasts. As the sun sank ever lower, the evening's dying rays cast a magical bright amber glow over the dunes. Nick and I glanced at our shadow twins perched improbably high on the elongated sticks our camels were walking on. Just as my bottom was telling me it didn't want to go any further, we arrived, as if by magic, on one of the highest dunes, for the perfect view west to the sunset. Samir had done this before. Nick and I took a few hundred pictures and then rode the short distance to our overnight encampment.

Mr Rama and Baloo enjoy a well earned rest

Two other hardened men of the desert joined us there. Simon and Wolf, both from Germany, were ending the middle day of a three-day desert experience. As we sat around the campfire well into the night, supping our beers, we exchanged stories of foreign adventures. Bizarrely, when we wandered a few metres out of our encampment area we could find a phone signal. Google maps informed us we were less than eighty kilometres from the Pakistan border. Samir brought us a meal that would have been excessive for twelve people, and what we couldn't manage was finished by Samir, Mahendra, our driver, Pranav the cook, and their dog. As well as providing entertainment, the dog mixed in with the chores by providing the pre-wash to our used dishes and mugs. To be factually correct, we only saw the dog licking out one mug.

After some rousing singing of traditional Rajasthan folk songs, as you do, we finally turned in for the night. We all snuggled down as the dying embers of the campfire gradually faded into the pitch-black night. A few sparks crackled and darted upwards into the night sky, as if in defiance, in a final mini firework show, and then all was inky darkness and quiet.

There were two woollen blankets between me and the Thar desert, and three blankets between me and the stars of Orion's Belt, which seemed to be immediately overhead in the darkest skies I've ever seen. Our chatter soon faded to silence, as if we were intimidated by the enormity of the starry heavens above us. Several bottles of Kingfisher beer and half a day in the desert also had something to do with it. It's not every day you can fall asleep in the desert, looking at the Milky Way... but there we were. I tried to keep looking at the stars, trying to appreciate the moment, but within minutes I'd succumbed and drifted off, snug as a bug in a rug (an unfortunate choice of phrase), even though it was only about three degrees centigrade.

~

A heavy dew covered our blankets as we stirred at around 7:30 am the next morning to the gentle sound of camels gurgling and snorting. At least I think it was them. We were in good time to scramble up the dunes to see the sun rise lazily over the desert. Samir appeared on cue with four cups of coffee and although nothing was said, all four of us knew we were playing Russian roulette – who had the tin mug licked clean by the dog? I took my mug of coffee for a short walk over the dunes and disposed of its contents in the sand. Behind the next dune, I heard what sounded like someone doing the same thing. I think we all had the same idea. At least the mugs were hot – just the thing to warm our hands with the temperature still not much higher than freezing.

Pranav served us a breakfast of Indian style porridge, fruit, and toast. Again, it would have fed a small army. We saddled up and set off for another hour of camel riding, ending up back in Samir's village... the one with the four old fellas from yesterday. I was really glad to get there. I'm not sure my anatomy is optimised for camel riding and my bum bones felt worse than when I'd cycled 1,600 kilometres from Land's End to John o' Groats. I wasn't the only one suffering. When we got back in the Jeep, Simon couldn't stop his legs shaking. Nick thought we should call him Shakin' Simon, especially as he was sitting beside the green door. We didn't mention it to our German friends – they wouldn't be old enough to remember old Shaky's 1980s hit.

We were back in the hotel in Jaisalmer by early afternoon. We showered and got changed before exploring the UNESCO World Heritage Jaisalmer Fort. The architecture was stunning. When looking around, tourists are challenged by a constant barrage of invitations to browse around shops. There were countless enquiries of 'Where you from?' and offers to sell us all manner of 'very good price' trinkets and clothes. The trick is to keep moving; a moment's hesitation implies you are interested in something and from that point, you're in trouble. Nick and I couldn't help but hesitate a millisecond too long when we saw a sign in a shop that read 'discount for dwarfs.' You would, wouldn't you? We paused, nonplussed, and the shop minder pounced. He was a nice man and chatted for a long time without trying to talk us into buying anything. He gave us a brief history of the fort and told us he was sad that some fantastic architectural features were, allegedly, being bought up by posh Mumbai hotels. Hesitatingly, I asked about the sign, and after a couple of stops for clarification, he informed us it was because of a bad throat condition that the shop owner has. Another 'lost in translation' explanation I guess, but I'm sure the underlying intention was well meant.

We had a beer and a pineapple lassi (yoghurt milkshake) in one of several cafés that offered 'the best views in Jaisalmer.' We got chatting to a twenty-two-year-old Indian lad who had recently completed a three-year university course. He was using his newly gained skills 'working in hospitality.' Further discussion revealed he was a barman. That made it seem strange when Nick had to show him how to use a bottle opener on his bottle of Kingfisher, but he was probably just starting out.

Nick and I had dinner on the roof terrace of our hotel again and shared the evening with our new friends, Wolf (an RB Leipzig football supporter) and Simon (a TSV 1860 Munich supporter). As usual, football provided a common ground for discussion between nations, but in wide-ranging discussions I recall covering Brexit, favourite curry dishes, deserted villages, bhang lassi (cannabis flavoured yoghurt drink), and potential improvements to camel saddle design. To answer your question, the German boys had found bhang lassi and tried it. Nick and I hadn't come across it, and after the account we had from Wolf and Simon, we didn't bother to go looking for it. We turned in at 10:30 pm, all packed up, and ready to move on early the next day to Jodhpur. It had turned out to be a magnificent hotel find in Jaisalmer, and at £27 for both of us for three nights, it was reasonably priced.

JODHPUR

Like a disturbing scene from a Rajasthani murder mystery play, Nick's torch beam picked out the shape of a body sprawled across the floor of our hotel. It was 6:00 am, and we wanted to check out. Fortunately, we didn't have to cancel our departure plans; it was just the night manager who'd fallen asleep on the job. He didn't look too pleased at being woken up, but he got his act together and summoned the hotel driver from the bowels of the basement. We were off to the station and on the next leg of our journey – to Jodhpur.

With more technical cunning than a North Korean cyber hacker successfully accessing the US nuclear missile codes (allegedly), our friendly hotel manager had somehow made an online booking for Nick and me, for two third class seats on the Jaisalmer to Jodhpur train that morning. After our pleasant train ride across the Deccan plateau to Aurangabad, Nick and I were hoping for the same type of experience again. In the event, it was even better.

Once aboard our train, an eight-person compartment was all ours to enjoy, so we could really spread out. We could even have a leisurely sleep, if we felt like it. And we felt like it. The six-hour journey went in a flash; we must have gone through some crazy Rajasthani time portal – but as we kept saying, either in full or in its abbreviated form: 'This Is The Subcontinent.'

As we rattled along eastwards, devouring the railway track at about twenty miles per hour, we watched the landscape gradually transform. As the rails and train wheels formed a duet to give us another soporific clackety-clack backing track, the dry desert gradually gave way to more greenery, and we entered an area that we were told by a local chap was the farming heartland of India. A quick Internet search didn't really back the claim up but let's not quibble over regional arable excellence. Agricultural, it certainly was, however. We passed countless fields of sweet corn, rape, wheat, mustard, and pomegranates. The fields kept coming; a mesmerising repeating pattern, synchronised with the beat from the train's wheels, for kilometre after kilometre. It wasn't quite counting sheep, but it had the same effect.

After a brief sleep, I caught up on some blog writing. Nick monitored our progress on his phone mapping app and provided a regular stream of interesting facts about places we were going through. There's no stopping him now he's entered the world of smartphones. For example, he informed me that our second stop, Pokhran, was the site of seven nuclear tests, the first in 1974, then six more in 1998. The first, and India's first, was given the slightly chilling name, 'Smiling Buddha.' A couple of stops later, we were in Phalodi, the site of the highest temperature recorded in India, 51 degrees centigrade for the record. Mathania, another stop, will become Asia's largest solar hybrid power project... and so the facts kept coming, an invaluable supplement to any journey.

We were soon in Jodhpur, the Blue City. By comparison

with many other developed cities, Jodhpur remains relatively unspoilt. The old blue buildings, many built from chittar pattha, a sandstone mined from the surrounding hills, provide an extremely photogenic foreground to the magnificent Mehrangarh Fort that towers over much of the urban area. The buildings were originally painted blue to signify that they were occupied by Brahmins, the highest caste in India. With a present-day population of just over one and a half million people, the city is the second largest in the state of Rajasthan. Historically it was the capital of the Kingdom of Marwar, but right now you're probably just imagining a pair of unusual tight-fitting polo trousers. The 'jodhpurs' design was adapted from a traditional style of Indian trouser called churidars, which are loose at the hips but tight around the calves and ankles. The story goes that Pratap Singh, the Maharana's son, came up with the design and the trousers were worn by his polo team when they visited the Queen of England in 1897.

Nick and I made our way on foot the short distance from the station to the hotel we'd booked for the night. There was still an entire afternoon left to explore the city, and our hotel owner, Jaggi, gave us all the information we needed to optimise our time there. His two top tips for our visit were the Umaid Bhawan Palace, and, of course, the magnificent Mehrangarh Fort. We stopped a tuk-tuk driver on the road outside the hotel and asked to go to the fort via the palace – no problem. For some strange reason, the driver stopped halfway to the palace, got his phone out, and transferred us to a tuk-tuk driven by his nephew. Perhaps it was something we'd said, but you just go with the flow.

The impressive Umaid Bhawan Palace is a beauty, and quite a stunner in its scale and grandeur. It would have been worth the trip just to enjoy an hour of its calm tranquillity, but the palace is so much more than just a refuge from the noise and bustle of the city. It is by all definitions a grand building and one of *the* iconic symbols of Jodhpur. Built between 1928 and 1943, the golden yellow sandstone building was the last royal palace to be built before Indian independence in 1947. It spreads over ten hectares and with 347 rooms; they say it is the sixth largest private residence in the world. Having just moved house myself recently, my first thought was – they should think about downsizing; that's far too much room in which to collect *things*. As well as being home to the Rathore Dynasty of Jodhpur, the palace is also a heritage hotel with twenty-five rooms, thirty-nine suites, and a museum. It's just the place to go if you're looking for stuffed leopards, a flag gifted by Queen Victoria, and an impressive collection of classic cars. There is, of course, much more, and the palace is well worth a visit. Like the City Palace and many others, it was a former maharajas' private property needing to diversify to pay its way.

As I mentioned at the very start of our trip, strange things seem to happen in India. Nick and I were just leaving the palace gift shop, and I had just about convinced myself (incorrectly, in hindsight) that I didn't need one of those stylish Jodhpur polo club shirts, when a young man in front of us calmly turned to us and said, 'Hello, do you remember me?' Neither of us did, and I immediately thought he must be a trickster, trying to engage us in conversation. 'We met on the plane from Aurangabad' he said, very matter of fact. And then it fell into place – he was the guy who tipped us off about the Uber app as our plane taxied to a stop at Udaipur. Nick and I were taken aback, but the other guy acted as if we met up every day. But let's just consider the odds for a moment. We previously saw him a week earlier, over 300 kilometres away. Since then, we'd travelled all over Rajasthan, in a country of over a billion people. Even accepting that we were all tourists, that was some coincidence!

'A palace that might have been built by Titans and coloured by the morning sun'... I wish I'd thought of that, but it's a description of our second stop, provided by Rudyard Kipling. Jodhpur's Mehrangarh Fort was a highlight of our five-week trip, along with the Taj Mahal, the Ganges at Varanasi, and the Golden Temple at Amritsar. With massive forty-metre-high red sandstone walls, the Mehrangarh Fort sits atop a 130-metre-high hill and towers over the spectacularly camera-friendly tiny blue buildings of Jodhpur city below. It is a jaw-dropping sight. My geologist friend Nick was just as impressed that they built the fort on a Malani Igneous Suite Contact, a unique geological feature representing the last phase of igneous activity during the Precambrian age in the Indian subcontinent. He loves that stuff.

Mehrangarh Fort, Jodhpur

Built in the 15th century, the Mehrangarh Fort is India's largest, and looks impregnable. The architects weren't taking any chances with the defences. There is a series of seven massive, fortified gates. Students of defensive fortification design will especially appreciate the last/first gate. Massive wooden doors, studded with anti-elephant spikes, were set at right angles to the main access way to prevent any possibility of a good run up and charge. Given sufficient soldiers and a few hundred elephants, you might get through one gate, maybe two on a good day, but seven?

As visitors go through the gates one by one nowadays, the story of the fort unfolds. On the second gate, for example, you can still see the imprints of cannonballs fired by attacking armies, and on the inner-most gate, the Loha Pol, or Iron Gate, visitors can see a grid of thirty-one ochre painted hand shapes. The small, pitiful, sculptured shapes are the farewell waves from former maharaja's wives. Naturally, it was bad news when a maharaja died, but it was especially so for his wives. They were required to coat their hands in ochre paint and leave a print on the walls of the fort before throwing themselves onto their husband's funeral pyre. The custom of sati, in which maharajas' wives dressed in their wedding finery before joining their husbands in death, has its origins in the Hindu faith, and was considered an act of devotion, symbolising closure to a marriage. Well, it would certainly be that.

The word 'sati' is thought to originate from the Sanskrit word *asti*, meaning 'she is true/pure.' The sight of the occasional sati horrified the early colonial incomers, and the British government outlawed the practice. It took until the Commission of Sati (Prevention) Act 1987, however, for the Indian government to ban the practice. The passing of the law followed the controversy surrounding the death of a teenage girl in Jaipur, but there have been cases of voluntary sati reported as recently as 2015.

Talking of horrific death rituals, I can't leave the story of the fort without a brief mention of the legend that surrounds its very origin in 1459. When the Maharaja Roa Jodha chose the site, he had a minor planning obstacle to overcome. Having cleared the hill of nearly all existing occupants, just one man remained – a hermit who refused to budge. No problem for a maharaja, of course, and he got round the difficulty by forcefully evicting the chap and providing him with alternative accommodation. Unhappy at his removal and, presumably, the lack of an appeals procedure, the hermit placed a 'frequent droughts' curse on the Maharaja's kingdom. Rao Jodha thought he'd been more than reasonable by providing the new home, but to overcome the curse, he had to bury a random local man alive in the foundations of the fort. It's unconventional when compared to modern UK building practice, but in the Maharaja's eyes it was the only way to proceed with the build. I couldn't confirm the fact, but I was told that to this day the state still takes care of the descendants of the poor local man buried in the foundations.

In 1971, the constitution of India was amended. The royal title of 'maharaja' was abolished, and with it went the associated royal powers and privileges, including the privy purse allowance. According to reports at the time, the downfall of the royal families caused mixed feelings. Some people saw the royals as glamorous leaders and held them in great esteem. Some people resented how royal riches were gained at the expense of thousands of lower-class citizens. There also seems to have been some resentment at the way many of the royal families sided with the British colonialists to further their own family interests. Maybe there was an element of payback in the changes to the constitution.

Gaj Singh II was the 29th maharaja of the princely state of Jodhpur and owner of Mehrangarh Fort. Like the rest of us, Gaj Singh II had little say in the life he was born into. Sent to Britain to be educated, he came back home to India in 1971, aged 23, to find himself stripped of the $125k per year privy purse but with an inheritance of palaces and forts and a (former) king's treasure to look after. Rolls-Royce Phantom II's aren't cheap to maintain. By opening the fort and palace to visitors and developing hotels, Gaj Singh II not only maintained his properties but improved them and made them accessible to thousands of visitors. The way the Mehrangarh Fort has been maintained, and the way it is managed today, is very impressive. It wasn't over-run with trinket stalls and souvenir sellers, like so many other tourist locations. There were just a couple of shops as you leave the fort, and they were quite stylish, and the sales staff weren't pushy. The place deserves top marks for that, and just about every other aspect; I take my turban off to everyone involved.

Nick and I used audio guides as we walked around the fort, and one of the first bits of history we were told about, as we made our way through the seven palace gates, was about the sati ritual and the unfortunate fate of the maharajas' wives. The architecture is as stunning inside as it looks from the outside. Just like the City Palace in Udaipur, all the rooms and articles on show oozed royal opulence from times gone by. It was stunning, breathtaking, and in places very over the top. If you're an Indian royal, you can do over the top, and they do it well. The Sheesh Mahal, also known as the glass palace, is an ornate white marble pavilion within the main fort. It's a stunning example of Rajput interior architecture. The entire surface of the walls and ceiling of the room are covered with pietra dura, sometimes called marquetry in stone, and an intricate and beautiful combination of coloured glass and mirrors.

We certainly saw things you don't see every day in Oswestry or Brora... chics, palanquins, and howdahs, for example. Chics are fine bamboo screens, embroidered with silk and impregnated with aromatic scents to waft agreeable smells through the ladies' quarters. It probably made a welcome change from the unpleasant smells emanating from the men's quarters. The museum had an impressive collection of palanquins (covered chairs or beds carried by poles on the shoulders of bearers), on which they would carry the Maharaja and his wives in luxury. Some required twelve men to carry them. Howdahs were the seats on which royalty would parade on elephants. They say the collection in the fort is unrivalled. For its imposing location, elaborate architecture and magnificent contents, the fort is an all-round awesome place.

After a few hours, Nick and I made our way down from the fort, through some back streets to find a step well that we'd read about. Step wells seem to be a feature of the hot, dry northern states of India, and many go back to the 2nd and 4th centuries. There were once thousands of them, but today – well, no one really knows. Their original purpose was to supply water from the deep water tables, but they are also thought to have been used as temples, community gathering points, and trade route service areas. They say the Toorji Ka Jhalra (Toorji's Step Well) that we visited is one of the most impressive in India – it was certainly impressive. It's an enormous hole in the ground.

The large sandstone structure is approximately thirty metres square at the surface, going down about seventy metres, depending on how high the water table is. The Toorji Ka Jhalra was built in the 1740s by the consort of Maharaja Abhay Singh, continuing a tradition of royal women building public water works. I imagine that involved supervising the construction, rather than wielding a trowel, but who knows.

Toorji's Step Well

The well descends to the water level in a frighteningly steep, symmetrical series of large ornate stone steps. They descend in a set of diamond shaped blocks. By the time you've climbed about halfway down to the water level, you become completely mesmerised. It's easy to think you're trapped inside one of Escher's impossible stairway drawings. You might be condemned to walk around a never-ending series of stone steps for the rest of your life, never reaching the surface, or the water table.

Nick and I arrived at Toorji's Step Well shortly after sundown and daylight was fading rapidly. After we'd been there for a few minutes, a few lights came on in the surrounding buildings to part illuminate the scene. The place had a relaxed atmosphere. We seemed to be the only foreign visitors there, but there were plenty of locals relaxing by the well. There were a few oldies like us (except they had dark hair and healthy skin tones), and there were some families taking selfies. Several canoodling couples sat on the stone steps giggling nervously, and a few teenage lads dropped by to hang around in the shadows with some whacky baccy.

Before the evening completely turned to night, Nick and I walked around the edge of the well and clambered down a few blocks. We got some photos and clambered back out again. Continuing our walk through the bright and busy backstreets, we then tried to find the Ghanta Ghar clock tower in the Sardar market area. The clock wasn't half as impressive as Nick's attempt to buy a turban in one of the many shops in the square that overlooks the clock tower. The deal broke down, however, because of the twin hurdles of price and head size. Nick would have compromised over head size, but he dug his heals in when it came to paying anything more than a mere pittance. We got a tuk-tuk back to the hotel, watched the closing overs of the second India v Australia ODI, and had a curry and beer for dinner while we reflected on another great day. We were getting into a routine.

BENGALURU

Growing up in Britain during the 1960s and 1970s, I was just about aware of the name Bangalore. It was somewhere in India, along with places like Madras, Delhi, Bombay, and Calcutta. They played cricket there. I'm ashamed to admit that was about the limit of my awareness until I was a lot older. Of course, it's a lot more than somewhere 'where they play cricket,' although that was what we were travelling halfway across the country for.

With a metropolitan population of over nine million, Bengaluru is one of the most populous urban areas in India. It lies at a height of 1,000 metres on the Deccan plateau in southern India – in the middle of the map of India, and about 1,000 kilometres from the pointy bit at the bottom, as the White-bellied Treepie flies. Although it goes back centuries, it's another city that grew significantly when first the British East India Company and then the British Raj were in charge. While the old city could develop under the nominal sovereignty of the Maharaja of Mysore, the British developed their own cantonment outside the old city during the 19th century. The two separate entities merged in 1949, shortly after independence, and became the capital of the new state of Karnataka. The name Bengaluru was adopted as the official name in 2006.

If you're a blooming computer geek who likes gardening programmes, are keen on your hard borders and hard drives, then Bengaluru is the place for you. It's known as both 'The Garden City' and 'The Silicon Valley of India'; the latter because it has the highest concentration of IT firms in the country. While a stroll around the city's delightful Cubbon Park was a nod towards ticking The Garden City box, Nick and I saw nothing of its famed IT industry. In fact, we saw very little of the city at all, apart from the airport, a hotel, and a game of cricket. Sorry Bengaluru, Nick and I will have to catch you again when we do our southern India tour (note to self, must tell Nick about that, and my wife, Jan). With that briefest of introductions to the city, I should warn the reader that the rest of this chapter features quite a lot of cricket.

In a country obsessed with the sport, Nick and I were looking forward to experiencing the phenomenon at first hand. As we are huge fans of the game, it was a very enjoyable aspect of our adventure. Not every reader or traveller has the same enthusiasm for the game, but this chapter is about more than just a game of cricket. It gives an insight into how much the game means to the people of India and why it is a key part of 'the Indian experience.'

Every country has its national sport; the English have their football, Americans love baseball, and the Welsh enjoy running at speed into their opponents and falling over. No country is as fanatical about its national sport, however, as India is with cricket (although hockey is the national sport). Cricket is very close to a national religion and the players are superstar celebrities, adored by their fans. The greatest batsman of his generation, and possibly all time, was Sachin Tendulkar, who retired in 2013. He scored the most runs in international cricket (15,921 – almost 20 per cent more than his closest challenger) and holds countless other records. Having someone who is, or was, the world's best, is something that makes the country proud, and millions of small boys have grown up wanting to be Sachin Tendulkar. Towards the end of our adventure, Nick and I (and Nick's wife, Ellen) ran the Kolkata 10 kilometres race. The start of the run was overseen by the great man himself and we could see at first hand how he was idolised (Sachin, not Nick). It was like the Pope waving to the masses in Vatican Square.

Cricket in India expresses patriotism, and it's something that binds people from all religious backgrounds. Everywhere we went in India, there was someone who wanted to talk about cricket and one of my fondest memories of the trip is playing street cricket with the locals in Kolkata. I expect they're still talking about my sweep slog for six onto the top floor of the ironmonger's shop (I exaggerate; it was only a drive for four).

When Nick and I began planning our adventure back in July 2019, an ODI was something we *had* to include on our itinerary. As luck would have it, there were three India v Australia matches due to take place during our five weeks on the subcontinent, and we set about getting tickets for the last one, in Bengaluru. With luck, it would be the decider after a win for each team in the first two games. We soon found out it was too early to buy tickets, and when they became available online in 2020, we still couldn't get any. Upon arrival in India, we tried again but had no luck. Like my battle to get train tickets, the attempt ended in failure.

When it was time for us to fly to Bengaluru, halfway through our trip, we were still without tickets and the game was completely sold out. That hadn't really gone to plan, but on the positive side the series was perfectly poised at 1-1. So, it was with slight trepidation that we set off from Jodhpur on day twelve of our adventure and flew 1,500 kilometres south to Bengaluru.

We awoke at daybreak in our Jodhpur hotel to the gentle hum of morning commuter traffic. That's if you equate the sound of a formula one grand prix grid, when the lights go green, with a gentle hum. As I lay awake and waited for Nick to re-join me in the world of the living, I spent a few more minutes than was healthy contemplating the sound profile of the traffic outside. I reckoned an analysis would show a standard bell-shaped normal distribution curve. In the middle would be the output from thousands of lawn mower engines and the puny but persistent horns from the tuk-tuks and smaller taxis. There is some unwritten agreement between drivers that means 60 to 70 per cent of all horns must be in use simultaneously. Down at the lower left end of the graph would be a few hand-operated horns, some bicycle bells, barking dogs, crowing cockerels and exasperated humans. Further right would be the buses, full to overflowing and belching black smoke and fumes – a particular health hazard as they heave themselves forwards after stopping at the traffic lights. At the right extreme would be the heavy-duty lorries (some on 500-mile journeys to deliver bricks) painted colourfully, like mobile fairground attractions. Some of those eardrum wreckers have pneumatically enhanced sound installations instead of horns, something akin to the organ at Blackpool tower pimped up with a Glastonbury centre stage sound system. You probably think I'm exaggerating.

We left the hotel at 8:45 am and were soon at the airport. Jodhpur Airport was the first international airport built in India, because of the Maharaja's love of flying. Our flight went smoothly, and the two-and-a-half hours soon passed. I sat next to an Indian chap who was taking his family back to his workplace in Singapore after a trip home. We chatted most of the way, mainly about jobs, family, Indian politics, the partition, the role of turmeric in Indian cuisine, and Indian relations with Pakistan.

When Nick and I arrived in Bengaluru, it felt pleasantly warm (26 degrees centigrade), after the cooler weather in Rajasthan. We tried the Uber app again and were directed to a huge taxi rank dedicated solely to Uber vehicles. There were three lanes of queuing cars and you picked which lane to wait at, depending on which grade of transport you wanted. It was a first for both of us. My Indian friend on the plane had warned me about the traffic in the city and he was right; it took us an hour and a half to travel the twenty-five kilometres to the hotel.

The hotel was excellent and with tremendous forethought on Nick's part at the booking stage, it was only about 200 metres from the M. Chinnaswamy Stadium, where the ODI cricket match was going to take place the next day. We were reasonably confident of being able to secure tickets for the match, being on the spot, but the chap on hotel reception didn't think we had much chance, which was an enormous disappointment – Nick and I thought those guys could fix anything... didn't he have any cousins?

We wandered up to the ground at dusk for a look around, hoping we might somehow get some tickets. There must have been a few hundred young lads hanging around the front of the ground, and we looked around to see if we could spot any who might be touts. Everyone we approached just said they were there because they'd heard the teams were due to arrive in the early evening... oh, and did we know the match was sold out?

As we were passing the formidable iron gates of the main entrance, they swung open to let a press car out. The security presence was formidable. Hundreds of officers, all dressed impeccably in sharply creased black trousers and light orange shirts, kept close formation, determined not to let anyone into the ground as the car left. As they slammed the gates shut, I asked one of the security men where the ticket office was, and if it was still open. 'Tickets all sold, Sir. There are no tickets,' he said, politely but firmly. Nick and I went into our best despondent old pensioners act. It wasn't difficult because we were despondent old pensioners. 'Oh no! we've come all this way. We just wanted to see your great Indian cricketers,' I said, looking dejectedly down at the ground, barely able to make eye contact with the guard. 'We're not sure if we'll get the chance again' (which was also true). Nick was playing an absolute blinder by wearing his 'I love India' bandana again. Barely able to speak as he fought to control his emotions, Nick told the security man how we'd saved up for months to fly out and support India. This information was delivered with exaggerated pathos but it was also true. The poor man took sympathy on us and waved us in.

I should add at this point that Nick had to go the extra mile by saying he came from England. I can imagine the shock and horror this will cause back in his Highland home, but fortunately for him, no one will ever read this. I teased him about the shameful abandonment of his Welsh/Scottish (depending on company and sporting results) roots, but he cunningly pointed out to me we had arrived in Mumbai from Heathrow – so technically he had come from England.

Anyway, the security man, with no words, beckoned us to follow him. So, we did. I'm not entirely sure what happened in the next ten minutes, or why, but we had another of Debbie's *crazy shit* experiences. I suspect Ganesha had something to do with it. Nick and I followed our new friend, passing queues of people trying to get into the main offices of the stadium. We were whisked through a trophy room full of silver cups and shields. At a brisk pace, barely able to catch our breath or take in what was happening, we sped through corridors lined with black and white photos of international touring teams. Nick and I paused briefly to admire the photos of the 1937 and 1957 (I think) England touring teams, pointing out individuals as if we knew who we were talking about.

We were hurried along and eventually approached what looked like a command-and-control room in the very nerve centre of the ground. Our friend told us to stay by the door while he went to speak to someone who we took to be his boss. They chatted briefly, occasionally flashing glances in our direction, and then we were off again. We were led into another enormous room that had a massive window with a perfect view of the floodlit stadium. The pitch looked so close and so green... like you could reach out and touch it. In the centre of the room, with an Indian Cricket Board blazer badge, was the man who seemed to hold the final decision. Nick and I still didn't know what was happening, and our security guard friend had hardly said a word to us. The head man gave a nod, and we were whisked out yet again, across the corridor to a room where a man sat behind a four-metre-long table, covered with an enormous pile of tickets. He politely asked which tickets we would like; we could choose anywhere we wanted in the stadium. We bought two medium priced tickets, in a bit of a daze, and were promptly escorted out of the ground again, even faster than we'd gone in. Somehow, we were the proud, and stunned owners of two tickets for the next day's ODI!

As we were shown the gates, we thanked our security guard friend profusely and tried repeatedly to give him some money for helping us, but he was adamant that he wanted nothing. Nick and I were nearly speechless. We were riding an incredible adrenaline rush, ecstatic that we were going to see the match and overwhelmed by the generosity of those involved. We sat down on some stone steps under a statue of Gandhi in the park next to the stadium to calm down and work out what had just happened. The security guy could easily have just stuck to his initial 'sold out' comment and made life a lot easier for himself. We can only assume it was kindness and a desire to do good that drove him, and we were so *very* grateful – and will be forever. What an experience! There will be some good karma coming that man's way, and there were a hundred overs of top quality ODI cricket coming our way.

On the day of the match, for once, Nick and I had plenty of time. We had an entire morning before we were due at the stadium to see the ODI mini-series decider. We planned to have a quiet walk around the pleasant Cubbon Gardens Park that was near to the hotel and opposite the cricket ground. In the event, the moment we stepped out of the hotel entrance, we were swept along in a human tide of Indian cricket supporters. Nearly everyone was wearing the blue shirts of their national heroes, and every other person seemed to have an excessively large Indian flag.

There was a solid wall of pavement entrepreneurs, shoulder to shoulder, lining the way to the stadium, selling shirts, hats, horns, flags, and face paint. Nick and I went all in. We both got kitted out with shirts and hats, and got Indian flags painted onto our faces. We didn't know when we'd be back, so it felt worth splashing out £5 each. We were quite a sight. Every ten yards, excited fans would stop us for selfies. Everyone, it seemed, wanted their picture taken with the two white oldies. By the time we'd met most of the 40,000 crowd, we realised we'd only seen two other non-Indian people. I guess we stood out a bit.

An enthusiastic supporter gets ready for the match

An Indian TV crew was broadcasting live from the crowded street, and they homed in on us. Nick gave them an in-depth analysis of the two teams, the pitch conditions, and the well-balanced state of the series. His words boomed out to the crowd through loudspeakers. The multitude soon built further to hear what the crazy foreigner had to say. This was Nick's moment; his fifteen minutes; his time had come. He didn't really need much encouragement, but he was spurred on when the interviewer told him the broadcast was going out live to the whole of India. Not everyone would be tuned in, of course, so it was probably only an audience of a few hundred million. Nick whipped what had grown to a sizeable crowd of several hundred into a frenzy by praising their sporting heroes one by one. 'Shami will get a hat-trick'... the crowd roared its approval, 'Sharma will get a century'... the crowd thundered its agreement, louder still. 'Kohli will score a century'... the crowd roared again, even louder. It was like watching Freddy Mercury work the crowd at Live Aid at Wembley in 1985. In a dramatic climax, Nick turned from the camera to face the fans. Fist pumping in time, he repeatedly roared 'India is great... come on India.' The crowd went completely delirious. That's ma boy!

Crowd successfully whipped into a frenzy, we just had to run the gauntlet of matchday security, and then we'd be in the ground and ready for a great day's cricket. Although getting through security isn't one of Nick's strengths, surely there wouldn't be any problem getting into a cricket ground. Our bags held just the essentials – water, hand sanitiser, toilet roll, binoculars, camera, sun cream, etc. Nothing controversial there. What were we thinking? We were told in no uncertain terms that no bags or cameras were allowed into the ground. Without wanting to push our luck too much, we sought clarification. Phones with cameras were fine, but not cameras. It would be possible to take some things in our pockets, but not in bags. There were no arguments; those guys weren't messing.

It was lucky we were still close to our hotel – we just went back. We fought against the blue tide of noisy supporters to dump our bags (and cameras) in our room. The toilet rolls would have to go also because they weren't allowed in the ground either. Thinking through the potential repercussions wasn't something to dwell on. We returned to the ground to tackle the security guys for the second time, fingers crossed. Completely counter to form, Nick sailed through in front of me. Also counter to form, they pulled me to one side – because I still had hand sanitiser in my pocket. I was told it wasn't allowed because I could throw it. 'Well, that would just be a waste' I protested, trying to convince them I had prioritised hand hygiene over a need to throw projectiles at other spectators. As the security guy stood shaking his head, once again, something, or someone came to our help. Although Nick had strolled through with his binoculars in his pocket, the security guys decided that the Indian chap behind me in the queue couldn't take his binoculars in... a totally random decision. Before I had a chance to ask the person behind me if he had any intention of throwing his binoculars when inside the ground, a noisy and acrimonious row broke out between him and the security team. While binoculargate was unravelling, with continued shouting and arm gesticulating, I slipped through and into the ground, sanitiser in pocket. The guard had bigger potential criminals to deal with.

Anyway, at last we were in. We found our seats in a sea of blue India shirts and soaked up the incredible atmosphere. For the next nine hours, there was a constant pulse of excited chatter, loud chanting, and singing. Between the overs, loudspeakers boomed out blaring dance music, which seemed totally appropriate and good fun. A regular stream of salespeople came around with popcorn, pooris (sandwiches), drinks, and ice cream. It was fantastic.

The match itself went almost completely to script. Nick and I speculated on what we thought would be the perfect outcome – it would involve Australia batting first, Steve Smith getting a century, and the Aussies getting a good but gettable total. India would then bat and tick off the runs by the forty-seventh out of fifty overs, with Virat Kohli stroking the winning runs to take him to his century. And that's almost exactly how it worked out. The only blemish on a perfect script was Kohli being bowled on eighty-nine, just short of his ton. All the rest went just as we'd thought; it was a perfect day of top quality international sport.

We left the ground swept along by a tide of sweaty bodies, in a sea of blue India shirts. We could have lifted our feet off the ground and been transported out of the ground. Even after such a long, hot day, everyone was very excited, and naturally they all wanted a selfie with the old foreigners decked out in their blue cricket tops and with Indian flags painted on their faces. India had won the game and the series, so what better excuse for a festival... they were partying like it was 1947.

We eventually got back to our hotel exhausted and elated. At the end of a near perfect day for Nick, he sat in the hotel restaurant, a dish of chungdi malai coconut curried prawns and rice on his plate, beer in hand, watching Liverpool beating Manchester United live on TV right in front of him. Could life get any better... well, yes, if his wife had been there as well, obviously. Apologies to the non-cricket fans reading this chapter, if any of you did, but I hope it has provided a glimpse of how important the game is in India. Right, back to normal tourist stuff in the next chapter, and our visit to Amritsar.

AMRITSAR

We were nearly two weeks into our adventure. Nick and I were leaving cricket-mad Bengaluru to travel back up to the northwest of India, to Amritsar, where we would be in the Punjab. It's a name sprinkled with magic from my childhood, and I tried to pass that magic on to my kids. I remember how, with one jab of his needle in the Punjab, Peter Sellers cleared up a brace of unpleasant tropical ailments while falling under the spell of Sophia Loren. Goodness gracious me, I'm showing my age again. As we could have predicted, our journey continued to be unpredictable and by the end of the day we had witnessed the ridiculous and the sublime.

Amritsar was one of the first names on our list when Nick and I sat down to design our travel itinerary in 2019. The city is the largest in the state of Punjab and was founded in 1577 by the fourth Sikh guru, Guru Ram Das. A new national boundary has appeared in the meantime, and the city now lies only twenty kilometres from the border with Pakistan. It is the epicentre of Sikhism, one of four major world religions that have their origins in India. It is also a place of pilgrimage and the site of the spectacular

Harmandir Sahib, Sikhism's holiest shrine, more commonly known as the Golden Temple.

India is officially a secular state. The principle is enshrined in the Indian constitution, which, by the way, is the world's longest, and is handwritten. As an outsider, and a traveller on a self-confessed supermarket trolly dash through the country, it's dangerous to pass judgement. I can only describe things as I've experienced them, and that experience is very limited. I was told that there is an article in the Indian constitution, for example, that bans the slaughter of cattle. Now at first sight, to a foreigner, that could be interpreted as contradicting secularism because it seems to support the Hindu religion. Others would argue that the constitution aims wider than that – the issue is also sacred to Jains, Zoroastrians, and Buddhists. Then again, perhaps the article is worded to support an animal rights position, irrespective of religion... although several billion non-exempt chickens and goats might take issue with that each year.

As well as Sikhism, India is the birthplace of Hinduism, Buddhism, and Jainism. With over 172 million followers, it is home to the third largest population of Muslims in the world. The Christian population of more than twenty-seven million includes Catholics, Protestants, and Oriental Orthodox Christians. The largest number of people who follow Zoroastrianism and the Baha'i faith are also found in India. Religion heavily influences people's lives; there are countless temples, and that's part of the fascination of the country. More than that, faith is often evident in the way people go about their day-to-day lives.

Hinduism appears to dominate daily life for most Indian people, but that's no great surprise with almost 80 per cent of India's population (that's over one billion people) identifying themselves as Hindu. With so many followers, there would seem to be an obvious political advantage in aligning to that way of life and culture, and indeed, since 2014, the ruling party in India has been the Bharatiya Janata Party (BJP – in English, the Indian People's Party) led by Prime Minister Narendra Modi. Their website describes how, within the principle of 'justice for all and appeasement of none' they believe in 'the Hindu identity and culture as the foundation of the country.' The BJP party appears to be riding the wave of popularism and nationalism that has swept around the world in recent years.

Nick and I still had the Hindu holy city of Varanasi on our itinerary. Also coming up was the Taj Mahal built by Shah Jahan, and Bodh Gaya, where the Buddha found enlightenment. There would be no shortage of world-famous religious sites to visit. We had faith in our itinerary. But to begin with, there is no better place than Amritsar to learn about Sikhism.

Sikhism started in Punjab in the 15th century, based on the spiritual teachings of Guru Nanak. In the mid-19th century, it spread to the rest of India and then further afield. Nowadays, it is the fifth most popular religion in the world, with approximately twenty-five million followers. Just over sixteen million of those live in India, with almost 80 per cent found in Punjab, so Nick, and I were in the very heartland of the religion.

It is possible to identify some elements of both Hinduism (the concept of karma) and Islam (the concept of one God) in Sikhism. The Sikh's goal in life is to focus on being at one with God; to live a good life a person should do good deeds and meditate. It's hard to argue with that part. Sikhs believe in 'the five K' articles of faith. Only those believers who have experienced the 'amrit' initiation rite can use all, but most Sikhs have one or more. A *kangha* is a small wooden comb used twice each day to look after a

Sikh's uncut hair, or *kesh*. Sikh men cover their kesh with a turban. Most people will recognise Sikh men by their distinctive and often colourful turbans. They believe that leaving their hair to grow naturally acknowledges and respects God's will. A *kirpan* is a short dagger, a *kachera* is an undergarment, and a *kara* is a bangle.

Our early morning taxi journey to the airport in Bengaluru, the flight, and the taxi to our hotel in Amritsar all went smoothly, except for one thing. Three-quarters of the way into our sixty-minute taxi ride to Bengaluru airport, Nick and I were speculating on how cold it might be when we arrived back in the north again. Brass monkeys featured heavily in the conversation. That triggered a train of thought in my head that rapidly de-railed as I remembered leaving my nice, warm down jacket and woollen scarf back in the hotel wardrobe. There was no time to go back. 'Ah bother' – is a rough translation of my reaction.

Not to worry; this is India. By the time we'd arrived at the airport I had phoned the hotel, they'd found the items and arranged for a courier to forward them to our hotel in Kolkata in ten days' time. An interim jacket for the cold north was going to set me back all of a fiver. Well done, Ganesha, you're still looking after us.

We arrived in Amritsar (population 1.1 million) at 1:00 pm after another uneventful flight. The entire journey had been routinely boring, which was great. I didn't even have the usual entertainment of watching Nick go round the security loop several times. I think he got all his drugs, small firearms, batteries, penknife and Bombay mix through with no hold-ups. I'm joking, of course... I don't even know if he had any Bombay mix.

On the taxi journey from the airport into the city, we asked the driver about the famous lowering of the flag ceremony at the Attari-Wagah border with Pakistan. I had seen a film of the colourful daily ceremony before we left home (*Michael Palin's Himalaya: Journey of a Lifetime*) as part of my pre-travel research, and it looked like something we had to see, if possible. We didn't have much time if we wanted to see it that evening, it seemed, and that would be our only opportunity. The following day we would be moving on again. As we headed for the city, and our hotel, Nick stepped up and negotiated with our driver to see if he could get us to the border in time for the ceremony that evening – what were we thinking?

A receptionist with the unusual name of 'Love' slowly checked Nick and me into our Amritsar hotel. There was some urgency, with our taxi waiting outside for the dash to the border, but you can't hurry Love. We threw our bags into our room and rushed back out to the taxi for the twenty-kilometre dash. We raced to the boundary faster than a Virat Kohli cover drive. I recall writing reassuring text messages to let wives, relatives, concerned individuals, etc., know that our visit to the border was perfectly safe. It was completely bonkers, but perfectly safe.

More by luck, and a spot of white-knuckle driving, than judgement, we arrived at the border checkpoint car park at 4:00 pm, in plenty of time to see *the* most bizarre of spectacles. Even by Indian taxi standards, our drive had been rapid. If I'd opened my eyes, it would have been scary, but our driver had done a great job and got us there in time.

The lowering of the flags border ceremony has taken place since 1959 and shows both the rivalry and friendly cooperation between the Indian and Pakistani border security forces. I'm sure it started out as something quite civilised, with the flags simultaneously lowered and respectful salutes being made across the border, but it has somehow morphed into a daily pantomime. Imagine a mash up between the Buckingham Palace changing of the guard, the TV programme 'It's a knockout' (for those of a certain age) and a Monty Python sketch. The loud and colourful spectacle draws crowds of up to 10,000 people each evening. Indian spectators on one side of the border and Pakistanis on the other cheer their boys on to acts of extreme silliness.

At the Attari-Wagah border, there is a normal-looking road, one lane either way, that crosses from India into Pakistan. A fence, running at right angles to the road, marks the national border. At the point where the road meets the fence, there is a substantial steel gate. Along each side of the road, for fifty metres on either side of the gate, they have erected terraced seating so spectators can witness the flag ceremony. It resembles a small football stadium with a public highway running through it from end to end. And why not?

Nick and I left our taxi in an enormous car park and followed the crowds to the seating area. We guessed it would be our last sight of the taxi. On our way to the seating area, we passed under the shadow of the biggest flag and pole either of us had ever seen. In March 2017, the Indian authorities raised a 40 x 26 metre national flag on a 110-metre flagpole. The mast alone weighs fifty-five tons. They say it can be seen eighteen kilometres away in Lahore. National rivalry reached new heights six months later when Pakistan raised a 122-metre high flagpole on their side of the border. It remains the eighth highest in the world (Jeddah, Saudi Arabia at 170 metres... before you ask). Fortunately, flag-wars stopped there. I guess both sides realised it was potentially a bottomless pit of expenditure for little gain. To carry on would border on the ridiculous. It was fifteen love to Pakistan; they had the highest flagpole.

Nick and I continued the short distance between the car park and the terraced seating, our way lined with an unlikely combination of military police and trinket sellers. Most of them were selling Indian flags, face paint, and bottled water (the trinket sellers). Buying a flag seemed obligatory. When we arrived at the seating area, Nick and I stood out like a couple of white-bread spam sandwiches on a plate of exotic Indian thali. That worked to our advantage. A petite military policewoman approached us and directed us to an area of seating designated solely for foreigners. It was the section closest to the border, so we had the best seats in the show. There were only a few other pale people there. During the wait of ten to fifteen minutes before the performance began, Nick and I caught our breath after our mad dash to get to the border on time. It gave us time to soak up the atmosphere. The crowds in the surrounding stands got increasingly rowdy and restless. On occasions, they spilled into our visitor's enclosure to get a better view but were immediately herded back by stern-faced military police with big sticks, lots of arm waving and ear-piercing whistle-blowing.

And then the show got underway. An Indian border guard acted as master of ceremonies, parading up and down the middle of the empty road in front of hundreds of spectators. He was a lean and handsome officer, immaculately turned out, with the improbable combination of Peter Kay's stage presence and the booming voice of Brian Blessed. I'm not sure he needed the microphone. To a background of deafening Indian dance music, he whipped the crowd into a frenzy, getting everyone to chant 'India' and 'Hindustan' in a repeating mantra. It was almost as good as Nick's legendary TV performance with the Indian cricket fans at the M Chinnaswamy Stadium.

When he sensed the time was right, the master of ceremonies gave a signal and waved a hundred or so people down to join him on the road to take part in a hypnotic, rapid pulse rave. The music was deafening and the rest of us in the stands were clapping and waving flags as we got carried along by the hysteria (note to self – next time get yourself into the rave section on the road). At 4:15 pm, the master of ceremonies gave the order for the music to stop, and the dance floor/road was cleared. Seated back on the terraces again, the crowd first hushed, then gasped, as the border gates dramatically creaked opened – there was an open road into Pakistan. A nervous quiet overcame the crowd. We fidgeted with expectation and waited for the next round of jeux sans frontières.

The Attari-Wagah flag ceremony

A group of elaborately dressed Indian border guards arrived at the end of the road, fifty metres from the open gate to the Pakistan border. Their immaculate uniform included a striking fan of red and yellow striped fore-and-aft feathers on their caps, like excited hoopoes. One at a time, then in pairs, and finally in groups, the soldiers marched along the road to the border, turned, and marched back. 'Marched' doesn't come close to describing the spectacle properly. The marching involved raising their arms and legs exaggeratedly high in the air, high kicks, pirouetting, and walking on their heels. And a lot more. Nick suggested it might have been the inspiration behind Monty Python's Ministry of Silly Walks sketch. No wonder Michael Palin went to check it out on his way to the Himalayas. If we'd seen it in any other country, we might have thought it was strange.

When they reached the border, the guards postured with all the drama they could muster. The crowd roared its approval, urging them to produce ever more outrageous gestures. The guards puffed their chests out, twirled their extravagant moustaches audaciously and waved their swords defiantly at the opposition, posturing theatrically with every well-rehearsed move. They had a little routine where they opened their eyes as wide as possible and then looked suspiciously out of the corners towards their counterparts. Such contempt, such arrogance; the crowd went wild. I'm not sure who was enjoying it more, the crowd or the soldiers. As all this was taking place on the Indian side, a mirror image performance was being acted out on the Pakistan side.

It was all carefully choreographed. We watched the smaller Pakistan crowd also going wild. Maybe on other days, they had more supporters, but during our visit it looked like India had home advantage and was making the loudest racket. The ceremony ended with both national flags being lowered and removed. The respective chiefs-in-command shook hands before the border gates slammed shut again. Both sets of guards retreated to the safety of their own territory, using their best strutting and posturing. It was all over. The crowd roared its approval and clapped loudly. It had all been totally crazy, but great fun to witness. My feeling was the Indian side had the greater flamboyance and noise – just. Fifteen all; new flags, please.

I'm so glad we witnessed the flag ceremony. The protagonists had put on a magnificent piece of theatre, but there was clearly a mutual respect. It was like they were saying 'We've both got a job to do guarding the border, but let's just acknowledge we're all in this together and have a bit of fun.' Perhaps the politicians from each country can learn from it. Maybe they could do a bit of face painting and poke fun at each other instead of issuing threats.

Back at the hotel over a beer, we discussed how to make the best use of our limited time in the city. Our plan was to visit the Golden Temple that evening and save the Partition Museum and the site of the Jallianwala Bagh massacre for first thing in the morning. The Golden Temple, or Harmandir Sahib, was only a ten-minute walk from our hotel, so off we went.

In hindsight, I'm slightly embarrassed by our itinerary. Not for the first or last time. We were on a whistle-stop tour that packed so much in, but we both felt those incredible places deserved more time and respect. It was a lesson learnt. It's such a conundrum when travelling – how much time to spend in any one place.

In the half-light of evening, we made our way through tiny streets packed with hundreds of colourful shops and food-stalls. Had we needed a set of saucepans, a sari, or a bag of cement, it would have been a wonderful opportunity to pick some up, but they weren't on our shopping list. As we neared the site of the Golden Temple, we entered a recently re-developed area. There we found unusually wide streets and well-paved roads lined with smart modern shops – and everywhere was shiny and clean… it wasn't normal!

It was just getting dark by the time we arrived at the

complex that surrounds the Golden Temple. The gradual build-up of hundreds of people, the darkness and the bright lights contributed to an atmosphere of expectation. Nick and I followed the flow of the crowds to the building that forms the perimeter of the complex. We deposited our shoes and socks in a hatchway, a bit like you'd leave your coat at the entrance to the theatre, and they gave us a tag with which to reclaim our shoes later. There were plenty of helpful people to show us what to do, and they seemed friendly. First, we each had to pick an orange scarf out of a large lucky dip box and put it on our heads. Second, we had to wash our feet (hadn't they heard about my fish pedicure?) in a public, very well-used foot bath like you'd see at the swimming baths, but probably minus the chlorine. These were both acts of respect and, of course, we were happy to go along with that. Suitably prepared, we went through an archway into the main quadrangle.

We caught our breath as we saw, blazing in golden light and shimmering above a pool of black sparkling water, the stunning sight of the Harmandir Sahib – the Golden Temple. It is a place of great beauty and, despite the crowds, sublime peacefulness.

The fourth Sikh guru, Guru Ram Das, founded the Golden Temple in 1574, and the original construction was completed thirty years later. Over the years, people from opposing religions have trashed or part-trashed it, but each time, devoted Sikhs have rebuilt better versions. What you see today is largely the result of a 1764 re-build and work done around the turn of the 19th century to decorate the Golden Temple with marble sculptures, golden gilding, and large quantities of precious stones. The glittering panels on the second level and the dome are covered with 750 kg of gold. It's another one of those 'you have to see to appreciate it' and we were lucky to be there – it was breathtaking.

The Harmandir Sahib – the Golden Temple

The Golden Temple complex is a collection of buildings forming a large square, with entrances on each of the four sides to emphasise that it is open to all. Inside the outer structure is an open-air pool of water or 'tank.' The 'Amrit Sarovar' tank, which translates to 'Pool of Holy Nectar' is almost 150 square metres and five metres deep. A walkway, nearly four metres wide, goes around the outside. A causeway, or pier, stretches out from one side of the tank to reach the sanctum in the centre. This two-floored rectangular building, with sides of just over twelve metres long and covered in gold foil, is the Golden Temple.

Sikhs call their temples gurdwaras (doorways to God). These are where birth, death, baptism, and marriage ceremonies take place, but they also serve as kitchens. They share vegetarian food with anyone who visits the temple, and this includes the Golden Temple. Every Sikh is required to visit the Golden Temple once in their lifetime, and it was clear to see what it meant to the pilgrims who were all around us. Nick and I followed the path around the pool and walked out on the causeway to visit the temple. We joined a long patient queue waiting to get in but towards the end, for some reason, they waved us through and fast-tracked us to the temple entrance.

Nick and I followed the flow of worshippers, very conscious that we were the outsiders, but still feeling comfortable and welcome. The interior of the temple is richly decorated with golden ornamentation, mirrors, and fine murals. The combined effect is indescribably beautiful. There were three levels to the temple. In the first, a Sikh elder was the principal focus. He sat cross-legged in front of a large open book, presumably *the* holy book, the Guru Granth Sahib. In a relatively small space, a few seated musicians and devoted worshippers flanked the elder. As our queue filed slowly through the room, many thankful pilgrims showered rupee notes into the space in front of the Sikh elder. There was a large open box to receive their offerings, but most notes fell short and landed on the floor. Two helpers were literally raking it in with long sticks. Like croupiers in a casino, the helpers scooped the notes into bundles that could be gathered and put into the box. It was a similar story, without the music, on the next two levels.

Towards the end of the procession around the temple, Nick and I were offered a simple rice meal, served on banana leaves and some water from the world's largest community kitchen. The stats are impressive; they feed up to 100,000 people each day in a dining hall that seats 5,000 people. At the time, neither of us felt justified in taking it, so we politely declined. We both felt that we didn't need it, so we should leave our portions for people more needy. In hindsight, we got that all wrong and now feel stupid – it wasn't about the cost of the meal; we should have sat down and shared a meal with the Sikh worshippers, to hear their views and share a conversation. I feel like going back already.

Before I leave the subject of the Golden Temple, I should briefly also mention Operation Blue Star and its aftermath because it represents a significant but dark chapter in recent Indian history. Following a breakdown in law and order in Punjab in 1984, the Prime Minister, Indira Gandhi, ordered a ten-day military operation to remove Sikh militants who were sheltering in the Golden Temple. The militants were promoting Sikh nationalism and fighting for an independent state. The militants were killed, but four months later, Indira Gandhi was assassinated in retaliation by two of her Sikh bodyguards. It's a very sad reminder of the nationalism and inter-religious tensions that exist to different degrees in most countries. Fortunately, Nick and I saw no evidence of that, and our impression as brief visitors was of somewhere where different religions live peacefully alongside each other – although it was impossible for us to judge properly based upon our brief exposure to the country.

Going with the flow of the crowd, we made our way out of the Golden Temple complex. We collected our shoes and walked back to the hotel. On our way, dodging the gauntlet of stall holders, our discussions focussed on comparative world religions and our vulnerability to a range of common foot infections. Back at our hotel, we dined on an excellent chicken bhuna, rice, dal and roti, washed down with a couple of Kingfisher Premiums. It had been another afternoon of sensory overload; the ridiculous and the sublime. It would take time to process what we'd seen and attempt to understand it.

~

After breakfast the following day, we headed by bicycle taxi for the Jallianwala Bagh, another sad reminder of Britain's inglorious past in India. The site is a large open public garden surrounded by high walls. There is one narrow opening to get in and out. Back in 1919, just after the end of World War One, it was the scene of a terrible massacre. It was a time of heightened tensions as Indian opposition to British rule was rising. India had contributed hugely to the British war effort and must have been hoping for some sympathy towards its claims for self-government in return. It wasn't to be, for almost another three decades.

As a sizeable crowd of unarmed and peaceful protesters gathered in the Jallianwala Bagh, British troops were ordered to open fire on them, and they only stopped shooting after ten minutes, when the ammunition ran out. As well as the shooting, many people lost their lives in the stampede, and they found hundreds of people dead in the well of the gardens. Between 400 – 1,000 peaceful protesters lost their lives. The British suppressed news of the massacre for six months, after which a commission of enquiry found the officer in charge, General Dyer, guilty of a 'grave error.' The House of Commons subsequently relieved him of his command, only for the House of Lords to clear him. He expressed no remorse and retired on a handsome pension, supplemented by a sum equivalent to over a quarter of a million pounds in today's terms, collected from a public campaign. To go with that, they presented him with a jewelled sword of honour. In contrast, the families of the murdered victims received compensation equivalent to approximately £37 for each life lost. The shock and outrage caused by the massacre, however, was arguably the beginning of the end of British rule.

When Nick and I visited the Jallianwala Bagh public garden, it resembled a building site. The place was being tidied up with new walkways, a fountain, and an impressive memorial statue. Despite the makeover for visitors, the sight of bullet holes in the walls, outlined with white painted squares, was a chilling reminder of the outrage that took place there.

We headed back to our hotel via the Partition Museum. After reading *Midnight Furies, The Deadly Legacy of India's Partition* as part of my pre-adventure homework, I felt reasonably informed about the story of the partition and I was looking forward to visiting the museum. I don't feel that the events surrounding the partition of India, when Pakistan was split off as a separate country at the time of Indian independence in August 1947, are well known in Britain. The statistics and sheer human suffering are on a frightening scale. A few brief lines here just scratch the surface of a complex issue. Britain's withdrawal from India comes across as a disorganised and rushed operation, with Britain desperate to leave. After 190 years of rule, Britain had sucked India dry; one study estimates it drained $45 trillion from the country. Having bled the country of resources and used her soldiers to fight in World War Two, Britain found itself heavily in financial debt to India, and by 1947 it was more than ready to get out. The Brits departed with indecent haste.

As professional mapmakers, the story of the 'new' boundary interested Nick and me. It never ceases to amaze me how so many of the world's countries are defined by dodgy borders. In simplified terms, the politicians had to decide what an independent India would look like. It would become two nations, mainly divided according to religious demographics. India would be the home for Hindus and Pakistan would be created for Muslims (in fact, the latter became two – East and West Pakistan). There was no simple way to partition India. As well as the religious divide, there were a few other complications, such as strategic roads and irrigation patterns to take into the equation. Any line would have been arbitrary and was always going to cause difficulties, especially for the people living in Bengal and Punjab. And then there was Kashmir, about which several chapters could be written.

Drawing up the maps sounds like a job that could take some time to do properly, even in the hands of an experienced team. Sir Cyril Radcliffe, a lawyer who had never been to India before, was sent out to come up with a solution in five weeks. The maps and census data available were out of date. He must have done the best he could, but he was put in an impossible position. He was also presumably subject to considerable political pressure. The maps weren't even published until after Independence Day, so the Indian and Pakistani public didn't know the extent of their countries as they were celebrating on the big day. Millions of Hindus and Muslims suddenly discovered they were in 'the wrong place,' even though the new countries were officially secular. Finding themselves on the wrong side of the new border, families had to hurry to safety. In the Punjab area, Muslims headed west, and Hindus to the east. The opposite was happening 1,500 kilometres to the east, in Bengal. Whole train loads of people were attacked, and the passengers slaughtered. Estimates vary, but something like twelve to fourteen million people were displaced and between 200,000 to 2 million people were killed. It was a bloodbath. It's likely that the legacy of the partition remains just below the surface in some places, such as Kashmir. As well as describing the historic events in chronological order, the museum takes a sensitive view of some specific aspects of the partition, such as the plight of women. It ends by focusing on the future and looks forward positively.

Well, it had been a heavy afternoon for a couple of

happy-go-lucky pensioner playboys, and a lot to take in. Nick and I were reeling from tales of bloody massacre and massive inter-communal violence. That's enough of the serious stuff for now, although it's food for thought and shouldn't be overlooked. It certainly opened my eyes to aspects of history that they never taught us at school. The history of the British in India got more horrific and shameful the more we found out. It's a wonder they allowed us into the country, and yet, everyone was so welcoming. Perhaps we should be a bit more generous with our taxi fare negotiations. We'd be back to the much lighter fun stuff the following day – you don't get much lighter and fun than a toy train!

Nick and I returned to the hotel and asked the receptionist, 'Could we check out please, Love?' The taxi driver who was going to take us to Kalka, which was the next leg of our travels, soon arrived and we were off again. It was about 180 kilometres by car and took us the best part of five hours to get there. It was a car journey my brain has somehow filtered out of my memory, especially as the last part was in the dark again. I think the horror was such that my neural networks shut down to protect themselves from long-term trauma. The one incident of the journey that I can recall was stopping off and looking around a brickyard... and why wouldn't you? Our journey at light speed must have slowed down sufficiently for the passing world to come back into focus for a moment. It was long enough for Nick to notice what looked like an abandoned brick factory, and ask our driver to pull over so we could investigate it. There seemed to be scores of them along that section of our route. The place was deserted but very photogenic, in stark industrial heritage terms. What was this weird construction materials sub-plot that kept appearing – brickyards, cement advertising, lorries hauling bricks?

Our plan was to stay overnight in Kalka and wake early to catch the UNESCO World Heritage Toy Train up to Shimla in the foothills of the Himalayas. It was having to work our schedule back from our pre-booked train journey to Shimla that gave us such little time in Amritsar. No, that's not really an excuse. We just got it wrong and didn't give ourselves enough time.

We arrived in Kalka shortly before 7:00 pm. Just enough time for me to buy a camouflage hoody as my replacement coat, ready for the mountains. What could be more stylish and appropriate for a sixty-five-year-old? On the upside, it only cost the equivalent of £6.50. Over yet another delicious and inexpensive curry for our evening meal, Nick and I discussed another day's sensory battering.

Our hotel wasn't amazing. In fact, it turned out to be the only accommodation dud during our five-week trip. Our beds were spongy and I'm sure we weren't the first to lie on those sheets. Nick reminds me that the pillow slips were pristine though; it's funny, the things you remember. Oh well, on the bright side we were only in those beds for a few hours – we had to be up by 4:30 am to catch the train to Shimla.

SHIMLA

Before independence, the building now known as the Rashtrapati Niwas (the President's Residence), on the outskirts of Shimla was known as the Viceregal Lodge. Viceregal means something relating to a viceroy, who is someone who governs a colony, country, or territory on behalf of their monarch. It's a sizeable grey sandstone property, built in 1888 in the Jacobethan style. It looks like a cross between a Scottish baronial castle and an upmarket hotel. In fact, at first glance you could mistake it for something from the Hogwarts franchise, or maybe a compact overseas branch of Harrods. What makes the place remarkable, however, is that for a while, back in the early decades of the 20th century, it was the building from which Britain ruled a fifth of the world's population.

Cool in more ways than one, Shimla was the hillside city to which the Brits in charge of India retreated during the summer months to escape the oppressive heat of Delhi. In the conference room of the Viceregal Lodge, you can still see the table at which Nehru, Jinnah and Mountbatten, the key decision makers of the moment, drank tea and discussed how India might look after independence. If the elaborate Burmese teak panelling could talk, it would tell tales of disagreements and historic events that would affect millions of people and change the map of the world (I'm a mapmaker so I can always bring the narrative back to cartography).

Shimla

Nick and I liked Shimla a lot. In those tumbling Himalayan foothills, where provincial India meets Victorian England, the air is refreshingly clean. They should bottle it. When you arrive, you just want to fill your lungs, especially if your journey to Shimla was via one of the more polluted major cities. The air is fresh, and everything looks 'clearer' than lower down. Looking around, it's like someone has taken a fine filter off your eyes. Everything seems that bit sharper in outline and colour. In fact, generally, it's very easy on the eye. The city has a lot going for it.

Shimla sits astride a mountain ridge, about ten kilometres long, and tumbles photogenically down the surrounding hills. Most of the streets in the tidy and picturesque city centre are traffic-free. The local authorities clearly want to keep the city clean. There are heavy fines for dropping litter, for smoking in public and for spitting. That last one must be hard to swallow. In the rest of India, spitting seems to be a national sport. I can't help but think they should persuade the International Olympic Committee to add it to the official list; India could have an unclean sweep of the medal table. I recalled the young lads in the station at Mumbai. I think they were already practising for the ten metre platform event.

Window shopping has a relaxed feeling about it in Shimla. Unlike many places in India, the shopkeepers (well, in our experience, all except one) weren't hyperactive salespeople trying to haul us off the street. The city has a microbrewery, a charming old theatre and nice coffee shops. But top of the list of its qualities is the location. Its mountaintop perch provides stunning views of the towering Himalayas and its foothills. The sunrises and sunsets we saw over the snow-draped mountains were just beautiful.

I'll return to Shimla in a few paragraphs' time. First, I need to get back to the start of the day in Kalka and our 4:45 am departure from the hotel. Once again, Nick and I had to wake the night porter to let us out of the building, which was easier said than done. If we'd had a bit more sense when we woke up, Nick and I would have checked for potential delays because we'd heard that snow had blocked the railway line to Shimla a few days earlier. It didn't occur to us... of course. We were on an old boys' adventure; we didn't do sensible. Getting washed and dressed by ourselves and out of our hotel room on time was challenging enough. Had we checked, however, we could have stayed in our beds for another two hours.

As we picked our way in the cold and dark through the

potholed back streets of Kalka, our brains slowly stirred into life for another day. We found the railway station and were told about our delayed departure. At least our train was still running; it was just going to be a bit late. Instead of the dubious pleasure of extra time in our soft and dirty hotel beds, we settled for a two-hour wait in Kalka station. An upgrade to the executive waiting room meant we could enjoy comfortable upholstered seats instead of benches. It came at a price though; we had to fork out the equivalent of twenty pence per hour for the privilege. That was something we hadn't budgeted for, but as usual, Nick worked his magic on the spreadsheet and reallocated resources from one of his contingency buckets. I took the positives; it was two hours I could use to write up my notes, which meant I'd be able to enjoy the train ride without distraction.

I'd booked the train seats back in the comfort of my house in Shropshire several weeks before we set off on our trip. It had been quite a battle, and I realised after my wasted morning in Jaisalmer that successfully booking the toy train tickets online must have been beginner's luck.

The toy train that winds its way slowly each day up to Shimla has earned its nickname because it is relatively tiny. The scaled down engine and carriages run on narrow-gauge track so it can negotiate the steep winding route through the mountains. There is another toy train that runs between New Jalpaiguri and Darjeeling in West Bengal. That's another one on my list now.

Judging by the pandemonium that broke out when the train arrived, Nick and I weren't the only ones who didn't know what we were doing or where our seats were on the train. Being a toy train, there wasn't much space in the carriages, especially as most people had luggage. Nick and I eventually battled our way through to a couple of seats and settled down for the journey.

Oh no, that would be far too easy. The train guard came through the carriage and decided it would be much better if he shuffled everyone around. When the dust had settled, Nick and I found ourselves in a completely different carriage with a new set of travel buddies – we were squeezed in with a group of excitable medical college students, like the proverbial sardines but also with luggage. They were off to Shimla for a three-night break as part of their post-exam stress relief therapy. The guard must have looked around at the demographic mix of the passengers at the station and thought that a couple of old pensioners would be the ideal travel companions for a bunch of hyperactive medical students. Nick and I were quite happy with the outcome; for all the bluster, they all seemed very polite and friendly. I guess they'd be what people refer to as Generation Z, in their early twenties, and for some reason, they conversed in English. They had a combustible mixture of post-exam delirium and rampant hormones; anything could happen.

Two hours after its scheduled departure, the train finally pulled away to great excitement from all aboard. Well, it was wild excitement, bordering on hysteria, in our carriage. In the rest of the train, things might have been a little more subdued. Slowly at first, the slope of the track increased. We left behind the litter covered outskirts of Kalka, and as we gained height, the amount of trackside rubbish gradually decreased. More of the upland greenery came into view, and it wasn't long before we were in the most stunning mountain scenery. As we ascended, it felt like you could taste the air becoming cleaner and see the colours even more vividly. The views were as spectacular as one would expect from what is widely recognised as one of the most iconic train rides in the world. The only thing missing was a running commentary from a pastel-jacketed Michael Portillo.

As Nick and I had observed in many other places along

our journey, for example, in the City Palace in Udaipur, the Generation Z kids were hard-wired to their phones and could take a photo in a flash. But mostly without a flash. During our five-hour slow chug through the mountains, our carriage-mates seemed to take a selfie or group photo at least every minute. Everything was *very* exciting. They treated Nick and me to lots of singing and lots of oohs and ahh's every time another amazing view opened up. Best of all, in case we couldn't quite hear them, the girls in the group screamed and screeched extremely loudly every time we went into a tunnel and the carriage was plunged into darkness. Such exhilaration! Lucky for us, there were only a hundred of those tunnels in the hundred-kilometre journey.

The toy train winding its way up to Shimla

As we neared the halfway point of the journey, we entered the longest tunnel on the trip. It stretches for over half a mile and when you eventually emerge from the darkness, you arrive at Barog, the only station at which we stopped on our journey through the mountains. As we approached the tunnel, the medical students got even more excited. Someone mentioned a tradition of passengers kissing in the middle of the tunnel in the darkness – I think he'd probably just made the tradition up that morning, but fair play if he had. It cranked the students' excitement level up another notch, to semi-delirious. Although the group had been playing musical chairs ever since we left Kalka, by the time we approached the long tunnel, Nick and I found ourselves with three female students sat opposite us. Perhaps I should just stop the story there and leave you to fill in the next part with your imagination.

Nick leaned towards the young women, and with his right index finger he carefully slid his glasses half a centimetre further up his nose to add gravitas to what he was about to say. There was a touch of Eric Morecambe about his delivery as, with great seriousness, he said, 'Excuse me... my friend here and I are both married and approaching middle age. I hope you three lovely ladies are not planning to smother us in kisses in the tunnel?' As luck would have it, they took him at his word.

Everyone got out of the train at Barog station to stretch their legs. Nick and I walked over to the end of the tunnel to peer into the darkness. We joined in a lengthy photo session with our student friends, and it was soon time to get back on board for the second leg of our journey. As we left the station, our luxury breakfast arrived. That's the benefit of travelling first class. The carefully packaged treat comprised three cold chips, two cold veggie croquettes, and twenty raw peas. We swished that feast down with a shot of chai (boiling water in a cup with a tea bag and powdered milk). It was nicely presented, however, and filled a gap. We took it in good humour; we weren't on the train ride for its gastronomic benefits.

The further we travelled, the more spectacular the scenery became, and the mountains became ever steeper. In the distance, they were snow-capped and, perched precariously on the ones we were travelling through, we occasionally saw tiny houses. As the track turned and twisted one way and then the other, we kept gaining more height. There were innumerable spectacular bridges as well as all those tunnels. The railway was a real feat of engineering. As with the other Indian trains we travelled on, it was possible to stand in the open carriage doorway and watch the world go by – great for photo opportunities.

We arrived in Shimla at 1:00 pm. We were well over 2,000 metres high. The sun was out, and it was nothing like as cold as we had expected. We had read reports of the place being cut off by snow only 24 hrs previously, but there wasn't much snow to see by the time we arrived. The snow was forecast to return by the time we were due to leave but as things turned out, we had two days of glorious sunshine for our visit. Our temporarily adopted Hindu god Ganesha seemed to be looking after us still. He has a reputation for removing obstacles... like snow.

Although it felt smaller and cosier, the city of Shimla has a population of approximately 800,000. It nestles, prettily, in the foothills of the Himalayas and is the largest city of Himachal Pradesh. In March 2021, the Indian government ranked Bengaluru and Shimla in the top two 'most liveable cities of under one million population in India.' For our trip, there was a cricketing connection between those two cities. I'll come back to that, but first I need to get back to our arrival in the city.

Nick and I left Shimla train station and found a taxi to take us to our accommodation. We had booked a homestay for two nights. It was a room let out by a local family and we would live and eat with them. The homestay arrangement is something we can recommend. When we arrived at their house after the short taxi ride, our hosts greeted us warmly. Once again, we seemed to have struck lucky. Our room had a balcony with spectacular views over the mountains. Pavan, the son of the family, was thirty-one and spoke very good English. As he showed us around the house and let us into our room, he advised, 'Keep the door to the balcony shut or the monkeys will come in... oh, and we get leopards here. They come to feed on the stray dogs.' No problem, I thought; it's much the same in Oswestry.

Pavan introduced us to Geetha and Sanjiv, his mum and dad. Pavan asked us how much we had paid for the taxi and seemed shocked when we told him 500 rupees (about a fiver). 'This is too much' he said. 'It should only be 300 rupees.' As if incensed on our behalf, Mum Geetha took up the case immediately and rang the taxi driver. She made her point with quiet assertiveness at first, and then with very loud assertiveness. It was relatively easy to follow the gist of the conversation, which concluded with the taxi driver promising to drop by and refund the overpayment as soon as possible. This seemed like exceptional customer care to us.

When we had settled in, Pavan took us on a whistle-stop walking tour of Shimla, taking in many of the main sights, including the old post office, an old half-timbered library and many other signs of colonial influence. We ended up in a lovely little coffee shop, where our generous host insisted on paying for us. Afterwards, Nick and I continued to explore the Mall, the Subzi Mandi (vegetable market) and the Lakkar Bazaar, while Pavan went off to find some ingredients for our evening meal.

There is a cable car in Shimla that whisks visitors up

Jakhu Hill, Shimla's highest peak, to the Vakhu Temple, dedicated to the Hindu deity Lord Hanuman. Nick and I arrived at the base station at 5:40 pm, timing our run perfectly so we could witness what was promising to be a spectacular sunset from the top of the hill. The man in the ticket office nonchalantly informed us that the cable car had closed for the day ten minutes before we arrived. Almost instantaneously we came up with a cunning Plan B, which involved witnessing the sunset from the warm and cosy bar of the Brew Estate microbrewery. We drowned our sorrow at not getting to the top of Jakhu Hill with a selection of wheat beer, red ale and stout. I don't think it was what we'd ordered, or in the quantity we'd ordered, but by the time we'd finished, we didn't really care what we'd asked for. The sunset was perfect, and we loved everybody.

We meandered our way back the mile and a half or so to our lodgings just in time for Pavan's mum, Geetha, to dish up a tasty chicken curry with aloo gobi and steamed rice. Our hosts were incredibly hospitable, and it was a treat to be with them. We discussed our ideas for sightseeing the following day and our plans for the next leg of our journey through India. Sanjiv, Pavan's father, gave us some good local advice and arranged a taxi for the morning. By the time we retired for the night, it was getting noticeably cold, probably close to freezing, and we were glad to have the luxury of electric blankets on our beds – not something you'd naturally associate with India, perhaps. They did the job, though, and we both slept snugly and soundly.

~

The next day we awoke with great excitement... well, eventually. We were expecting another heady day of adventure and exploration. Still on a high from our ODI exploits in

Bengaluru, the day ahead promised to reach even greater cricketing heights.

When you first saw the name Shimla at the beginning of this chapter, I'm sure your first thought will have been, 'Wait a minute... isn't that just a two-hour car ride from Chail, site of the highest cricket ground in the world?' And you'd be right. Not that anyone would be daft enough to go there.

Nick and I awoke to a magnificent vista of the distant, snow-capped high Himalayas as we stepped out onto our balcony. Swinging effortlessly through the woods and across the adjacent buildings was the troop of monkeys we'd been warned about. They looked like they were on the lookout for easy pickings from naïve foreign visitors, so we quickly closed the bedroom doors behind us.

After a homely homestay breakfast of fried eggs on toast, our taxi driver, Govindrum, picked Nick and me up at 8:00 am. Getting from A to B in the Himalayan foothills is a bit more difficult than back on the Deccan plateau. It can be tortuous. As the red kite flies, the distance from Shimla to Chail must be about twenty kilometres, but by car it's more than double that. The trip involves countless switchback bends up and down steep pine-clad valleys. The first half of the journey was mainly downhill, and according to the altitude app on my smartphone, we descended from 2,200 metres in Shimla to 1,400 metres at the lowest point. Then we started the slow ascent. For the first hour of the journey, I sat in the back, with Nick in the front – standard procedure. I tried to jot down some notes for the daily travel blog that I was writing. The other reason for concentrating on my notes was that it distracted me from looking at the driving and the near vertical drops alongside many parts of our route. What crazy lengths some people go to for a world best. Anyway, the cunning plan went the way of most cunning plans, mainly because of the constant battering from a road that seemed to be still under construction for most of the way. Those frequent vertical jolts were supplemented by regular sharp lurches left and right as contact with traffic coming the opposite way was avoided at the last second. After an hour, I felt sick and gave up writing. If it was going to be my last ever journey, I might as well try to enjoy the spectacular mountain scenery.

I mentioned my blog writing to Nick and before long, we'd upgraded it to a book, a Netflix series, DVD and a blockbuster movie. We speculated on who might play us in the lead roles. We agreed that Lee Mack and David Mitchell might be suitable contenders if we based it on our sense of humour, as long as David Mitchell didn't mind shaving all the hair off his head. Then again, with their near photographic likeness, George Clooney and Daniel Craig might be more obvious choices for the roles.

After just under two hours of swerving and bumping, twisting and turning, we reached the village of Chail. The initial signs weren't promising. A notice at the start of the road that led to the cricket ground said it was closed to the public. To roars of approval from Nick and me, our driver nonchalantly drove straight past it – yes! ... we liked his style.

It turned out that the cricket ground was in the centre of a military camp. Undeterred, our driver drove on – he seemed to think it would be alright. After a half mile or so we reached a security barrier – ha, maybe our quest was over without a sight screen being sighted. As we pulled up at the gate, the soldier standing outside the guard box didn't even bother looking up from his phone. He eventually acknowledged our presence and after a brief exchange with our driver, he handed over a form for us to fill in. Paperwork completed, he raised the barrier for us, and we were on our way again. Most things in India seem to involve filling out a form – another legacy of British rule. We drove into the military camp and at the highest point, there it was: at 2,250 metres and 2,209 metres above Lord's Cricket Ground was the highest cricket ground in the world. Nick and I speculated if the pitch would take spin. Contain yourself reader.

There was one slight problem. There was no way of getting into the ground. A high chain-link fence topped with barbed wire surrounded it, and each gate we came across as we walked around the perimeter was locked. There were several signs saying that access was not permitted. What were they trying to say?

'We seem to be in a Gilbert Hill situation,' said Nick as we strolled around the ground looking in desperation for a way in. 'Surely we haven't come all this way to be foiled at the last moment – there must be a way in somewhere.' I felt duty bound to bolster his morale with a bit of laddish banter. 'It's about as difficult to find as a Glamorgan T20 win, Nick.' This didn't help.

Although the military camp we were in the middle of seemed almost deserted, we bumped into someone else wandering around the ground and he confirmed that it was not possible to see the pitch itself. Car sickness, near-death road incidents, vertigo and brain rattling vibration for two hours... for this! 'Bother...' comes nowhere near our actual vocabulary for describing our frustration.

Nick and I continued our walk around the boundary fence anyway, and from each of the gates we came across, there were excellent views of the ground and the pitch. We took some photos and continued our perambulation of the perimeter. At one point, we noticed that a bit of the supporting wall had fallen away from underneath a section of the chain-link fence, leaving a human torso-sized hole... if the human was a lean, athletic sort. Nick and I looked at each other, and we each raised an eyebrow in unison. 'We've come a long way to be here, Nick,' I said. 'Yes Mark, I don't know when we'll be back,' he replied. We speculated that if someone was sufficiently determined, they could wriggle under the barbed wire of the fence and get in. That way, they'd get a close-up view of the pitch and feel the thin atmosphere of a unique cricket ground... the highest in the world. If anyone was to do that, they might hang around for a few minutes, take a few pictures of the popping crease and maybe a couple of selfies, with the scoreboard as a background. What a wheeze that would be.

Nick and I brushed ourselves down after our disappointment, as you must, got back into the car, and prepared for the return journey. Our flirt with high-altitude cricket wasn't over, however. We stopped off at the village of Junga on our way back to Shimla and we witnessed the final two balls of the Himachal Pradesh Government Education Department's twenty overs' innings against the Public Works Department. It was enough time to see a nail-biting misfield on the boundary and a run out. We chatted with the Public Works boys between innings, and they seemed confident of knocking off the required runs. We posed, borrowed bats in hand for the obligatory photos with the lads and got on our way again.

We continued our journey back to Shimla, and with my head up this time, I could enjoy the lush, pine-clad mountain scenery bathed in beautiful sunshine. For most of the way, the road was barely more than a single track and the spectacular views over the sheer drops at the edges were, of course, unimpeded by safety barriers. Despite the health and safety issues, admiring the gorgeous view to the side was preferable to looking ahead and watching a stream of near-death incidents.

When we got back to Shimla, our driver dropped us off at the Rashtrapati Niwas (the old Viceregal Lodge) and we risked some boiled eggs and potato pattie street food while we waited for the next guided tour.

As the Viceregal Lodge, the building was the summer residence of thirteen Indian Viceroys, the British Raj leaders who governed the whole of the Indian subcontinent between 1888 until independence in 1947. The building was clearly a statement by the Brits to any Indian visitors. It said 'Look! We're in charge here and we can afford all this splendour!' (800 staff and luxuries such as electricity and a clever wax-centred fire sprinkler system). Nick and I were the only foreigners in a group of a twenty or so visitors. Our guide was thoughtful enough to give Nick and me an initial briefing in English, before our group set off, and he then told us about each room, one by one, after he'd addressed the main group in Hindi.

There were three take-away memories for me. First, the photos of all the leading actors in the partition talks. Those black and white images were so evocative of that historic period. Second, we stood next to the table where Lord Mountbatten, Gandhi, Jinnah, and Nehru drank tea and discussed the imminent partition in 1947. For me, this was spine-tingling, especially after reading *Midnight's Furies* as part of my pre-adventure homework. The atmosphere of the room made it feel like we were there at the time of the talks. It felt like the protagonists could walk back into the room at any moment. That would have caused a stir. Third, and maybe not charged with the same degree of geopolitical and historical significance, Nick and I were told that we were standing on the watershed between the Ganges and the Indus (back to the cartographic narrative). In theory, drops of rain or snowflakes landing on the Rashtrapati Niwas have a 50/50 chance of heading west and ending up in the Arabian Sea south of a Karachi, or heading eastwards and ending up in the Bay of Bengal near Kolkata. To me, that's amazing, although I understand if no one else gets excited about it.

Nick and I headed back to downtown Shimla and booked train tickets for the second half of the next leg of our trip – to Agra – for the following day. We still had to arrange bus tickets for the first leg of the journey, but our homestay host had assured us he would arrange that for us. We headed for the cable car again and with the advantage of our previous day's experience, we could time our run perfectly to catch the last ride of the day up to the Jakhu Temple. At 2,455 metres, the hill is impressive enough, and then the colourful statue of Hanuman stretches up another thirty metres. I'd like to report that there were magnificent views back to Shimla below, but the views, although impressive, were partially obscured by pine trees. We walked back through the woods, in the half-light of dusk, towards the bright lights of the city. As was tradition by now for our stay in Shimla, we stopped off for a pint at the microbrewery, leaving after just one drink this time.

A series of little roadside fires illuminated our way back through the main streets of the city. People selling tourist souvenirs had set up their pitches every few yards and lit little log fires to keep out the cold, which Nick reminds me, was by then bitter. It looked like someone had strung up a set of fairy lights to guide our way back, and it just added to the already charming atmosphere of the city by night. We stopped off at several stalls. I bought some little woollen booties for my granddaughter, Lyra. Although they cost very little, the seller insisted that I took some change. I felt a rush of remorse as I walked away, realising how little I'd paid to the mother and daughter who'd made my presents. They sat serenely, knitting by their little log fire with a small blanket spread on the ground on which they'd neatly arranged their hand made clothes. The flickering light lit up their beautiful scarlet and gold saris and they looked up at us with big eyes and huge beaming smiles. Further along, Nick tried on several hats and admired the scarves on display – but I could write that about everywhere we went in India. Nick and I hurried on, conscious that we needed to be back at our homestay in good time for dinner. Once back, we again enjoyed delicious home cooking and delightful friendly discussions with our hosts.

Anyone going to Shimla in January should expect some very cold weather, with a likelihood of overnight freezing. Thanks to our electric blankets, Nick and I had another toasty night's sleep, but the following morning our high-altitude sojourn in Shimla would be over; we were heading for Agra. The plan was to get the bus to the city of Ambala, in the state of Haryana, where we would pick up an overnight sleeper train to Agra, via Delhi.

~

Our hosts advised Nick and me to turn up for breakfast 'past 9:30 am' – whatever that meant. Like a couple of typical Brits abroad, we turned up at 9:30 on the dot. No one was to be seen. We waited another hour before our host family emerged, and fair enough, that *was* past 9:30 am. It was worth the wait; we were greeted like family members again and treated to our scrumptious breakfast of gobi paratha – cauliflower pancakes with lashings of pickle. We then had more waiting to do, while our hosts worked out every possible permutation for getting us to Ambala, and then went about phoning around to buy tickets for us. We didn't really know what was going on (no change there then), but the relaxed morning we were expecting, looking around Shimla, somehow disappeared. That's how it goes, but we were grateful that our hospitable hosts were going to so much trouble to arrange our travel for us.

Pavan took us into town by car. Picking up our bus tickets involved a roadside handover that felt like something out of a spy movie. I was just wondering if I'd have to trot out my migrating Siberian gulls' line again when our host asked us to get 1,100 rupees in cash ready. The car slowed down and we pulled up next to someone, probably one of Pavan's cousins, standing by the side of the road. The window was lowered, and the exchange took place. You go with the flow. It seemed a world away from buying a bus ticket at a conventional bus station back home in Blighty... but much more fun.

Adrenalin junkies who are bored with the best that Thorpe Park or Alton Towers can offer could do worse than invest 550 rupees in a bus ticket for the journey from Shimla to Ambala. The tickets we had for the 150-kilometre, white-knuckle ride were for a 'Volvo bus,' which we were told was the safest and most comfortable of the two options available. While we waited in Shimla bus station, Nick and I chatted to a young scientist who had travelled to the city for a job interview. Travelling from Delhi had required an overnight stay in Shimla, which had added to her expense. She was told she was one of hundreds being interviewed, and the interview took less than five minutes. She was rightly upset and felt she had been misled; she thought the company was just going through the motions. It led to a brief but illuminating discussion on Indian women's participation in the job market, and in society in general. Our fellow passenger thought that large elements of the Indian community still believed that a woman's place was in the home; in fact, in some parts of the country there was even a stigma attached to a woman being at work instead of staying at home, to look after the family, and attend to household chores (I should add this isn't restricted to India, of course). There is a perception among some Indian families that having a daughter will be more costly than having a son – a bride's family may have to pay a dowry to the groom or his parents. Parents may also believe that a son is more likely to look after them in old age because a daughter is likely to run off and marry, and then care for her own children and husband. Violence and the risk of sexual assault in public places, on public transport, and in the workplace are even more serious issues, discouraging Indian women from participating in the workforce. It was desperately sad to be told that domestic violence in India is widely accepted for cultural and religious reasons. Our brief discussion was a tiny insight into a huge topic, but just as we were getting more deeply into the subject, and our job-seeking friend was opening up to us, the bus arrived, and we parted company. We'd touched on a delicate and disturbing subject and, although it shouldn't be ignored, it's not one to explore in depth in a book like this. Our fellow bus travellers' views seemed consistent with many disturbing press reports and other sources. It's something that should be talked about.

The Volvo bus *was* comfortable. It had large reclining seats, plenty of legroom and air conditioning – not really a priority, however, with the outside temperature hovering around five degrees. There was no toilet, of course, which strangely becomes more of an issue when you're in your sixties, although the driver stopped for a couple of comfort stops during the six-hour trip.

We should have realised what the journey was going to be like when the conductor walla came through the bus dishing out what he called 'hill sickness' bags. He also gave us a bottle of water each. Looking back, it was a journey of two halves; the first half took us through the mountains down to the plain, the second took us over the flatlands.

Luckily, for the mountain section, we had the scenery to distract us, and from time to time we could see the tracks of the toy train we had travelled on two days earlier. About 80 per cent of the mountain road section of our journey seemed to be a 'work in progress,' a label that might describe many parts of India we saw. We passed or drove through mile after mile of construction works. We lurched from side to side as we snaked our way down the mountains. Just like our taxi ride to the cricket ground, we were getting rhythmical left-to-right traffic avoidance jerks to go with the vertical jolts induced by the construction sites and poor roads. The sick bags were there for a reason, although fortunately we didn't see anyone using them.

Looking back, now that the nausea is a distant memory, it wasn't so bad. The second half was even quite comfortable. We arrived in Ambala at 'past 6:00 pm' and everything was still going to plan. Earlier in the journey, we'd asked the conductor walla where the train station was in Ambala, and when we arrived, the bus driver took us slightly off their normal route to drop us off by the side of a busy dual carriageway, close to the train station – now that's excellent service! An overnight sleeper promised to be another new experience, and we were looking forward to it.

Ambala is a major route intersection with important road and rail connections. It is also a major grain, flour milling, cotton and sugar trading centre. Nick and I didn't see any of that. We enjoyed four hours there, our time divided equally between finding somewhere to eat, eating, crossing that dual carriageway, and finding the right platform in the train station.

We had our evening meal (we both had dal makhani and vegetable pilau) in a less than spotless food establishment. I can't quite bring myself to use the word restaurant because it implies so much more. On our journey through India,

Nick and I soon learnt that there was no correlation between an Indian food outlet's appearance and the quality of the food. Cost was no guide to quality either; it had all been good. In Ambala, the meal was unbelievably good, but it felt like we were playing Russian roulette with Indian food bugs and bacteria. Nowhere in that cafeteria seemed remotely approaching clean. The dark brown grease encrusted light switches and power sockets looked like they carried DNA from at least two decades of previous customers. I say again, though; the food was superb! We shared a table with a chap called Manvad from Delhi. He told us he was on a business development trip trying to find buyers for the lightweight backpacks his company makes. Like almost all Indian people we met on our travels, Manvad was extremely friendly. He left us his phone number in case we got into any trouble, saying 'Please just phone me. Wherever you are in India, I will help you. Next time you must come to my place to visit some villages and see another side of India.' He also offered to throw in four hours of Hindi lessons to enrich the experience. How amazing is that?

We made our way to the station. By now it was dark and everywhere seemed incredibly busy and noisy. Nick reckoned he'd never been anywhere so busy. The city seemed to be in a permanent rush hour. Somehow, we crossed a dual carriageway under a flyover. We stopped in the gap between the carriageways to look at a compound full of rats. It was a fenced off enclosure under the flyover between busy traffic lanes, holding half a dozen goats and a few sheep. I know it sounds crazy, but somehow it seemed perfectly normal. There were also hundreds of rats that popped up comically from their tunnels, scurried across the ground to grab some goat feed, and then scurried back. It was like splat the rat without the splatting. When the novelty of watching them wore off, Nick and I headed for the station, found our train and carriage, and settled in.

Anyone could wander through the carriage's central thoroughfare, which had bunk beds parallel to it on one side and at right angles to windows on the opposite side. The seats were covered in a blue vinyl-type material and were fairly comfortable. Our berths were on opposite sides in middle level bunks. We stashed our bags under the lower bunk bed and settled in. It wasn't quite the luxury of our first two railway journeys in India. This time, we didn't have any pillows, sheets, or blankets. This wasn't a problem for the other passengers around us because they knew the system and had brought their own. Nick and I settled down in our respective bunks, fully clothed. I used a couple of shirts for a pillow and a tee shirt for a blanket. There was an electrical socket above the window between us at the head end of the bunks. We both used it to charge our phones. It felt freezing because we were the first compartment in the carriage, close to the join with the next carriage – the join that was open to the outside world and the cold night air. We had air conditioning in the form of an icy blast that picked up the smell of the toilet on its way from the open carriage doors to our bunks. Nick's solution to this was to wrap his nice warm Shimla scarf (250 rupees) around his head, invisible man style, to lie down and turn his back on the rest of the carriage. The physical and mental battering of another day in India caught up with us and sleep came easily.

The relative calm of our draughty and urine-scented freezer cabinet soon changed when we arrived in Delhi. There was pandemonium as what seemed like several hundred people, their luggage, and a random selection of small farm animals filed through our train compartment. Brought back to a few of my senses by the racket, I peered through half-opened eyes towards Nick. His face was expressionless, but I knew something was wrong. 'That's not good,' he said, leaning on one elbow and holding up one end of his phone charger lead. There should have been a Samsung mobile phone attached to it. We did a rapid sweep of the bunk beds and the surrounding floor, but Nick was immediately sure that someone had taken his phone. By then it was a Galaxy far far away. I was lucky; I still had mine. It must have been tucked under my pillow just enough to be safe, or maybe the culprit was more partial to the Android operating system.

Despite all the seats and bunks being full, more people kept coming into our compartment, presumably without tickets. Maybe it was a *Guinness World Records* attempt we hadn't been informed about, to achieve the most people in a train compartment. As the train pulled out of Delhi station, things began to settle down. A few people went off to see if they could find seats elsewhere and we were soon down to just thirteen in our eight-person compartment. The five extra bodies stood around or sat on the bottom bunks, nudging the slumbering occupant to one side. It seemed the accepted passenger protocol was to chatter as loudly as possible or play loud Bollywood dance music on phones. Nick and I scanned the carriage, looking carefully at each of those phones, but they weren't his. Eating and throwing food on the floor was optional, but a practice enjoyed by many of our fellow travellers. Added to the dance beat sound mix, like a looped Indo-rap backing track, was the regular piercing cry of 'chai' from the wallas walking through with flasks of sweet milky tea.

Although Nick and I kept possession of our bunks in the turmoil of Delhi station, the once peaceful compartment no longer lent itself to gentle slumber. Anyway, after 'the incident,' I couldn't sleep anymore. I was on constant alert, and everyone suddenly looked suspicious. Although Nick's initial description of the chai leaf isn't suitable for print, he took the loss on the chin, saying 'Well, it was on charge in the open, and it was probably quite a temptation if you're as poor as most people we see.' It was still disappointing, though, after all the kindness and goodwill we had encountered up to that point. You can go anywhere in the world and have your phone nicked, though. Nick saw it as an opportunity to get a new one. Little did we know at that point how much fun that was going to be. In the meantime, the sun was up, we'd arrived in Agra, and we had a theft to report.

AGRA

Quoting from Nick's diary, he writes, 'Treating my phone loss philosophically, we arrived at Agra station to a beautiful sunrise at 8:30 am.' And that's how it was. We'd arrived, and we were on a mission to report a theft. We had zero expectation of ever seeing the phone again, but Nick needed to get something in writing to support his insurance claim.

Reporting a theft can't be that difficult, can it? Life is too short to recount the process we went through. Both the planet's stock of trees and the reader's attention span would be too limited, so a brief precis will have to suffice. Nick and I soon identified the station's administration office and after a few enquiries, were escorted around several more offices and a car park before visiting more offices and finally the police station. After explaining the problem, the police officer on duty instructed Nick to write out a statement. Although you'd think Nick would have known what had happened, the police officer insisted on dictating how the events unfolded to Nick so he could write it down. It had to be in capital letters and include the important detail that the theft occurred at Ambala. Presumably, that put the problem in someone else's patch. While the only person of authority was being distracted, I had a wander around and checked out the police cells. Had things not gone well at Gilbert Hill on our first full day in Mumbai, we might have seen the inside of one already. Let's say they were functional, and I had no desire to see one again, but anyway, back to the main plot. Report written, we were told to return at 5:00 pm. This would give the police department sufficient time to do the paperwork and provide an official document for Nick to give to his insurance company. After that, getting a taxi to our hotel was straightforward.

Agra is a city of over 1.5 million people, in the state of Uttar Pradesh, and is another of the major road and rail intersections in northern India. The millions of tourists who visit each year, however, don't go there to admire its communications infrastructure. Keen followers of this book's construction related sub-plot will be interested to read that Agra is home to India's leading infrastructure company, with a market capitalisation of over sixty billion Indian rupees. Not even that, nor Agra's renowned leather goods, cut stone, and handwoven carpets, will be the number one attraction for most tourists, however. They go to see the Taj Mahal.

To only visit the world's most iconic and famous building, however, as many people do, is to overlook so much more – not that I'm one to preach about whistle-stop tourism. The city was the seat of Mughal Empire power from 1526 to 1658. During that time, they built the Agra Fort, Taj Mahal and Fatehpur Sikri, which are now all UNESCO World Heritage sites. I think a Mughal themed tour would be an excellent idea for a future adventure.

India is a country that depends on tourism. Supported by eleven million foreign visitors, the travel and tourism sector contributed over 9 per cent to the national Gross Domestic Profit in 2019, keeping over eighty-seven million people in work. That's well over the entire population of the

United Kingdom – just employed in tourism. As well as the obvious tick-list of famous sights that Nick and I were working our way through in India, several niche themes have enjoyed rapid visitor growth in recent years. These include specialities such as adventure, medical, wellness, sports, eco, film, and spiritual tourism. The travel sector, like most, was struck severely by the global COVID pandemic in 2020. Tourist numbers dwindled, hotel occupancy plummeted and half the jobs in the sector disappeared within a few months. The most symbolic sign of the crisis came on March 17th 2020, when the Taj Mahal was closed to tourists. Just six weeks before that, not realising how the world was about to change beyond all recognition, Nick and I arrived in Agra to visit the world's most recognisable building.

Our taxi driver dropped us off at our hotel in the narrow backstreets. We quickly stashed our backpacks in our room and headed for the hotel's roof garden to get some breakfast. There was a glorious view over the city rooftops, and across to the Taj Mahal, about a kilometre away. Its huge white dome and minarets were bathed in mid-morning sunshine. We seemed to have chosen well again.

As is normally the case in India, the hotel staff included a fixer, complete with a comprehensive set of near relatives. Nick told the hotel fixer about the unfortunate phone incident and asked about finding a replacement. 'No problem, Sir' was his instant reply. He then gave us a phone number to call at 6:00 pm that evening – 'You will get new phone, Sir.' It reminded me of our cloak and dagger money transfer on the Shimla roadside, and I couldn't wait to see how our evening rendezvous would turn out.

Our friendly hotel fixer then escorted Nick and me to a nearby travel agent, where we booked tickets for the next few days of our trip. He then recommended a taxi to take us on a tour of the city in the afternoon. We wanted to see some of the main sights of Agra but thought it best to leave the Taj Mahal for the following morning so we could see it at its majestic best – at sunrise.

Our taxi driver, Yousaf, appeared within ten minutes, complete with a city guide called Murad. We hadn't asked for a guide; how much was that going to add to the price we'd already agreed? 'Oh, you will pay me no money, Sirs. You pay me what you think... or not at all, that's fine; it's completely up to you.' This seemed a typically flexible Indian arrangement, but like the hard-nosed, experienced international travellers that we are... we took him at his word. Murad explained that the first stop on our tour would be Agra Fort. We would then visit the 'mini Taj Mahal' and end up at the Mehtab Bagh, or Moon Garden, on the opposite side of the river to the Taj Mahal.

It's a pity so many visitors make a beeline for the Taj Mahal and miss what is one of the most impressive and historically significant forts in India. Mughal emperors ruled India for over three centuries and built Agra Fort in the year 1573, under the reign of Akbar. The twenty-one-metre-tall red sandstone walls tower skywards and form a one-and-a-half-kilometre long perimeter around the fort. This was their military command-and-control centre and the administrative hub from which they governed the empire. The emperors had their own bathing ghats (stairways down to the river), when the Yamuna River used to flow alongside the eastern edge of the fort. The Fort must be on the short list of the best in India, alongside the likes of Jodhpur, Udaipur, Jaipur, and Jaisalmer. Nick and I had the briefest of stops at Agra Fort and feeling very guilty with our use of drive-by tourism, we drove on to the tomb of Itimad-ud-Daulah, a building more commonly referred to as the 'mini Taj Mahal.'

A few words on the Mughal Empire... but again, this is

the very lightest of touches that barely skims the surface of a rich and complex history. The Mughal Empire ruled most of India during the 16th and 17th centuries, and we still see many aspects of its legacy today. Babur founded the empire when he moved into India in the early 1500s from territories that are now in Uzbekistan. He was a descendant of Genghis Khan, so invading other people's countries and expanding empires was in his blood. Fast forward a few generations and the Mughal Empire was in control of most of India. The Mughals introduced an organised central government, Persian arts, crafts and architecture, religious tolerance, and a structured education system (what did the Mughals ever do for India?).

Although Muslims had been in India for hundreds of years before the arrival of Babur, the first Mughal Emperor, it was the spread of the Mughal Empire that marked the widespread adoption of the religion across the region. The Mughal ruling class was Muslim but there were many Hindu and Sikh subjects throughout the empire. Today, there are more than 200 million Muslims in India. But back to the Mughal Empire – as well as consolidating Islam across a wide swathe of South Asia, it also spread Islamic (and particularly Persian) arts and culture – and the Taj Mahal is its most famous artistic legacy.

Jahangir, the fourth Mughal Emperor, ruled from 1605 until his death in 1627. He was a larger-than-life player in the story of the Mughals and provides our introduction to the story of the Taj Mahal. Widely recognised as being well educated, Jahangir was a patron of the arts, but he also enjoyed fighting and conquering. According to our guide, Jahangir was even more fond of the bottle. So much so, his wife, Nur Jahan (one of seven), ended up running the empire herself. Her father is buried in the tomb of Itimad-ud-Daulah, and after Agra Fort, the tomb was the second stop on our afternoon's sightseeing trip. The mausoleum is a small-scale version of the Taj Mahal, which was built a few years later. Maybe it was a practice piece.

Jahangir's son, Shah Jahan, built the Taj Mahal in honour of his beloved third wife, the Persian Princess Mumtaz Mahal, first lady among hundreds in his harem. He was completely besotted with his wife and was so traumatised by her death that his beard is said to have turned white overnight. Stress can do that. My beard was similarly transformed when I saw Southampton lose 9-0 at home to Leicester earlier in the season.

It seems Jahan became completely obsessed with the Taj Mahal project, and when he started building a second mausoleum for himself, which was going to be a black marble version of the Taj Mahal, his son, Aurangzeb took over in what sounds like a military coup. He exiled Jahan to house arrest in Agra fort. The whole mausoleum thing had become completely out of control. In today's terms, the cost of the Taj Mahal would be approximately $1 billion. The country was being ruined because of one man's obsession and personal agenda. It wasn't the first example of that, and it will probably not be the last.

Jahan's son Aurangzeb, must have thought he could spend the Taj Mahal project money on better things, like conquering more lands. He is said to have killed off his older brother to clear the path to the throne, and it's likely that Aurangzeb's extremism began the decline of the Mughal Empire. The British deposed the last Mughal Emperor in 1858 and opened a new chapter in India's history.

The last stop on our hasty tour of the city was the Mehtab Bagh or the Moonlight Gardens of Agra. This relatively overlooked gem occupies a deserted area of floodplain on the opposite side of the Yamuna River to the Taj Mahal. I'm not sure Nick and I would have found the gardens on our own, so maybe it was good to have a local guide after all. It was well worth visiting the site for its completely tourist free views of the world's most famous building. The site was quite scruffy and partly overgrown, but even more attractive because it was so quiet and natural.

Babur, the first Mughal Emperor, constructed the original gardens in the mid-16th century, so they pre-date the Taj Mahal. Our guide told us that Shah Jahan saw the gardens on the opposite side of the river and decided to build his own mausoleum there – a black marble twin of the Taj Mahal. Although hard evidence that the second Taj was going to be built is hard to find, I like the story. Considering Shah Jahan's obsession with neatness and symmetry, the idea of two opposing buildings either side of the river, one white and one black, feels romantically right and even plausible. What a sight that would have been!

Tour over, Yousaf drove us to a restaurant that he recommended. We invited him and Murad to join us – it was our treat. Yousaf wanted to stay in his car, but Murad made up for our driver's absence by eating for both. When it was time to say our farewells, we gave our guide a generous payment, despite his early protestations that he wasn't doing it for the money. To hell with the expense, we wanted to show our appreciation. He immediately told us we hadn't given him enough, so we paid him more.

Our ride back to the hotel was via the police office at the railway station, where Nick picked up his official stamped statement written out in Hindi. We returned to our hotel, via an English wine shop, and at the prescribed hour we rang our mystery contact to sort out the new phone for Nick. Our man arrived shortly after and invited Nick and me to jump on the back of his motorbike. We raced off at breakneck speed to find the phone shop. With no helmets, we tore through the tiny streets and alleyways of the old city part of

Agra. Somehow, we dodged the tuk-tuks, pedestrians and cows, but it felt like one of those movie chase scenes – where piles of cardboard boxes and startled chickens go flying into the air to the sound of loud screams, high revs and screeching tyres. We sixty-somethings know how to have a good time.

The phone shop was somewhere deep within a labyrinth of small streets and alleys that were teeming with bright lightbulbs, household goods and evening shoppers. It's another story that could fill several chapters, but I'll give you the summary version. The deal to buy the phone took nearly three hours and involved most of the shopkeeper's extended family, cups of tea, some serious negotiating, a lot of paperwork, and Nick having his photo taken several times. By the end of the evening, we were part of the extended family, and Nick had a new phone. We just had another *Mad Max* motorbike ride back to the hotel to survive.

~

The rhythmical wailing of the Muslim call to prayer provided a fitting alarm call to stir Nick and me for our visit to the Taj Mahal. We were up at 6:00 am and on our way to catch the sunrise. More than seven million tourists (pre-COVID pandemic) descend upon the Taj Mahal each year to see what has been voted the best of the seven modern wonders of the world. According to one source I read, only half a million of those are non-Indian. At first sight, that seems unlikely, but that ratio seemed about right from what Nick and I saw on our visit. There were surprisingly few non-Indian visitors. People arrive at the UNESCO World Heritage site with high expectations. Even though it is arguably the most famous and iconic building in the world,

I kept my expectations in check. I was prepared to be disappointed. I expected to be whelmed, nothing more.

Nick and I bought our tickets and were provided with some fetching blue plastic bag overshoes. We grabbed a couple of bottles of water and began to zig zag our way along a lengthy queue. Before too long we arrived at, and entered, the main entrance archway. We saw that famous view across the gardens and ponds to the iconic ivory-white marble mausoleum. Even after seeing countless photos of the Taj Mahal before, to see it in that half-light of morning, in the flesh – well, it's an absolute jaw-slackening stunner! I'm not sure why it is so breathtaking.

Early morning at the Taj Mahal

It must be a combination of the graceful lines, the symmetry, the garden/river location, the space, the beautiful white marble, and Persian decoration. Of course, the romantic story behind it helps. The impact was helped by being there at dawn as the mist rose from the Yamuna River and partially draped the Taj Mahal. The mist came and went in a game of peek-a-boo for an hour until the sun broke through completely, unveiling the full beauty of the building. I would build something similar for my wife, of course, but I'm not so well resourced with vacant land and building materials.

As I have already mentioned, the Emperor Shah Jahan had the Taj Mahal built in honour of his beloved third wife, the Persian Princess Mumtaz Mahal. She died in 1631, aged thirty-eight, while giving birth to the couple's 14th child. That's quite an output for nineteen years of marriage! Construction of the Taj Mahal involved 20,000 artisans, using 1,000 elephants, and was completed approximately twenty years after the death of Mumtaz Mahal (the exact figure varies slightly according to sources). The site occupies seventeen hectares, with the tomb of the princess providing the main focal point on the riverside. Mughal buildings had mainly been constructed using red sandstone prior to the Taj Mahal, but it was Shah Jahan's idea to use white marble, beautifully and intricately inlaid with precious stones. The basic design elements are Indo-Islamic. An enormous dome covers the tomb, which stands on a square plinth. Four minarets, each forty metres high, are positioned with perfect symmetry either side of the tomb. They lean outwards slightly so they won't damage the rest of the building if they collapse because of an earthquake. The Taj Mahal is one of those rare places in the world where no number of words can do it justice. I would never manage that, and I've probably used up too many already trying.

As Nick and I walked around, we couldn't believe the number of photos being taken. All right, the Taj Mahal is special and worthy of a few pictures, and we must have taken a fair few ourselves, but it seems Indian tourists are obsessed with them. With the influence of social media these days, it's difficult to get out of the mindset of having to get the killer photo, and instead to just enjoy the moment and take everything in. But then again, we're all guilty of it. We took our time looking around the building and grounds, and went into the museum, which most people seemed to neglect. After a delightful few hours, we ambled back to our hotel and popped up to the rooftop for some breakfast, with the Taj Mahal still in view.

Nick and I bumped into one of the few foreign tourists we came across on our Indian travels. Ryan was an outgoing American millennial who, during his five months touring India, seemed to have been everywhere. There was a binary simplicity to his view of the world; everything was 'fuckin' shit' or 'frickin' awesome.' To be fair, he could add subtle nuance by coming up with other combinations of those four words. The three of us compared notes on the places we'd seen since we arrived, and our itinerary for the rest of the journey. I told Ryan we were heading for Lucknow next, which he immediately told us was 'fuckin' shit.' That was something I must have missed in the guidebooks. Trying to find something more positive, Nick then asked him about the best place he'd visited so far – good thinking Nick. Ryan stared into the distance and his eyes went misty as he recalled his time in Varanasi: 'Oh, the fuckin' Ganges man... and all those dead bodies... frickin' awesome.' I was mentally questioning his visitor attraction criteria by this point but didn't see any need to change our itinerary, which included both Lucknow and Varanasi.

Considering it involved Indian driving, our five-hour coach journey to Lucknow was relatively uneventful. We drove on the best roads we'd seen in India, and the coach was comfortable. We drove for hours through flatland scenery, with plenty of wetlands and fields of mainly rape, wheat, rice, and fruits. The land was low-lying all the way, especially, as you'd expect, in the area where we crossed the Ganges. We stopped around halfway for a comfort break at a motorway services type place. About an hour later, the coach pulled over to the side of the road and a dozen fellas got off to wee by the side of the bus. I can't imagine that happening with National Express on the side of the M25.

We got to Lucknow on time, a pleasant surprise that forced Nick to roll out the obligatory 'We're not late... we must be in luck now!' Just before we arrived, I received a text to tell me they had cancelled our coach to Varanasi in a couple of days' time, so we needed to find the ticket office to get a different bus booked up. I mention that task in passing like it's a five-minute job. You'll have worked out by now that in India, it's never like that. I'll spare you the details; you can only expect a reader to wade through so many long rambling accounts of Indian bureaucracy. After we'd got replacement tickets, it was a quick taxi ride to our hotel, a shower and out for dinner.

The hotel was very plush and had a lovely old colonial feel to it. It was a quite a sizeable, whitewashed Edwardian style building with a grand porch and entrance. The interior was clearly designed and furnished for a high class of occupant. We had splashed out seventeen pounds per night (each), which by then was top of the range for us. It was very nice, and we had high hopes for an impressive evening meal. One of the two dishes we ordered was goat stew, and our immaculately tailored waiter brought it to the table on a little trolly, in an impressive silver tureen. He served me first, scooping up a piece of goat's leg-bone covered in green-brown sauce. When I say goat's leg-bone, it was almost just that – a bone, there was very little meat involved. The waiter deposited this in my bowl with the clunking sound you'd expect from a heavy bone meeting a China bowl. He said, 'This is good, Sir.' He must have seen the look on my face, so he followed up with a quick 'Very good for you.'

He dished out the same to Nick and then disappeared.

Being elderly Brits, we are hard-wired not to complain, but when the waiter returned he insisted on asking us if everything was alright. 'Well, yes, sort of, but no, not really.' The chef was summonsed, and he told us the dish was very popular. 'It is local speciality, Sirs,' he told us, adding, 'The bones make very splendid sauce.' We didn't want to make a fuss or make anyone feel bad, but we made a note to ask for an off the bone meat dish next time. Over the rest of the meal, Nick and I recapped on another remarkable day. The following day, we had the treat of remaining the entire day in Lucknow, and then we'd move on to Varanasi.

LUCKNOW

In Lucknow, Nick and I had the luxury of a lazy morning and a lavish breakfast. By lazy morning, I mean one where we didn't have to set the alarm for silly o'clock to catch our next bus/plane/train. We pigged out on the hotel breakfast to see us through the day, even though it cost more than some of our overnight accommodation.

Suitably stuffed, we got a taxi and headed for 'The British Residency.' What sounds like a luxury gated community for ex-pats is, in fact, the site of the siege of Lucknow, the catalyst for the end of the East India Company ruling India and the beginning of British colonial rule.

The siege took place in 1857 as part of the Indian mutiny, or the first Indian war of independence, depending on who is describing it. British accounts describe heroic acts of defiance against rebels, while Indian versions describe its people as freedom fighters and martyrs against imperial oppressors. The winners write the history books and when I was at school, we were told of heroic acts of defiance against rebels. It seems reasonable to want your country back, however, if some foreign power comes in and plunders your national assets.

Anyway, politics aside, the site is a vivid reminder of a significant chapter in India's history, however it is described. If we chop the last few hundred years of Indian history into outrageously simplified bite-sized chunks, we have the Mughal Empire dominating India from around 1526 to the mid-18th century. From the early 1700s, Britain gradually replaced various European colonial interests, and then the British Crown ruled the country from 1858 until independence in 1947.

What's mind boggling about British control before 1858 is that it was a private company, the East India Company, that governed India. What began as a commercial trading venture gradually transformed into empire expansion on behalf of Her Majesty's Government. The story is remarkable. There had been nothing like the East India Company until then, and there has been nothing like it since. Imagine a company owning and running a subcontinent – it's crazy, but it's what happened.

A group of well-connected British merchants originally set up the East India Company, laughably also known as the Honourable East India Company, in 1600. Queen Elizabeth I granted them a royal charter to trade with the East Indies and India. It was possibly a genuine commercial proposition to begin with. A couple of decades earlier, she had commissioned Sir Francis Drake, her favourite pirate, to plunder Spanish ships, so Good Queen Bess was quite comfortable with her subjects travelling overseas and using imaginative trading methods.

The original remit of the East India Company was to bring home commodities like spices, silk, and cotton. Spices were big business in those days. They were small in volume and high in value – and there was a lot of dodgy food and many unpleasant smells around in 17th century Britain.

From small beginnings, profits were good, and expansion was rapid.

Fast forward 150 years and the private company had, through partnerships with the regional rulers of the princely states of the Mughal Empire, established bases in Madras, Calcutta and Bombay. In doing so, they elbowed out their French, Dutch, Spanish and Portuguese trading rivals, which the British government was quite happy to see. Apart from spices and cotton, there was big money to be made from drug trafficking and slaves... it was very profitable, if not honourable.

The public/private business partnerships with various princely states entailed investing in some strategically placed forts to protect trade routes. Before they knew it, the East India Company had built a private army. Backed by 250,000 mainly Indian soldiers, the company had considerable negotiating power. They took their original remit to trade with the region to the extreme by taking control of large parts of the Indian subcontinent and colonising parts of Southeast Asia, Hong Kong and China. A simple mistake to make... let's call it mission creep. The company also had state support from the British Government, which saw India as strategically important in the ongoing power struggle with its European rivals, especially the French. At its peak, the East India Company handled approximately 50 per cent of world trade, making it the most powerful corporation that ever existed. Google, Tesla, Microsoft, and Apple are minnows by comparison.

Robert Clive, who later became Lord Clive, is credited with establishing the military and political supremacy of the company over the subcontinent following the battle of Plessey in 1757. His power was enormous and when he returned to Britain, his fortune of £23 million at today's value made him one of the richest men in Europe. It enabled him to buy his way into parliament. He went back to India in 1765 and then returned to Britain after two years with the equivalent of another £40 million. He is quoted as saying 'When I think of the marvellous riches of that country, and the comparatively small part that I took away, I am astonished at my own moderation.' Right Bob; what an absolute hero! The East India Company's influence in India lasted for over 250 years by which time a small island off the north-west coast of Europe had taken over half a continent.

An uprising by Indian soldiers in 1857, culminating in the siege of Lucknow, was the turning point for the East India Company. After the siege, the British army took over military control, and colonial rule over the Indian subcontinent lasted from 1858 to 1947, a period known as the British Raj. The East India Company was dissolved in 1874 but in a nice twist of fate, what remained of the corporation was bought in 2003 by Indian investors.

Back to 1857 and Lucknow. A potential uprising had been simmering for a while amongst the many thousands of Indian soldiers, known as sepoys, who had been recruited into the East India Company's army. Apart from their unease at fighting their compatriots, they felt that British rule was undermining Indian cultural traditions, particularly their Hindu religion and the caste system. Poor terms of service, poor living conditions and low pay didn't help. Many accounts point to the introduction of the Enfield rifle as the tipping point and the catalyst for the mutiny.

The story goes like this: the cartridges for the new rifles were covered in grease to make them easier to load. The grease included pig and cow fat. As part of the procedure for loading the rifles, the cartridges had to be bitten (possibly the origin of the term 'biting the bullet'). The Hindu sepoys were non-cow eaters, and the Muslim sepoys were non-pig eaters. Both groups were therefore offended by the new practice. Not content with insulting two major religions in one go, the army also used brutal methods to impose discipline. The mutiny began at Meerut on the 10th May 1857, extended to Delhi the following day, and rapidly spread further.

Lucknow was the capital city of the state of Avadh, or Oudhh, (now part of the modern Indian state of Uttar Pradesh) which was under the control of the East India Company. The man in charge was Sir Henry Lawrence. He was based in a complex of buildings known as the Residency. The enclosure extended over thirteen hectares and contained a mixture of residential and administrative buildings. As the unrest grew, 855 British soldiers, 712 loyal sepoys, 153 civilian volunteers, and 1,280 non-combatants retreated from various locations around the city into the compound. Beginning on the 25th May, a force of around 8,000 rebels, which grew eventually to over 20,000, besieged the compound for nearly six months. It must have been terrifying for the civilian wives and children, who presumably had little say over their circumstances.

An initial British Army relief force got through to the Residency by 25th September, but they suffered so many casualties on the way they could only join forces with those already there. A second force got through by 19th November to relieve those under siege and restore British control of the area. They evacuated the surviving soldiers and civilians from the Residency, which was then abandoned. Around 2,500 people were killed on the British side, but the fatalities on the Indian side are unrecorded. The fighting was fierce. Twenty-four Victoria Crosses were awarded to soldiers on the last day of conflict – a record in a single day.

Ironically, the Residency compound today, overlooking the wide meandering River Gomti, is an oasis of peace in the madness and noise all around it. As you enter the site, you leave behind the smoke and congestion of the city and enter a green and beautiful sanctuary of meticulously maintained gardens and lawns. There was only a handful of other visitors while Nick and I were there; we nearly had the place to ourselves. Nearly… the calm quietness and greenery seem to be a magnet for the young lovers of Lucknow – somewhere for a quiet canoodle.

The site still contains the remains of most of the buildings that existed in 1857, with the main 'Residency' (the building that used to house the governor of the state) now converted to a museum. Nick and I watched a ten-minute film that told the story of the people besieged, and their eventual relief. Back outside again, it wasn't hard to imagine the scenes from all those years ago; the buildings are still pockmarked from bullet and cannon fire.

The Residency in Lucknow

Nick put his archaeologist hat on as we slowly wandered around. He rummaged around in the ruins and gardens and found a few pieces of porcelain lying on the ground. What stories they could tell. It was a thought-provoking place. Being there amongst the ruins somehow made the events of 1857 come to life and left us thinking of how horrific they must have been for both sides.

The quiet solemnity of the gardens and grounds of the Residency, including the cemetery, must have affected us. We both seemed to leave in reflective moods, lost in our own thoughts about the siege and the people involved. It had been another significant enhancement to my rather incomplete fourth year history GCE education.

We crossed a busy dual carriageway to stroll alongside the River Gomti for a while, enjoying another opportunity for some quiet greenery and open space in the riverside gardens. Despite gorging on a sumptuous breakfast before we left our hotel, we yielded to temptation in the form of some local kakori kebabs. Lucknow is renowned for its Awadhi cuisine – an amalgam of Northern Indian cooking traditions with those of Central Asia and the Middle East. Kebabs are a feature that have spread worldwide but I suspect the post night club and six pints variety back in Britain have little in common with the Lucknow delicacies.

The dish goes back centuries to when hunting parties would chop up the day's catch, marinade it and cook it over an open fire. Kakori is a village near to Lucknow and it gives its name to a type of kebab that is well spiced but very soft and tender. Local stories tell how the melt-in-the-mouth kakori variety was produced for Begum Hazrat Mahal, the brave but toothless wife of Nawab Wajid Ali Shah of Lucknow. She was one of the most prominent figures of the Indian independence movement. She led her people to seize control of Lucknow from the East India Company and took charge of the regional state after her husband was exiled to Calcutta.

Our kebabs were exquisite, the flavour undoubtedly enhanced by the time, the location, and the melancholy of our morning's viewing. It was spiced comfort food. We toasted Begum with a swig of bottled water before negotiating a tuk-tuk ride to our second tourist target of the day, the Bara Imambara.

An imambara is a Shia Muslim meeting hall and bara means big. The Mughal Empire was an amalgamation of various princely states, and the Muslim rulers were known as Nawabs. Asaf-ud-Daulawas was the fourth Nawab of Awadh, and he built the Bara Imambara in 1784. It was part of a relief project for a major famine that struck the area in that year.

Our tuk-tuk driver dropped Nick and me off at the entrance to the imambara, which was quite an architectural spectacle itself, but just a warm-up for the main act. We walked through the impressive archway into the main grounds of the complex. For a second or two we stood transfixed, staring in awe across the gardens and fountains at the stunning grand design and scale of the main building. The Bara Imambara complex also includes a large mosque, a labyrinth (the bhool bhoolaiya), and a step well. More about the labyrinth later, but I need to mention that the central hall of Bara Imambara is said to be the largest arched hall in the world. I can't resist a longest, fastest, oldest etc., so I was easily pleased, ticking another one off the list. For the record, the central hall of the imambara is fifty metres long, sixteen metres wide, and fifteen metres high. The building has four storeys, all very different, and without going into detail, there are many unusual aspects to its construction. My guidebook described the architecture as '...the pinnacle of the Persian/Islamic influence in India,' and I'll go along with that. It certainly seemed to take the architectural features we'd seen elsewhere on our travels to a new level, with countless ornate onion domes, turrets, minarets, and lots of flamboyantly styled windows. It felt like the architects of the time had sat around and said, 'Come on guys, let's see how far we can push this one.'

We entered the Bara Imambara complex, unsure whether we needed to buy a ticket. There was a pay booth, but everyone seemed to walk straight past it, so we followed the crowd and did the same. Nick and I looked around the huge central hall for a while, staring up at its towering, vivid green and white walls and the impressive crystal chandeliers hanging from the ceiling. And yes, the hall really was huge. There were quite a few other visitors, and we took a recommendation from one of them to hire a guide before we ventured up to the labyrinth. I would advise anyone to use a guide for this part of the building... unless you're happy to spend a day or so finding your way out.

We followed our guide, Mahtab, up some very well-worn stairs in one corner of the building. We trailed behind him and his torchlight along countless dark passageways, and up and down many flights of steps. Eventually, we emerged on the roof of the Bara Imambara. There were amazing views of the complex and the city beyond, to the river.

Mahtab then said we would go back down via the labyrinth. We set off along yet another dark and narrow passageway. Before long, we came to an open doorway, offering alternative routes. Mahtab told us which way to go, but when the next choice appeared, our mischievous friend took great delight in asking us to go first. He let us choose which way to go. Using his torch, we stumbled from passageway to passageway along a dark maze of tall and narrow, whitewashed walls... we were well and truly in the labyrinth. This tourist trap has a thousand passageways and nearly 500 identical doorways. The multi-layered fingerprints of thousands of previous lost souls decorate the nearly white walls, especially at the corners, but they don't point to the way out. At each junction, when we chose a route, Mahtab let us go ahead five metres or so before saying 'Wrong way!' We'd look back and see his broad smile beaming through the darkness. He must have played the same game many times each day, but he was clearly enjoying himself. There are two theories about the labyrinth. The more interesting one is that it was designed to confuse raiders, giving the occupants time to escape. The more sensible one is that the three-dimensional honeycomb of passageways was constructed to spread the weight over the great hall, which was built upon marshy ground. With a lot of help, we eventually emerged in the great hall again, said our farewells to Mahtab, and headed for the exit.

It would not be that easy, however. Every few steps, another Indian family, or group of friends, politely asked if we would appear in their selfie. The other visitors couldn't get enough of us; we were celebrities again. I stopped counting when we went past twenty photo-stops. We certainly stood out; we only saw one other white person in our two days in Lucknow. Perhaps they'd all read Ryan's (the millennial we met in Agra) review of the city.

On our way out of the building, back to the street outside, we had to walk through an archway and past what looked like a ticket check desk. We marched past, like everyone else. A second or two later, a serious-looking man in uniform appeared at our side. 'Excuse me Sirs, I am from the tourist police. Do you mind stepping to one side, please?'

As we walked slowly over towards his desk, I was rapidly trawling through my extensive database of innocent traveller abroad excuses. I was tossing up whether to go with the forgetful pensioner angle or play my 'parents met in India' trump card. Before we had a chance to protest, he pointed to an open book on the desk. My thoughts went into overdrive – this must be where we have to give our details before being severely admonished, fined heavily or led off to the cells... maybe all three. I wondered if it would be possible to get word to the British Embassy. An image of Nick and me appearing from an Indian jail in ten years' time, little more than pale and dishevelled skeletons, flashed before my eyes. It was a re-run of a vision I'd inexplicably also seen flash before my eyes at Gilbert Hill and Chail cricket ground.

The police officer opened the book and handed me a pen. He said, 'We are very honoured to have you visit our site Sir. Would you mind putting a few words in the guest book to let us know how you found everything. We are constantly looking for ways to improve and your comments are very valuable.' Using some sort of mystic sixth sense, he seemed to know our cartographic background, and gave us both a free map. It was another example of the kindness and great generosity we came across everywhere in India. What a nice man and what an amazing place to visit.

~

In Lucknow, we were approaching the end of week three of our trip. We had stuck to our original agenda very well. We only had to make one significant change; giving up a trip to Rishikesh, where the Beatles hung out when they went all hippie, to give ourselves more time elsewhere. It meant we could avoid a long run of consecutive days' travelling. Our adjusted agenda meant we had two relaxed mornings in a row in Lucknow. I caught up with some admin – updating the blog and the expenses spreadsheet, while Nick went for a 10-kilometre run in a local park and visited a nearby Commonwealth War Graves cemetery. We had another late blowout breakfast to see us through the day, because we weren't due to arrive in Varanasi, our next destination, until late that night.

We made our way back to the Lucknow bus station and boarded our 3:00 pm Volvo coach for the seven-hour trip. There's not much to report on the coach ride itself except that we survived it (noteworthy in itself) and that it was again, thankfully, very comfortable. Having changed our schedule, Nick and I talked again about the revised agenda for the rest of our trip, and we lapsed into some schoolboy repartee. Mention of Rishikesh had put us both in Beatles mode. I commented to Nick, 'This is turning into a bit of a magical mystery tour.' 'I know,' he said, 'this bus ride is a bit scary; I wanna' hold your naan.' I tried to remain positive: 'We can work it out. I'm sure it will come together,' to which he responded with, 'It sometimes feels like we've been travelling eight days a week.' 'Hang on Nick,' I said, 'we need to bring our construction theme to the playlist... Yesterday, all my rubble seemed so far away.' 'Let it be!' said Nick, before bringing our giggly session to a close with, 'You'd better copy some of this crap down – you're supposed to be a paperback raita.'

Three men acting as 'cabin crew' supported the bus driver. One of them checked our tickets five minutes into the journey and then did nothing else for the next seven and a half hours. Another one popped up when it got dark and wiped the windscreen with a greasy rag every half an hour. We'd noticed on multiple occasions that drivers don't seem to know about, or use, the front screen hot air demister. Maybe they just don't work. The third man stood up every now and again and shouted out place names loudly, presumably in case people wanted to get off, or maybe as a public information service to let us know how well the journey was progressing. The driver produced a masterclass in horror-show driving. All the normal rules were torn up and cast to the kerbside, as per every other driver in India, but this guy had might on his size. No one was going to mess with a ten-ton bus hurtling towards them at sixty miles per hour. This was a heart in the mouth, play chicken with other drivers, tour de force.

After an hour or two of that behaviour, you stop reacting – like when you initially gasp for air and hyperventilate when you immerse yourself in cold water at the seaside but then slowly acclimatise to the new normal. It's the same with a long-distance coach ride in India. After a while, you watch with numb indifference and fatalistic acceptance as the driver pulls out, once again, to overtake on a blind bend or in clear sight of a stream of traffic coming the other way. His rationale seemed to be that occupation of the road was ownership – he'd truck on through expecting that everyone coming the other way would dive out of the way, and we'd get through. And that's exactly the way it went, for kilometre after kilometre. Call me old fashioned but my body has remained arranged in a relatively standard format for more than six decades. It might not be perfect, but it has served me well and I'd quite like to keep it in its current configuration a bit longer. By the way, the Indian government could save a lot of money by scrapping all road signs, traffic lights and white lines... they are completely pointless.

Stress levels (mine, not the driver's) went up a notch or two when it got dark. The odds of hitting something while we were on the wrong side of the road suddenly seemed very short. Whether a lorry, a bicycle, or maybe a horse and cart was coming the other way with no lights obviously never crossed our driver's mind. I imagined the scene as the sun rose at dawn to illuminate the carnage – hundreds of kilometres of roadside verges across northern India littered with a trail of upturned motorcyclists, broken tuk-tuks and dead dogs.

The road for the first half of the journey wasn't too bad, but for the second half, it was terrible. We went through sections of road under construction that were no better than rough farm tracks. Amazingly, to begin with, our driver slowed down slightly. He was performing the same circus stunts as before, but only at half speed. But then a local bus had the audacity to overtake us, and our driver wasn't having that – afterburners were engaged and we were away again. I don't know how the bus' suspension survived, but it is a great testament to Swedish engineering.

We arrived in Varanasi half an hour late. Our driver couldn't have been trying hard enough. Our drop-off spot was on the edge of town and we had to find our hotel. While Nick checked out the Uber taxi options, a nice Slovakian girl called Merrica approached me. Well, that's what her name sounded like when I asked her. Maybe she thought I'd asked her which country she'd last visited. She was another rare white face and fellow traveller. She came over to ask where we were heading for, and if there was any chance of sharing a lift. Her hotel was quite close to ours, so we all set off together. I phoned our hotel to let them know we were coming because they had told us earlier that we would need help to find the place.

The taxi driver dropped us off in what looked like a dark and empty street – apart from an aromatic sprinkling of trash, excrement and stray dogs. Merrica strolled off, as if she knew where she was going, leaving us in a dark and deserted ghost town. Uncomfortably, for two former mapmakers, we didn't know where we were, or where to go.

At that moment, two men emerged from the shadows and introduced themselves. They smiled a lot, seemed friendly and mentioned the name of our hotel. The signs were positive, so we followed them. Our path to the hotel felt like a community recycling/sewage works variant of the

Lucknow labyrinth. We had to negotiate a path through piles of dog, cow and human excrement, heaps of rubbish of all kinds, and sleeping dogs. The smell of decomposing garbage lingered in the air and blended with the acrid aroma of stale wee. A quote from Rudyard Kipling sprang to mind: 'The first condition of understanding a foreign country is to smell it.' Even if he didn't have this place in mind when he wrote those words, they seemed very appropriate. Welcome to Varanasi.

Eventually, we arrived at our hotel. There were more friendly smiles and a warm welcome. The guy on reception showed us to our second-floor room. It had a balcony and there was just enough light from surrounding buildings to see an amazing view of the River Ganges drifting past slowly down below us. Thanks, Ganesha, you did us proud once again! We ordered a couple of beers, sat out on our balcony and looked out over the Varanasi ghats (stepped riverbanks) to the majestic River Ganges, flowing serenely past.

VARANASI

Where do I start? I've travelled to sixty countries on four continents, but I've not seen anything quite like Varanasi. I feel intimidated at the thought of even attempting to describe the place, but this will be a short chapter if I don't at least give it a go.

Built on the banks of the River Ganges in Uttar Pradesh, Varanasi (also known as Banaras and Kashi) is one of the oldest continuously inhabited cities in the world, which means somewhere around 6,000 years old, although the figure varies according to sources. Whatever the inhabitants have been doing all that time, they haven't spent much of it improving the road, sewage, or waste disposal facilities. But to focus on the deficiencies of the city's transport and water infrastructure would be to miss the point. Varanasi is first and last a sacred place – the spiritual capital of India. I defy anyone to go there and not be moved.

Varanasi is the Hindus' most holy city. Every devout Hindu hopes to visit the city at least once in their life, and to immerse themselves in the sacred river. The name Hindu is derived from the word Indus – the name of the river beside which Hinduism originated. Although Hindus worship the single deity, Brahman, they also recognise thousands of other gods and goddesses. They believe that living creatures have a core spiritual soul called atman, which in turn is part of a supreme soul. Also central to their beliefs is the concept of a continual cycle of life and death. Karma relates to the law of cause and effect, in which our actions affect our current and future selves. By living a good life, Hindus strive to follow the concept of dharma – a religious and moral framework that dictates an individual's conduct.

Varanasi

Hindus believe that dying in Varanasi releases them from the eternal cycle of life and death reincarnation (they call the release moksha), and many head there when they feel life ebbing away. As well as a magnet for its spirituality, the city attracts those seeking creative and artistic inspiration. It's a one-off. In 1897, the author Mark Twain described Varanasi as '...older than history, older than tradition, older even than legend, and looks twice as old as all of them put together.' Hindus go a step further. They believe that Lord Shiva and his wife Parvati stood in Varanasi at the moment time started. I love that image – the city and its religion as old as time itself.

It's very unlikely that anyone's first view of India will be Varanasi, and that's a good thing. The city is something you need to build up to. Everyone warns you that India is an assault on the senses. In Varanasi, it's like someone inside your brain has turned up all the sensory receptors to maximum, and then somehow tweaked them up a bit more. The input is overwhelming. Images of death, fire and smoke are forever etched into my memory, as well as soaring colourful buildings, squalor and filth, the magnificent (but filthy) Ganges, enthusiastic singing, and chanting... and seagulls. But I'll come to that later; I should do the descriptive bit first.

I'll begin with the River Ganges because it is central to the story of Varanasi. The Ganges just misses out on the list of the ten longest rivers in the world, but it is of enormous importance to India and its population. Apart from the economic aspects of supplying water for drinking and agriculture, the river has immense spiritual significance for Hindus, who comprise the vast majority of Indian people. The source of the river lies at an elevation of 3,892 metres in the Himalayas. It emerges from the foot of Gangotri Glacier, at Gaumukh (at the top and fairly central on the generalised triangular map of India) and sets off on its 2,500 kilometres journey to the sea. After heading west for a while, it drops to the south before curving in a gentle arc to flow along an enormous river plain between the Himalayas and the Central Highlands. It spews its sediment and detritus into the Indian Ocean through the world's largest river delta.

By the time it gets to Varanasi, India's longest river is over halfway to the sea in the Bay of Bengal. It has already become very wide, and the flow is gentle. From the beginning of time, the river has drifted slowly and serenely past Varanasi. A seven-kilometre line of eighty-eight ghats runs alongside the river as it flows past the city. They are stepped embankments made of stone slabs that drop into the water, from which pilgrims perform ritual ablutions and present offerings to the holy river.

Behind the ghats, spectacular buildings tower up, the colourful architecture reflecting the city's rich and varied cultural history. Most regions of India seem to be represented in the architecture of the buildings behind the ghats. They come in all states of repair but mainly biased towards the lower end of the condition range. High-rise Mughal style buildings, with impressive balconies and domes, jostle for space alongside crumbling ruins, Hindu temples and Muslim mosques. It's a mesmerising kaleidoscope of building styles and colour. Away from the waterfront, a dense warren of winding alleyways waits to entrap you in a maze of assorted waste products, dogs, cows, monkeys, and rubble. Some ghats are used for Hindu cremation ceremonies and the cycle of bodies being delivered and cremated goes on twenty-four hours a day. As you attempt to take in the sights and sounds, you notice the smell – there is an aroma that hangs in the air. It's a slightly acrid combination of the quick and the dead, but mostly the latter. It's brutal – but compelling.

On day twenty-two of our adventure, Nick and I were both early risers. As the city of light was coming to light, there was pandemonium somewhere outside the bedroom window. The noise was coming from the river. It sounded like the deafening cacophony of a flock of lesser black-backed gulls – more Grimsby than Ganges. Unlikely though, because Varanasi is about 700 kilometres from the sea.

I jumped out of bed, as much as a sixty-something can

perform such a feat, and threw back the curtains to see what all the fuss was about. A fine mist hung over the river. It was a tranquil early morning scene – apart from the noisy racket. The rowdy alarm call turned out to be the deafening cacophony of a flock of lesser black-backed gulls. To be more precise, they were Siberian gulls. Spurred on by reports of rich pickings from Varanasi tourists, these hardy birds raise the effort to fly south each winter from their home in northern Russia. It seems the lure of free Indian takeaways on the Ganges is sufficient motivation for them to fly all that way, via Mongolia, China, Tibet and the Himalayan mountains. They go home in March, completely stuffed. That's partly due to the increasing daytime temperatures by that time of year, but mainly because their body weight would prevent take-off if they delayed their departure slots any longer.

One of the touristy 'things to do' in Varanasi is to get up at dawn for an early morning boat ride to see the sunrise through the mist. With a few handfuls of bird food, you can get yourself surrounded by hundreds of hungry seagulls. It makes a nice photo, but you take the inevitable risk of a potential aerial bombardment. By now Nick had stirred as well, and he stumbled half asleep to the window. We both watched the events unfolding below. His first mumbled words were: 'They seem to have flown south early this year.' I looked at him through narrowed eyes... 'Don't you start!'

The view, looking across the river, was beautiful. An improbably large orange sun sat on the horizon. The first rays of sunshine were filtering through the mist over the holy river as it lazily made its way past. A handful of boatmen were vying for the custom of several groups of confused tourists on the ghat below us. Their excited chatter seemed to echo in the mist and mingled with the cries of the gulls. Never mind the fare negotiations; the impatient birds wanted their breakfast. Out in the middle of the river, one of the small punt-like boats slowly drifted downstream with the current. It was surrounded by hundreds of gulls that circled and screeched. They swooped down towards the boat, flapping their wings furiously as they tried to hover and grab some food. The boatman looked on and encouraged his crew of three tourists as they scattered the bird food and tried to take selfies in the cloud of gulls.

Well, that was us awake then. Nick and I made our way up to the hotel rooftop balcony and planned our day with the help of a masala omelette and chai for breakfast. The boat ride could wait until the evening; we had probably left it too late to see the best of the morning anyway. Instead, we'd take the entire day for an unhurried look around the city... which mainly meant a slow walk along the eighty-eight ghats alongside the river.

There were countless other people out and about as we set off and ambled our way along the ghats. A few were visitors, but most were locals. The sun was rising, and so was the temperature. Every ghat has its story, its own significance and history. Some are famous battle sites, some are pilgrimage destinations and others are reserved for cremations. Many of them appeared to be used for worship and celebration, but all were being used for more functional purposes. On every ghat there were men, women and children bathing in the holy river. Some were standing up to their waists in the water, just quietly taking their morning wash, oblivious to everyone around them. Others paid quiet homage to their ancestors and gods, offering flowers and rose petals in their own little ceremonial worlds.

We walked slowly on, ghat after ghat. More bathers, more ceremonies. The green/brown soup in which the devotees were bathing didn't look enticing; it is one of the most polluted major rivers in the world. Apart from the ashes of the dead, the river is the dumping ground for tons of rubbish and agricultural chemicals. Only a third of Varanasi is connected to the sewers, the remaining waste goes straight into the Ganges. The Ganges acts as a sewer for the 450 million people who live in its catchment area and the Mother Goddess is slowly dying.

Despite that, about one billion Hindus have bathed in their holy river and many continue to do so. After cleaning up in the 2014 elections, Prime Minister Narendra Modi introduced a 'Clean Ganges' programme. The national government set aside roughly 200 billion rupees ($2.8 billion) to spend between 2015 and 2019 on new sewage treatment plants, new electric crematoria, and a programme of building household toilets. Although some improvements have been made, it's an upstream struggle, and critics complain that the advances don't match the promises made, and the budget allocated is too small to tackle the problem seriously. In 2018, an environmental activist died after going on hunger strike, trying to get more government action to clean up the river. Nick and I passed a Hindu holy man squatting cross-legged and chanting. He was sitting in something that was a cross between a micro temple and an information centre. His aim was to bring attention to the problem of the polluted river. Let's hope he succeeds. I was just grateful to come across another person who looked older than me.

Every now and again, we had to sit down for a few minutes to take everything in. We saw several dead animals float by – water buffalo, goats, dogs, or maybe pigs. Difficult to tell. It's hard to imagine any animal life existing in the river, but at one point we saw a green snake swimming past, popping its head up occasionally, as if to check it was still on course. The locals told us we were safe because although the snake's bite is lethal, they only bite on Tuesdays and Sundays... and it was Wednesday, so that was OK.

By late morning, Nick and I had arrived at the Manikarnika Ghat, where legend says the funeral pyres have been burning for 3,000 years. Before the COVID pandemic struck, they used to cremate up to 300 bodies each day on the Manikarnika and Harishchandra Ghats... depositing nearly a ton of ashes and partially burnt flesh into the river. It's an uncomfortable watch, but no one says you must. I'm not sure if it's true, but Nick and I were told that mourners don't mind outsiders watching the funerals because it teaches people about the Hindu religion. Everything we saw was very solemn and respectful, but to tell the truth, it *did* feel uncomfortable, and it *did* feel like an intrusion. For each family, this was their private grief, and it felt wrong that the funeral ghats had become something else for tourists to tick off their 'must-see' lists.

For a Western visitor, death is something uncomfortable. In our culture, it's something we don't want to face, or even discuss if we can avoid it. In India, death seems to be part of day-to-day extended family life in a way we outsiders can't understand. There was a handful of Western-looking people on the ghat, but the locals just came and went, walking past without a second look, like it was just another day... which I guess it was for them.

As Nick and I watched the scene unfold on the Manikarnika funeral ghat, both out of our comfort zones by a long distance, a local guy came over to describe what was happening. In hushed tones, he patiently told us about the ceremony. After about five minutes, he invited us to contribute to the cost of wood for people waiting in the local hospice to die. It seemed plausible, and we gave him some money. We heard later that this was a common way of getting money out of visitors... and the cash didn't always find its way to the hospice. Our rupee recycling friend told us that not all Hindus can be cremated. Dead children, sadhus (holy men), pregnant women, and people who die of snake bites (presumably bitten on a Tuesday or Sunday) are instead set adrift on the River Ganges on wooden rafts. Hindus consider the children and sadhus to be pure, so they don't need to be cremated, but we didn't get the full story behind the pregnant women and snake bite victims.

From what we observed and were told, the cremation process went as follows. The mourners bring the deceased body to Varanasi, where it travels the last part of the journey to the ghats on a bamboo litter, a type of lightweight stretcher, held head high. They drape the body in white sheets (for men) or red/gold ornate sheets (for women). As we watched, a new funeral group arrived at the ghat. The people carrying the body were chanting, 'God is the truth' in Hindi. Some family members scattered marigolds over the body, which was taken to the river to be totally immersed. Then they took it up the steps to the place of cremation; the higher up, the higher the social standing of the deceased.

We were told that Hindus believe that for a body to enter the gates of heaven, it must be cremated in the presence of a member of the Dom caste. According to Hindu mythology, Lord Shiva cursed the Doms when a member of their community tried to steal an earring from his wife Parvati. To gain forgiveness, the Doms had to agree to become the keepers of the flame. It is both sad and ironic that these people only get respect from the rest of society when they do their traditional job as custodians of the cremation grounds – forced to make a living from the dying.

Back to the funeral ceremony. The wood for the pyres is carefully weighed to make sure they use enough, but not too much (because it is expensive). This seemed to be quite a side industry. There were many little buildings around the ghats housing a man, a set of scales, and massive piles of neatly stacked logs piled up to five metres high. The wealthy families use teak, sandalwood, or other expensive hard woods. Poorer families use cheaper varieties. When they get to the ghat, the Dom shows the mourners where to go. The family removes the drapes from the body, and the Dom anoints it. A member of the family then walks around the body five times, representing the five elements of Hinduism. The chief mourner, whose head should be freshly shaved, then takes the flaming torch from the Dom to ignite the wooden pyre. Cremation takes around three hours, and the family watches and waits until the end. The Dom then presents the relatives with the ashes, which are given up to the sacred Ganges. Nick and I watched with uneasy fascination as some untouchables sieved the ashes from the riverbed to retrieve any gold jewellery or teeth that may have survived the flames. Our guide told us that the recycled gold is used to purchase wood for poor families.

Nick and I picked our way to the top of the steps from where we could look down on the whole ghat. The sight was something I'll never forget. Eight pyres, each about two metres high, were ablaze. Each one had a draped body on top. Beside each one, family members were mainly standing in respectful silence. Some were quietly chanting. It was very dignified, but also incredibly sad, and we didn't want to stay long. The smoke from the fires swirled around the ghat, at times quite dense and obscuring the view. It filled the air and quite a bit of our lungs.

Each deep in our own thoughts, we left the burning ghats and headed towards the dense maze of alleyways that ran away from the river. The narrow passageways were full of wood sellers and Hindu temples. Crowds of mourners, traders, and people just going about their daily business ambled their way to and from the river, sharing the thoroughfare with lethargic cows and dogs, and frisky monkeys. Every now and again, Nick and I had to stand aside as another party of mourners came bustling through the packed narrow lanes; another body held shoulder high and on its way to eternal liberation.

Our thoughts had been scattered with the smoke. Seeing death pass me in the alleyway and watching the grieving relatives on the ghats was both intensely moving and thought-provoking. There is, as far as we know, one long, or short, life for each of us... for whatever purpose – what's it all about?

Nick was jolted back into the current world when he realised we were close to a restaurant he had been reading about. It was on the recommended list. He's always one jump ahead when it comes to the search for the next spice hit, and amazingly, deep in the labyrinth of narrow alleyways, we had stumbled upon the place he had identified as a potential lunch stop. His mixed outpouring of joy / relief brought me back to earth as well.

The area we were in was thick with yoga studios and craft workshops. The café/restaurant was small, but it had a snug and homely feel and we were the only two people in it. Everything was cosy and relaxing, especially after our morning of extraordinary sights and deep thoughts. The café walls were painted in soothing rose red and light blue tones. There were beautiful tapestry cushions on the floor to sit on and gentle sitar music provided a calm background. It gently filled the air, did a circuit of the room and then spilled out through the open door into the adjacent alleyway. The soothing music was just what our pummelled senses and battered feelings needed. The food and music were sublime, and still feeling a little emotionally tender, I wasn't in a hurry to leave.

Refreshed and revived, we continued our walk along the

ghats. One thing you get used to in India is people coming up to you to engage in conversation. When we first arrived in Mumbai, I was very suspicious. After a while, I became ashamed of my knee-jerk reaction. Everyone was so friendly and just seemed happy to chat. Unfortunately, that changed in Varanasi – but then it is a tourist magnet.

On two occasions, Nick and I were 'befriended' by locals who told us immediately they weren't guides and didn't want any money. Good, that was sorted out then. After each of them had hung around with us for about half an hour, they showed their hand. Would we like to contribute to their education or maybe visit a relative's clothes factory? You could be generous and say they were being entrepreneurial or opportunistic. After all, we were the wealthy Westerners. It didn't feel comfortable, though. After the morning we'd experienced, I felt in need of a bit of emotional stability. I didn't want the additional decision-making overhead of trying to double guess what each stranger's intentions were. And so, when opportunist number three hooked up with us, I'm afraid to say I ran out of convivial chat. As we strolled along slowly, I dropped back and let Nick deal with the guy. I knew Nick would be fine, he's compulsively sociable, and I kept them in sight in case my old pal needed back-up. About forty minutes later, the guy walked away, and I caught up with Nick to get the story. It turned out the fellow was gay and searching for some male company, and more if he could get it. After a long introduction of small talk about Varanasi, he had declared his intentions. Nick had politely told him that wasn't his thing, but sympathetically discussed with the stranger how it was to be gay in India. Anyway, the guy must have considered anything less than an instant rebuff to be encouragement. He was persistent, and Nick had to diplomatically bring things to a conclusion when he was invited to buy them both a drink.

There are no official figures, but according to government estimates, there are 2.5 million gay people in India. Rights activists and statistical probability suggest the true figure is much higher. From what Nick was told, they aren't accepted by large parts of the community, making it difficult for them to meet openly and form relationships. Nick was told that discrimination against gay and trans people remains common in what is still a socially conservative country. It's another aspect of cultural tradition that will take a long time to change. Given that lack of acceptance, it is perhaps understandable that the guy we met must take his chances with the foreign strangers who keep turning up in his city.

We continued our ramble along the riverside. No one bothered us when we left the more popular ghats behind. The images we were seeing were far removed from our normal day-to-day existence, and the weird and wonderful just kept coming. Every now and again we came across sadhus, or holy men. Wow, you don't see many of those back home – although there are up to five million in India. If you haven't seen one of these guys, you need to do an Internet search to find an image – or go to India. They are the most hardcore of Hindus and are revered by other Hindus. They let go of all material belongings and attachments to society, for example, family, possessions, money, and sex... such is their dedication and conviction in their beliefs. Their aim is to achieve the fourth and final Hindu goal of life, moksha (liberation), through meditation and contemplation of Brahman. It's a similar lifestyle to that of Buddhist monks – the goal is to meditate your way to enlightenment. Sadhus usually dress in modest ochre or saffron coloured robes, symbolising renunciation, and cover themselves in white and grey sacred ash. They live in absolute poverty and depend entirely on the kindness and donations of strangers.

These guys represent the very opposite of our typical Western way of thinking in which we concentrate on competition, selfishness, wealth accumulation, buying the next new shiny thing, and the accumulation of stuff in pursuit of happiness. Many visitors who see them will not *get* the sadhus, but I can't help admiring them. They don't judge wellness in how many Twitter followers they've got. Their measure of happiness is not calibrated in Facebook likes. Maybe the sadhus are the ones who've got it right and the rest of us are the saddos.

There's just one part of the sadhu lifestyle that I haven't got my head around... we can't all be them. In relying on the rest of the world for support, isn't there some selfishness inherent in their selflessness?

We made our way back to our hotel, still in a bit of a daze from the sensory and emotional onslaught of the day. What we needed was a nice, peaceful boat trip. Washed and changed, we re-emerged from our hotel, ready to go again. We made our way to the riverside and, as sunset approached, we hired a boat and boatman for an hour and a half to see the city from the river. It was one of scores of small punt-like rowing boats available, big enough for two passengers in relative comfort and four at a push.

Our oarsman took us slowly upstream, a steady pull against the gentle current. We reached some funeral ghats, but not the famous ones we'd been to earlier in the day. By then it was becoming dark and small fires seemed to appear all along the ghats, into the distance. With the dramatic flames leaping up and illuminating the surrounding buildings, and the cries and shouts from the riverside, we gazed upon a Biblical scene – although I might be confusing my religious references. Our guide eased his boat around slowly to go back with the flow. We picked up a nice bit of pace on our way downstream to the Dashashwamedh Ghat,

Varanasi's oldest. The name translates to the ghat of the ten sacrificed horses. According to Hindu legend, Lord Brahma created the ghat to allow Lord Shiva to return from a period of banishment. The Dashashwamedh Ghat is one of the 'pilgrim ghats' and during the daytime, it is one of the most popular for quiet meditation. By evening, however, the scene is transformed as hundreds of people gather for the nightly Ganga Aarti – the spiritual ceremony to worship the River Ganges.

Aarti is a ceremony in which dias (oil lamps) are offered to God. It can be done to a deity in a temple, or in the case of the Varanasi Aarti, it is done on the banks of the Ganges to Mother Ganga. The use of the oil lamps is said to denote the light of spiritual knowledge and the illumination of truth. If camphor is used to light the lamps, it eventually burns away without trace – representing the destruction of the ego in the light of true knowledge. Or, according to other sources, it is the illumination of the self in union with the universe. Either way, it had to be worth a look after the emotional day Nick and I had been through; the Ganga Aarti has become a regular nightly spectacle for pilgrims and tourists alike.

Our captain had cleverly positioned his craft centre-stream to catch the maximum of a moderate flow downriver. As we approached the ghat, he steered us towards the riverbank where scores of other boats, and their excited occupants, were gathering. Our boat became wedged in a solid raft with all the others, forming a giant floating extension to the ghat. There were hundreds of visitors, mostly Indian, to witness the aarti from the river, and even more were gathering on the ghat itself, where the colours, lights and sounds were already pushing the sensor dials up towards maximum again. At one point, a young lad jumped from boat to boat with a pot of paint to apply free bindis (a dot on your forehead to express spirituality) to everyone.

There were no questions asked or fee involved, it just happened.

Like the Attari-Wagah flag ceremony at the India-Pakistan border, although nothing like to the same extent, I suspect the Ganga Aarti ceremony has been enhanced as a performance over the years to reach the spectacle it is today. The ceremony has become so large over the years that it is now split into two halves, performed side by side, each with two sets of holy men and their helpers performing synchronised ceremonial worship. A row of saffron-robed priests stood on large plinths. They held large oil lamps, which they swung around theatrically. The overall scene was a palette of reds and yellows, with fire and lots of dazzling bright lights. The fragrance of incense and camphor, and a hint of smoke, mingled in the air. The activity gradually increased in intensity, over forty-five minutes or so, becoming dramatically noisy, and full of movement. As the ceremony reached its climax, the bells in the temples rang, and the air was full of singing, chanting and cheering. It looked like large sections of the crowd ashore were swaying gently in unison. The launching of hundreds of small candles and flowers on lily pads, which drifted down the river in a floating mass of flickering lights provided a charming end to the ceremony.

The Ganga Aarti had been impressive, but I just wondered if the spectacle had become a bit of a tourist show and lost some of its original spiritual significance – but then it would be hard to maintain the intimacy of the occasion with so many participants, and we ourselves had added to that. We slowly untangled our boat from the floating pontoon, and a small flotilla of craft dispersed up and downstream.

Back at our hotel, over spicy chicken korai, buttery chicken paneer, and creamy mushroom masala, we reflected on the sensory battering the day had provided. There was a lot to discuss. We did a summary and comparison of world religions, majoring in Hinduism, and considered the power of faith. There was no avoiding some deliberation about death, which led Nick, who has no children, into a thoughtful reflection on the long-term future of his football programme collection. Varanasi had left as big an impression on us as it had on Ryan, whom we'd met in Agra. We drank a couple of beers – we needed them.

BODH GAYA

Bodh Gaya (sometimes written Bodhgaya or Buddha-Gaya) is a small town in Bihar state, northern India. On the face of it, there's not much to do there. When Nick and I were doing our research, we found that number three on the list of places to visit in Bodh Gaya was a café – the Be Happy café. A short stroll from that eatery, however, is the Mahabodhi Temple, which marks the spot where they say Buddha attained enlightenment. Because of that, Bodh Gaya ranks alongside Amritsar, Jerusalem, Mecca, and the Vatican City as one of the world's most important pilgrimage sites.

With the good fortune that had been with us from the moment we landed in Mumbai, (ignoring the unfortunate phone incident), our arrival in Bodh Gaya coincided with the first of three days of the annual Bodh Mahotsava music and dance festival. Performers were converging from nine countries including Japan, Nepal, Laos and Taiwan. As if that wasn't enough, while we were in town, several thousand Buddhist monks were homing in on their most spiritual global location to pray for World Peace. Monks were everywhere.

But back to Varanasi. Although we hadn't asked for it,

the hotel staff had given us a 4:00 am alarm call. By then, Nick had already experienced many alarm calls during the night. Something unpleasant had found its way into his digestive system. Luckily for him, he'd finally got off to sleep at about 3:55 am. The Imodium was doing an excellent job, though, and Nick bravely trotted off to the taxi in reasonable shape to tackle the day ahead.

The hotel staff had kindly made us some breakfast and wrapped it in foil for us to take with us into the cold and dark of the new morning. We carefully negotiated the murky network of alleyways, which appeared to have been carpeted with a fresh layer of excrement overnight, to find the main road, where we had a rendezvous with our taxi, and made our way to the station. By then, the roads around the station were already grid-locked with traffic, and the air was filled with noise, dust and pollution. Where was everyone going?

Our 5:40 am train was the overnight cross-country express coming down from Jammu, up in Kashmir, and going to Kolkata in West Bengal. That would be thirty-six hours for those doing the entire journey. We had to evict two individuals who were asleep on our berths, but it was all very amicable, and the rest of our journey passed without incident. I even got a pleasant couple of hours' sleep. We emerged, four hours after boarding, and still with a full complement of phones, at Gaya Junction railway station.

Gaya is a city of half a million people in an agricultural region, and a pilgrimage site for Hindus, Buddhists and Jains. We were heading for Bodh Gaya, however, which was a further twenty kilometres away as the tuk-tuk rattles. We dodged the puddles as we picked our way across a potholed station car park to a group of tuk-tuk taxis. A fierce open-air auction ensued as several drivers scrapped over the prospect of a nice little earner. With a deal done, Nick and I arrived at our hotel almost an hour later, in the town of Bodh Gaya. Showers and a change of clothes were the priorities once we'd checked in, and then we were good to face the rest of the day.

Once again, we had struck lucky; thanks again, Ganesha! High user ratings and the words 'spotlessly clean' caught our eyes when we chose the hotel online, and we weren't disappointed. It lived up to the description and everyone there was extremely friendly. It seemed to be entirely staffed by adolescents, which seemed quite unusual until Nick and I were told the story behind the hotel. A Swiss guy called Jean was running it on behalf of a combined Indian/Swiss non-government organisation (NGO). He told us they were using it to provide apprenticeships for the young people of Bahir state. The hotel provided a year's practical training and then the students were given work placements... to give them a leg up in the hospitality business. The hotel was spotless, and the students were an absolute delight. They couldn't do enough for us and were charming, respectful, and keen to help.

The NGO was supporting young people in a country where less than 5 per cent of them receive any vocational education. Although over 95 per cent of children attend primary school in India, only 40 per cent attend secondary school. The dropout rate reflects financial constraints and the traditional need for boys to help their family with economic activities. For girls, there are cultural expectations relating to early marriage, and a lack of local schools to which they can travel safely. It's an unfortunate situation in a country which boasts a long and rich history of providing education.

Approximately 7,000 years ago, there was something called the Gurukul system of schooling. It was a residential system, where students lived with their teacher, or Acharya, until their education was complete. As well as a range of scholarly subjects, the students learnt how to live a cultured and disciplined life. The University of Nalanda, the remains of which were about eighty kilometres northeast of where Nick and I were staying in Bodh Gaya, is one of the oldest in the world, predating England's Oxford University by a few hundred years. It was one of the first great universities in the world. With a capacity of 10,000 students and 2,000 professors, the university was huge, and its dormitories accommodated students from across all of Asia. Its library held over nine million manuscripts. While Britain entered the dark ages, India had an international university in which it was possible to study theology, logic, philosophy, medicine, astronomy, and grammar.

As in every other walk of life, education was something about which British rulers of India thought they knew best. Concerned that religious sentiment could affect its business and diplomatic influence, the East India Company discouraged Christian missionaries from teaching. However, the Charter Act of 1813 made the company responsible for the nation's education and the schools and colleges that they opened over the following forty-four years operated on an English model. When there was controversy about how the 1813 Act should be implemented, Thomas Babington, better known as Lord Macaulay, arrived in India in 1834, tasked by the Governor-General to come up with finding an answer. The outcome was the famous 'Macaulay minute.' The historian George Trevelyan writes that Macaulay exhibited 'vehemence, over-confidence, and the inability to recognise that there are two sides to a question or two people in a dialogue.' Some things never change; that description sounds like many current British Members of Parliament. Taking a balanced view of the situation, Lord Macaulay forced himself off the fence by declaring, 'A single shelf of a good European library was worth the whole native literature of India and Arabia.' His famous minute proposed using only the English language and teaching methods in Indian schools. This still influences Indian education today.

Since independence, there have been many commissions and policy reports. Today, the deficiencies in the education system are well recognised (poor literacy levels, high dropout numbers in secondary schools, gender parity problems, quality standards). There is no problem in identifying the future needs – sufficient supplies of local facilities, trained staff, training for the subjects needed in the digital society (genomics, machine learning, artificial intelligence etc.). There are policies to overcome the problems. The challenge lies in political priorities and funding... like most countries.

Back to the positive example set by our hotel students in Bodh Gaya – they were a real credit to themselves, their families, and the people for whom they worked. At the end of our trip, I looked back at that hotel as the one I most enjoyed visiting.

By the time we were hosed down and ready to explore the town, it was getting on for midday. Nick and I wandered into town and found our way into an enormous playing field where the Bodh Mahotsava music and dance festival was taking place. In the centre of the field was a massive marquee that was being used for the performances. Inside, it had a stage at one end, and the rest of the space was filled with seating. Around the periphery of the field were stalls selling traditional arts and crafts and a range of food and drinks. Drawn by the loud noises coming from the marquee, we went to see what entertainment was on offer. With abysmal timing, we walked in just as a group of exotic looking female dancers were leaving the stage. We had to make do with a man who sounded like he was singing in some pain, with a similarly agonised bongo drum accompaniment. It was difficult to tell if the bongo guy and the singer were on the same musical page, but that might just be sour grapes on my part because we'd missed the exotic female dancers.

As we had experienced so many times on our trip, Nick and I caused a bit of a stir. We walked down the wide centre aisle that divided the seating area in the marquee and soon found ourselves in a series of group photos. We rarely get such celebrity treatment back in Oswestry or Brora. Someone important looking, who seemed in charge, guided us to a seating area reserved for monks and senior monks. Well... you just go with the flow. Thinking about it, with his shaved head, maybe Nick was mistaken for a monk. Perhaps they thought he was a senior monk, and I was his assistant. Anyway, we were honoured, and we stayed for nearly an hour, relaxing and enjoying the performances.

When we felt culturally fulfilled, we headed for a nearby café that Nick had identified during his research. The food and drink were both excellent, but there was a nasty surprise in store. The waiter informed us that the state of Bahir is 'dry.' Oh, no! ... What a state to get into! After several minutes of panic-filled discussion, the waiter commented: 'It may be possible to get some drink.' It seems there is always an underground market for alcohol if you know who to ask... you just have to ask the right cousin. We left the café and headed for the Mahabodhi Temple; there were headier things to consider than black market beer. We had only gone about fifty metres, however, when the waiter from the café suddenly appeared at Nick's shoulder. Furtively glancing around, he asked for Nick's phone number and promised to look into the beer issue and phone back with further intel later in the day... or maybe tomorrow. Oh great, I thought: another cloak and dagger operation to file alongside the Shimla bus ticket and Agra phone acquisitions. In the event, the waiter did phone Nick back. The going rate for a black market can of beer was 500 rupees, or about a fiver. I believe the possibility of a deal was on the table, but to protect my sources, I'll have to report that I'm not sure what the outcome was. We found out later that the going rate for a bottle of beer is the equivalent of two day's wages for a waiter. That's a sobering thought.

On our way to the temple, we had to go past the music festival site again. Easier said than done, however, and we got sucked in by the joyous sounds and sights of the place. The temple would have to wait until the following day. We relaxed to the cultural vibe of the event with a couple of ice creams – a butterscotch flavoured Cornetto and an almond Magnum. It doesn't get much more cultural than that.

At the hotel in the evening, our delightful student apprentices welcomed us back like family members and we chatted at length about our afternoon's activities. They served a delicious thali – a selection of small Indian dishes with a couple of rotis each. There was even a little dish of sweet rice for pudding. With teas or coffees, the whole blow out came to just under the equivalent of £3. We retired relatively early, in that it was before midnight. It had been a long day, once again full of new experiences, and the next day promised further enlightenment.

~

Over breakfast, Nick and I chatted again to Jean, the Swiss hotel manager. He was coming to the end of his six months stint teaching and guiding the young Indian students at the hotel. He told us about his experience in the hotel, and in India generally, which seemed to align well with what we had encountered on our travels.

Having been distracted by the festival the previous day, visiting the Mahabodhi Temple was the primary aim for our full day in Bodh Gaya. The temple sits next to the very tree (well, a tree from a sapling taken from the very tree) under which they say Buddha sat when he attained enlightenment. Neither Nick nor I are religious, but our experiences at the Golden Temple in Amritsar (the Sikhs' most holy place), Varanasi (one of the Hindus' most holy places), and now Bodh Gaya, were eye openers and thought-provoking insights into the devotion, sometimes fanatical, of believers. No matter what you believe, a visit to these places opens a window into the lives and thinking of millions of people. Whether Buddhism is a religion, by the way, could occupy many pages of discussion. It depends on your definition. Let's go with it being spiritual and leave it there.

Siddhartha Gautama is better known to the world as the Buddha. He developed Buddhism in the 6th century BC and it grew alongside Hinduism, with which it has some common background and characteristics. The Buddha rejected the concept of atman, which is central to the Hindu belief in birth and rebirth. Hindus believe that atman is the universal self, or soul, which gets transferred to a new life when a person or creature dies or attains release (moksha) from the constraints of existence. If I've got it right, Buddhists believe that nirvana – release and escape from the suffering of our lives – can be obtained by leading kind and good lives and in the process benefitting others in the world.

The place where Buddha attained enlightenment in Bodh Gaya is regarded by Buddhists as their most holy site and 'the navel of the earth.' One tradition claims it will be the last place to disappear when the world ends, and the first to appear when the world emerges into existence again. If our planet had been destroyed as Nick and I were eating our breakfast, we might have been two of the last people left on earth. That was another sobering thought, as, once again, was the implication for the future of Nick's football programme collection. Fortunately, the catalyst most likely to trigger a global disaster was still being held in check by the Imodium that Nick had taken earlier. The world's population of seven billion was safe for another day.

The town centre was a fifteen-minute stroll from our hotel. The walk took us past the eighty-foot high Great Buddha, the largest Buddha statue in India when the Dalai Lama consecrated it in 1989.

The eighty-foot Buddha statue in Bodh Gaya

It had taken seven years and tens of thousands of masons to construct the statue from sandstone and red granite. Keeping things uncomplicated, the local people have nicknamed it 'the eighty-foot Buddha statue.'

As well as being huge, it has a simplistic beauty. The

gardens that surround the statue help to create a calm and peaceful space that lends itself to quiet contemplation. Nick and I took our time to walk around the gardens and contemplate. At least partially chilled, we completed our walk to the town centre. As we got closer, the number of monks around us steadily increased until hundreds of them filled the pavements and most of the road. As we closed in on the Mahabodhi Temple, we realised we were going against the flow, against a considerable tide of purple and orange streaming in the opposite direction. The monks were returning from the temple after their early morning chanting. I had an unsettling burst of déjà vu for a couple of seconds... it was like approaching Fir Park five minutes after full time with a capacity crowd of bald Motherwell supporters coming the other way.

The Mahabodhi Temple Complex at Bodh Gaya comprises the fifty-metre-high grand temple (also known as Awakening Temple), the sacred Bodhi tree, and six other sacred sites linked to Buddha's enlightenment. It is one of four holy sites related to the life of the Lord Buddha. The others are Lumbibi, his birthplace, Sarnath, where he first taught, and Kushinara, where he died. Just for good measure, and to tap back into the ongoing construction materials sub-plot, the Mahabodhi Temple is one of the oldest brick temples in India. My mind briefly speculated on the availability of bricks and the regional distribution network that might have been in place during preceding centuries.

As Nick and I approached the temple complex, I remember noticing what a glorious day it was; warm and sunny, but not too hot. The approach was partly wooded and conspicuously clean. We deposited our phones (none are allowed inside the compound) at the first of two security checkpoints (no hold-ups this time) and joined the hundreds of pilgrims, worshippers and visitors filing their way into the temple complex. They were mostly men, and without being scientific about it, I'd estimate there were maybe 10 to 15 per cent women. Once inside, it was a beautiful sight. A perimeter wall encloses a large flower-filled garden area, criss-crossed with pathways, with the huge, ornate, and imposing multi-storied temple at the centre.

The Mahabodhi Temple at Bodh Gaya

The colours were the first thing that hit us – so beautiful. There were so many drapes of strung flowers and plates and cups of flowers, mainly orange and yellow marigolds, and of course, a good spread of lotus blooms. The overwhelming vision of colour was remarkable. Hundreds of mainly purple cloaked monks had set up temporary camp around the temple, some staying for several weeks or even months at a time. There were innumerable, purple-checked mattresses, mostly unoccupied, wedged into every available space. There was not a spare pitch to be had anywhere.

There was a calm atmosphere. Many worshippers were performing devotional exercises. They would stand upright with their hands together in front of their faces. Bringing their hands to their chest in the praying position, they would then, from their toes, collapse forwards, sliding their hands along the ground. They'd stretch out as far as they could before standing up again and repeating the routine. There were many variations on this theme. Most of the people had gloves or rags to protect their hands from the thousands of repetitions. Some had brought their own boards, the size of doors, which were angled upwards, and some had clickers in their hands to count how many repeats they'd performed. There was an OCD aspect to this which I simultaneously found pointless and admirable. I guess the idea is to do something so mind-numbingly repetitive and boring that the mind goes elsewhere. Other pilgrims were performing a mobile version of the routine on an artificial grass surface around the temple. Presumably beginning at the entrance to the complex, they moved forwards a body length each time, falling to the ground, and then standing up, homing in on the temple entrance a couple of metres at a time. Unusually, during our travels in India, we noticed some monks were even older than us.

The path around the temple takes you past the famous Bodhi tree. This area was very busy, but people kept moving past slowly so others could get close to see the tree. Next to it, and joining the temple, is a polished sandstone platform known as Vajrasana (the enlightenment throne of the Buddha). It marks the spot where Buddha sat and meditated. Nick and I chatted to a monk from Nepal who came to Bodh Gaya every year. It was his duty and non-negotiable; something he had to do. I'm not sure if I've ever met anyone so completely at ease and relaxed with the world. Whatever he was on, divine or earthly, real or placebo, it was working, and I quite wanted to visit whatever place he'd found.

Nick and I removed our shoes and made our way inside the Mahabodhi Temple. We saw, as in the Golden Temple in Amritsar, pilgrims being given handouts of food. There were only four or five Westerners around the temple in what must have been a crowd of many hundreds of people. We had been in the temple complex for a couple of hours by then and the sight of the food distribution must have made us hungry. We headed out of the temple complex to seek out the shady roof terrace of the Be Happy café. Because we're crazy dudes who roll how we like, we chose the most un-Indian meals of pizza and Greek salad – just for a change.

Wandering back to the festival site, we spent some more time in our allocated monks and senior monks seating area, and more time posing for people's photos, before looking around the rest of the stalls and shops. There was an interesting piece of theatre underway on an outdoor stage, being performed by a youthful team of actors. Although we couldn't understand what was being said, the message of the story seemed clear; girls *can* say no to fellas. It was a play to highlight women's rights. That's what it looked like because it mainly involved a chap, at first annoying a young girl, then being more of a nuisance, then chasing her around and trying to grab her. It culminated with her turning on the guy and knocking seven bells out of him with her shopping bag. She didn't hold back – the guy took a hell of a beating. I looked around the audience as we all applauded and saw approving nods and big smiles on the faces of some young women. They couldn't quite bring themselves to fist pump in public, but I'm sure that's what they were feeling.

Back home in the Highlands of Scotland, Nick is chairperson of Clyne Heritage Society and he's always up for a bit of heritage, cultural history, or archaeology. After our visit to the festival site, we headed for the Bodh Gaya archaeology museum. We had read about its excellent collection of Hindu and Buddhist relics, coins from the Mughal era, and stone sculptures. First, we had to get in though. On the other side of a pair of locked gates, between us and the museum, stood a security man. He was waving a double-barrelled shotgun around in a cavalier manner while telling us the museum was closed on Fridays. We were inclined to believe him. It was a bit like the situation at Gilbert Hill but in any language a brandished shotgun provides considerable weight to someone's point of view.

Instead, we had an amble around the town, taking in a fascinating, large, tented Nepalese market, a bookshop, and a look at the river Falgu. The river flows in the same way that an old-fashioned egg timer does – it's just sand. It was a reminder of one of India's (arguably the world's) most pressing problems – water shortage. The statistics are alarming. More than half of India's population has no access to safe drinking water and about 200,000 people die every year from lack of access to safe water. It's an economic as well as human need; almost every sector of the country's economy depends on water in some way, especially agriculture, which sustains two-thirds of India's 1.4 billion people. The Government of Narendra Modi has introduced a plan that aims to provide piped potable water to every rural household by 2024.

I sat on the riverbank for a few minutes' resting while Nick walked across the sands to the centre. His inner geomorphologist drew him to explore more of the river without water. I watched Nick pass a temporary allotment of crops that would undoubtedly be washed away when the first monsoon rains swept through. Sat next to me on the riverbank, at a suitable distance thankfully, was a pretty, young woman in a beautiful golden sari, who was meticulously picking nits out of her mum's hair while smiling contentedly.

As Nick and I walked away from the river along a narrow shady street, we passed a small building beating to the rhythm of some heavy industrial machinery. The doors were open to allow the air to circulate, and we could see a guy pouring mustard seeds into a funnel on top of a large, greasy, clunking piece of industrial heritage. Pistons flew up and down, wheels spun, belts were driven, and ram rods rammed. About ten feet away, at the other end of the greasy green machine, mustard oil poured steadily into a large grubby can. We gestured to the guy to ask if it was alright to go in and have a closer look. He showed us around and, above the din of the machinery, told us how it all worked. The system was very basic, and very old, but it worked and must have poured out millions of litres in its lifetime.

We had another meal in our hotel that evening, and our brief stay in Bodh Gaya was just about over. It was time to go through the routine of setting the alarm clocks again, this time for the morning train to Kolkata and our rendezvous with Nick's wife, Ellen. Our journey through India was reaching its east coast terminus.

We were about to leave Bodh Gaya on another long train journey, this time to Kolkata. Somewhere in the skies over India, Nick's wife Ellen was also on her way to Kolkata. Over breakfast, Nick was following Ellen's progress on his flight tracker; such are the wonders of modern technology. Ellen had left Inverness for Heathrow the previous day and via a change at Delhi she was due to arrive in Kolkata by early afternoon. Spookily, it looked like our paths were going to cross, separated by about 8,000 metres, somewhere around Bodh Gaya. We eagerly anticipated looking up into the clear skies to wave as she flew past.

We left our hotel after an excellent 7:00 am breakfast served to us by our lovely student hosts and walked towards the town centre to find a taxi for the journey back to Gaya Junction train station. There, we would pick up the Poorva Express for the 500 kilometres journey to Kolkata. It was scheduled to take eight hours. We flagged down a tuk-tuk and Nick began the lengthy business of negotiating a fare. Without, for once, recourse to whiteboards, Nick's pension statement, or reference to Maslow's theory of needs, a deal was eventually struck. We loaded our bags and jumped in. Oblivious to the high-level haggling being carried on eight kilometres below her, Ellen had passed overhead at 500 miles per hour without us seeing even her vapour trail. 'Where's Ellen now, Nick?' I asked. He gasped with momentary panic as he found and consulted the relevant app. 'Ah, bugger!' he said, 'It looks like she's just shot past.'

The subject of Indian signage popped into my head as Nick and I sat on the platform, just about to depart from Gaya Junction station. During our three weeks in India, Nick and I had seen countless signs that had made us laugh out loud or just raise our eyebrows in wonder. It was a case of the English translation being open to different interpretations. We could guess what most of them meant, but others, like the discount for dwarfs sign in Jaisalmer, left us bamboozled. In Udaipur, there was an advert for 'Golden Shower' that I really hoped was for a plumbing company. Others shouldn't be repeated in print. My favourite was in one of the train toilets. The sign read, 'Do not soil the seat Western style.' This one was especially disappointing for me, as I was just about to tie my horse up and put a cowboy hat on.

Once again, our experience with Indian Railways was good. But also, once again, our quiet compartment for six was over-run by twelve people halfway through the journey. And once again, they seemed to be medical students. It must be a condition of our ticket – there has to be some medical or construction related thread on each journey. When we arrived in Kolkata, we found that our train carriage was the furthest from the main station building. Our walk along the platform must have been at least 499 of the 500 kilometres journey. We soon found a taxi and sped to our hotel, where Nick was greeted by the open arms of Mrs L, and all was well with the world.

Prior to going out to India, the three of us had each filled out an online entry form for the annual Kolkata 10 kilometres run, which was due to take place the day after we arrived in the city. By the time Nick and I arrived, Ellen had already found her way to the nearby park where registration for the run was taking place. Although Nick and I only had about an hour to spare before registration closed, the park was only a ten-minute walk from the hotel and, fortunately, we had a guide. Not wishing to break with tradition too much, we followed up with a curry, washed down with Kingfisher beers from the local English wine shop. As athletes, dedicated to our sport, this was the perfect preparation for the challenge ahead of us. An early night beckoned to prepare for the Kolkata 10 kilometres run early the next morning.

KOLKATA

It was day twenty-seven of our *Journey through India*, and we were in Kolkata. Just like every other morning during our five-week trip, the sun was trying to force its way through some high-altitude haze. January is definitely a good time to visit India if you're from Britain. In most parts of the country, the early mornings are pleasantly cool, but by midday it feels like a pleasant summer's day back home.

Oh Calcutta! ... or Kolkata, as we have called it since 2001. The city is a north-south urban rectangle, sitting on either side of the Hooghly River, in West Bengal. It's on the north-eastern coast of India just to the west of the Ganges delta (the world's largest), and eighty kilometres from the border with Bangladesh. The nation's third largest city is also its oldest port. While extended families slept on the pavements each night outside the hotel where the Lindsays and I were staying, elsewhere in the densely populated city of just under fifteen million people, there were nearly 10,000 millionaires and at least four billionaires... unless they were away that night.

The city has played a prominent role in India's history over the last 500 years. Beginning with the East India

Company and throughout the height of the Raj in the 19th century, Calcutta was the capital of British India. Calcutta University, the first modern Indian university, was founded in 1857. The city became the centre of Indian arts and literature and earned a reputation as the cultural capital of the nation. From my background reading before our visit (especially *Midnight's Furies*, by Nisid Hajari) I was aware of the city's historic role in the struggle for national independence. In August 1946, the year before independence, the three main religious groups, Hindus, Muslims and Sikhs, argued over what the new independent state would look like. The disputes erupted into street brawls and then into a cycle of bloody clashes. Within months, the fighting was out of control, resulting in more than 5,000 fatalities. The British attempted to control the riots while negotiating a deal that would get them out of India as fast as possible. It was all a bit rushed. We read in the Partition Museum in Amritsar that when they published the map showing the border between India and newly created Pakistan the day after independence, hostilities broke out unchecked across all of India and the death toll rose to millions.

Partition took place shortly after devastating food shortages in the region. The 1943 famine is a desperately sorry episode. Approximately three million people starved to death. That's over six times the British Empire's casualties in World War Two, while Britain's wartime Prime Minister, Winston Churchill, watched on and refused to send food supplies to the region. He blamed the local population for 'breeding like rabbits.' The man who said 'I hate Indians, they are a beastly people with a beastly religion' was quietly confident that history would judge him kindly because he intended to write it himself. The combined effect of the famine and partition severely strained the economy of the region and Calcutta's pre-eminent position waned after the British departed.

Earlier, in 1912, India's then capital moved to Delhi. Unhelpful politics and economic decline dragged Calcutta backwards and by the 1970s, the city became synonymous with urban decay and poverty. The situation has improved in subsequent years, however, and today Kolkata is the prime business, commercial and financial hub of eastern India. The city is home to major industrial sectors including steel, heavy engineering, mining, minerals, and everyone's favourite – cement.

Kolkata is a city of contrasts. The desperate poverty that Agnes Gonxha Bojaxhiu, better known as Mother Teresa, sought to address in 1950 when she established 'The Missionaries of Charity,' still exists at one extreme of the economic scale, to counterbalance the millionaires and billionaires. Apart from the economic extremes, the city still has a reputation as the country's artistic and cultural capital. Upwardly mobile financial types are expanding the middle class, while cool hipsters pursue the east coast movie dream. The architecture is a confused mash up of grand colonial-era designs and quirky Bengali-European styles. Skyscrapers stand tall in the business/commercial sector, while elsewhere there are overcrowded residential blocks, slums, and scattered nuggets of Mughal, Hindu and old English influence. A generous sprinkling of parkland around the city offers a welcome break from its bustle and heat. Visitors to the City of Joy typically head for the flower market, the Hooghly River, the various museums, and Mother Teresa's House. I say 'typically' because our sight-seeing list was less conventional; read on for an account of the Kolkata tourist path less travelled.

Nick and I had another early start that morning, but for once, we didn't need to dash to an airport or train station.

Our coast to coast trip was over, but we weren't heading home immediately. There was a 10 kilometres run to enjoy, and we had time to look around Kolkata. Finally, we planned to make a mad dash over to see a piece of *old* India – Chattogram, formerly Chittagong, which is now in Bangladesh. Before that... did you hear the one about the Englishman, Welshman and Scotswoman?

The Lindsays and I skipped breakfast; sporting heroics demanded the sacrifice. Having found our way to the race registration area the previous evening, it took us all of ten minutes to get to the holding area for the start of the 2020 Kolkata 10 kilometres race. Like typical Brits, we followed the instructions to the letter, and arrived a full hour before the off. We were already in our running kit, so there was nothing to do... just hang around, do a few loosening exercises to look like we knew what we were doing, and wait for 15,000 runners to join us. They gradually did, in dribs and drabs, mostly in the final ten minutes leading up to the start. There was a friendly atmosphere, with the usual excited chatter, apprehensive stretching, and nervous giggles you witness before the start of a mass-participation run. As we walked around, we went through small invisible clouds surrounding those runners who had been a bit heavy-handed with the muscle heat rub. It smelt like a proper run.

As the start time approached, we could see people gradually shuffling their way into a narrow funnel of flags that led to the start line. We joined in and filed our way slowly in a long column of nervy but enthusiastic competitors. The sheer number of runners was slowing everyone down, but there was another reason why everything was taking so long. Standing on a high podium next to the start line was the internationally famous Indian cricketer Sachin Tendulkar. He dropped the flag to begin the race, and then waved to the competitors for the next fifteen minutes as they slowly shuffled over the start line, everyone applauding the great man as they went past. And why not? The man is a sporting legend. He made his international cricketing debut at sixteen, made a hundred test centuries, captained his country to World Cup victory and was the most prolific run maker of all time. He is arguably the biggest cricket icon the game has ever known, and his status in India is something akin to a god. They have quite a few already, so why not one more? The Little Master was enjoying the occasion and waved back enthusiastically to the runners.

Just as we'd seen everywhere else on our travels in India, mobile phones were out in force. Everyone had to get their photo of Sachin. Some people stood awestruck, finally remembering to get their photo at the last second before the crowd swept them along. The younger ones, lifelong occupants of the social media world, somehow ran along, perhaps backwards, angling their phone at arm's length to get the perfect selfie, which included them smiling, the crowd, and Sachin.

You might wonder why all those athletes had phones. Well, of the 15,000 runners, we only saw a handful of 'serious' runners. There could have been more; there probably were, but nowhere near us (obviously). The three of us were still together as we approached the start line, and I'm sure I saw Sachin's face light up with joy when he saw a trio of elderly white people. We hardly saw anyone else over fifty and hardly any other non-Indian runners.

Once over the line, we went our own ways and were soon lost in the crowd; Nick sped off like the Jammu Tawi Express train. Ellen and I were more like a couple of stopping trains on the suburban commuter route. I think the guard had left my brake on. The run had attracted a lot of occasional runners, and some weren't even trying; they were just happy to wander slowly around the ten kilometres and enjoy the party atmosphere. There were groups of friends going around together, with streamers and balloons, having a party on the run. Most people were treating it as a fun run; it was just a walk in the park. Cheering crowds lined large sections of the route and every few hundred yards there was a band, or group of spectators, applauding, trying to raise the tempo and encourage the runners.

By the end of the run, the temperature had risen to around twenty degrees, but thankfully, the last part of the run was through shady parkland. It was all over before we knew it. We all had good runs (thankfully, in the athletic sense, on this occasion) with Nick easily smashing the hour, and Ellen and I achieving respectable times. Had there been awards for such things, we would probably have picked up medals for first and second men over sixty, and first woman over sixty... because I think we were the only ones in those categories. The three of us staggered back to the hotel in triumph. We showered, changed, and set off to explore the city's cemeteries!

I should explain that Nick and Ellen had already been to Kolkata several times as part of a cemetery survey project. For this trip, they'd chosen three graveyards to visit from a list of over twenty. Who knew there would be so much choice? I was well up for that. I can happily while away an hour in a graveyard. I know it seems weird, but I like the quiet, respectful atmosphere, and there is so much to learn from the stories told on the gravestones and tombs.

We headed for South Park Street cemetery, which is quite a spectacle, with its huge ornate gothic tombs and mausoleums in the style of Highgate cemetery in London or Pere Lachaise in Paris. It opened in 1767, and by the time it was full in 1830, it was the largest Christian cemetery outside Europe and North America. Today, it provides a cool and shady oasis amongst the chaotic urban craziness of

Kolkata. It's easy to lose your way in the photogenic warren of walkways that intersect the rows of tombs, towering trees, shrubs, and vines. Shafts of sunlight filter through the canopy of vegetation to spotlight their favourite monuments and headstones. Stand still and listen – it's a few hectares of tamed jungle in the heart of an urban jungle, and it's deadly quiet. For a few seconds, in that calm air of colonial superiority, you can glimpse life... or death, at the time of the British East India Company.

The cemetery fell into disrepair after the partition in 1947. Since restored, it's now a heritage site, protected by the Archaeological Survey of India and a dedicated band of volunteers. In its day, the cemetery wasn't available for the ordinary folk of Kolkata. The 2,000 or so tombs contain mainly British officers, Civil Servants, senior staff from the East India Company, and their families. Many of them were victims of tropical diseases, such as cholera, for which there were no medicines or cure. It's sad to see how many died in their twenties or younger. A good number of the city's current generation of teens and twenty-somethings come to keep them company each day. Like the gardens surrounding the Residency in Lucknow, the South Park Cemetery seemed to be a magnet for the young loved-up couples of Kolkata to go for a quiet saunter and canoodle.

We moved on to the Lower Circular Road cemetery. Unlike some of the other cemeteries around the city centre, this one is still in use. Our brief stop was long enough to find the grave belonging to a descendant of one of Nick and Ellen's neighbours from back in Scotland. We even volunteered for a bit of graveyard maintenance while we were there, risking physical injury while clearing some African oil palm trees from the top of a grave.

On the way to collect our hat-trick of cemetery visits, we came across the Karaya Road Cricket Club... that is... a match taking place in the middle of Karaya road, one of the city's commercial side streets.

Undistracted by the occasional vehicular or bovine interruption, two teams were completing twenty overs a side in the middle of the road, with great passion and enthusiasm. The players were all male, but there was a wide age range. I couldn't work out whether participation was based on cricketing expertise or the willingness to take on a moving tuk-tuk while chasing the ball to the boundary. It was all very serious. They were using a tennis ball, but the bats were real. They used three proper stumps wedged into a wooden block at just one end of the imaginary tarmac pitch. The wicketkeeper whipped the stumps out of the way and replaced them each time someone inconveniently interrupted the game by using the road as a road.

We arrived at a possible turning point in the game. A heated argument had broken out over a potential wicket and emotions were running high. The batsman was refusing to move from the crease. He argued that in catching the ball off a steepling shot towards the sewing machine shop, the fielder had stepped over the boundary line. It was a fair point. We had seen the fielder scramble over the bonnet of a parked car and then stand on its roof to take the catch. The car marked the boundary of the pitch, so on a technicality, the batsman was not out and had scored six runs. Seeing our delight as spectators (the rapturous applause was the giveaway), the lads honoured me with the opportunity to face a couple of deliveries.

Right then! My chance to show these rookies how the game should be played. The fielders closed in, sensing an early dismissal. I attempted to tap down a few irregularities in the road surface at about the point where the ball would bounce 'on a length' to make it look like I was serious. Their captain shielded his mouth as he discussed some tactical adjustments with his deputy. He set an attacking field with a gully and two slips. That left a few gaps in the field, if I was bold enough to take them on. It was like a tactical game of chess between two masterly cricketing brains.

Preparing to drive down the road

I used the first ball as a sighter and prodded a quick single. The bowler looked nervous (not) as an excited murmur of anticipation ran along the pavement, in and out of the ironmongers, and back out onto the road. I got in line early for the second delivery and stroked an elegant four off the back foot between two tuk-tuks on the off-side boundary. The fielders and spectators rewarded both strokes with generous applause. These guys obviously recognised a stylish stroke maker when they saw one. I think there might have been a few mutterings of 'Wow, that was Sachin-like'... in my head.

After two deliveries, I retired, unbeaten, stumps undisturbed. I handed my magician's wand of a bat back and let the local lads get on with the proper action. I suppose for completeness I should add that the bowler de-tuned his standard 100 miles per hour unplayable missiles to nicely placed underarm dollies for this old man. Good on you lads, it was great fun, thanks!

Sadly, Nick had missed what would undoubtedly have been the second-best highlight of his trip to India because he'd been off in search of a toilet. He caught up with Ellen and me just as the last of the applause was dying down – as I was going round shaking hands with the fielders and posing for selfies. We moved on.

The day had somehow disappeared, and the sun was setting as the three of us looked around our third graveyard – the Scottish cemetery. That was the cue for the local mosquito community to come to life, so we headed back to the hotel. We were all exhausted anyway. We'd almost walked another 10 kilometres since running our 10 kilometres.

We set aside day twenty-eight to see some Kolkata sights that weren't cemeteries. I was happy to hand the planning to Nick, as he was familiar with the city from his previous visits. I had a bit of shopping to do first, though. Panic set in when I realised that I'd be back home by the end of the week. I'd been wearing the same trousers for four weeks and it was about time they were washed. An oversight in mission planning meant I had no back-up trousers, so I needed a cheap, temporary pair to wear for a day while the others were laundered. Not wishing to waste too many hours trawling the pavement vendors of Kolkata, I went for the first ones I found. You've probably spotted my mistake already. They were neither long enough nor ample enough around the waist, but the pavement vendor said, 'Will stretch, Sir, no problem.' The guy didn't seem keen on me dropping my kecks on the pavement to try his new pair for size, so I parted with my hard-earned 450 rupees (£4.50), and dashed back to the hotel to find a shoehorn to put them on.

Good for a laugh was my first thought, or maybe going through my Bee Gees repertoire. My unfamiliar look certainly kept Nick and Ellen amused... and I'm sure anyone else who caught sight of a white pensioner in a pair of hipster skinny jeans with elastic ends to the legs. A Kipling quote came to mind: 'Many wear the robes, but few walk the Way.' Only in my case it would be '... but few walk that way.' The trousers did the job... well, you could tell by the way I used my walk. My main pair of trousers got a much needed wash, and I paid Nick handsomely for reassurance that all photographic evidence of me wearing the new trousers had been destroyed. Let's move on swiftly.

Nick had worked out a brilliant Kolkata sightseeing schedule. The three of us squeezed into a tuk-tuk and headed for the Mallick Ghat, at the south-eastern end of the Howrah Bridge, the giant grey Meccano construction spanning the Hooghly River. By the way, three in the back of a tuk-tuk isn't really a squeeze; it's just comfortable. It's about nine people, a sack of rice, a set of saucepans, and half a dozen chickens short of full capacity.

We arrived at the colourful chaos of Kolkata flower market by mid-morning. It was open air and perhaps the size of a very narrow football pitch. It was already in full bloom.

The Kolkata flower market

It's possible that some people there knew what was going on, but to the outsider it just looked like a confused pot-pourri of humanity, mud and petals – a blurred bouquet of mainly white and brown, yellow and orange. A constant stream of traders arrived from all directions, with huge white bundles on their heads. Occasionally, a dangerously overloaded truck would inch its way through the crowds of people and flowers, with huge wobbling white sacks of blooms piled high on the back. The bundles were thrown to the ground when the truck stopped, and hundreds of garlands of marigolds spilled out into the mud. Buyers swarmed around like bees and haggled to snap up the new arrivals.

They mainly use the garlands for weddings, functions, or temple offerings... and sometimes a romantic Welsh tourist might buy one for his wife. We picked our way through the floral mayhem and worked our way up to the bridge. From there, the view was even better; it was possible to see the entire extent of the market.

We continued over the Howrah Bridge, which is one of *the* iconic sights of the city. Anyone who has been to Kolkata will have the image of that bridge in their heads right now. The towering steel construction officially opened in 1943, when it was the world's third longest cantilever bridge. About 100,000 vehicles, and over 150,000 pedestrians, use the bridge daily. The Kolkata Port Trust has to routinely clean and re-paint the bridge in an ongoing battle with a corrosive cocktail of bird droppings and human spit.

The Lindsays and I walked from Kolkata, on the eastern side of the river, to the more industrial Howrah side. Ahead of us was the Howrah Junction railway station, the country's oldest and one of the busiest train stations in the world. Each day, over two million passengers use the twenty-three platforms to get on and off over 600 passenger trains. We were on our way to visit the Railway Museum, and after that, the Botanical Garden. Contain yourselves. The first was a short walk from the end of the Howrah Bridge. Don't worry, I'll keep the account brief; it was shut.

Disappointed but undeterred, we took a twenty-minute tuk-tuk ride to the gardens. They were also shut, as was everything else in Kolkata, it seemed, on Mondays. Our consolation was a half- hour-long circuitous bus ride back through tightly packed streets to Howrah town, for the equivalent of ten pence, and then a ferry across the river. While we waited for the ferry to arrive, we watched local people coming down to the river to bathe and wash clothes in the muddy waters by the riverbank. We watched as a middle-aged man, dressed completely in pristine white linen, was led into the shallows by half a dozen friends. A brief ceremony involved him being totally immersed several times while everyone chanted. Two members of the party rang small hand bells. When the chap emerged from his third or fourth dunking, someone handed him back his sunglasses and there was joyous applause and laughter. Everyone involved seemed genuinely elated by the experience, but I'm not sure that bright white outfit would ever be the same again.

To keep this concise, I'll fast forward to the following day. We tried both visitor attractions again, and they were both open. If you're interested in old trains, the Railway Museum will be heaven. There must be just about every conceivable type of train from India's railway history represented in an enormous expanse of landscaped grounds. Its nicely laid out and kept us amused, and interested, for a couple of hours.

Kolkata's botanical garden (correctly entitled Acharya Jagadish Chandra Bose Indian Botanic Garden) is an eight-kilometre tuk-tuk ride from the city centre. One hundred and ten hectares of gardens sit on the northern bank of the Hooghly, where you can calmly watch the river meander its way through the city. Using specimens from five continents, they originally laid the gardens out in 1787, making it one of the oldest botanical gardens in India. The website I consulted entices visitors with the prospect of seeing 'about 12,000 living perennial plants and millions of dried out plants gathered from world over.' You can see why we found it irresistible.

We can thank the Kolkata botanical garden for an aspect of British daily life that many of us take for granted. They say the garden's staff introduced Chinese tea plants to India back in the days of the Raj, laying the foundations for the country's modern tea trade, and our daily cuppa. The highlight of our visit, however, and surely anyone's, is their famous banyan tree (ficus benghalensis). Some claim it puts all other trees in the shade by having the largest canopy in the world. When Nick told me the 250-year-old 'Great Banyan' tree had a circumference of approximately 330 metres and a spread of more than four acres (the size of a small copse), I must admit I was sceptical. The Great Banyan is not how you imagine a normal tree, though. It doesn't have a tall central trunk, and then branches that spread out for hundreds of metres. In fact, its original trunk, which grew to a diameter of fifteen metres, was struck by lightning in 1925 and became infected by fungus. They removed the sick part to save the rest. The tree continued to grow and expand its spread. What looks like hundreds of separate tree trunks that spring up and join the network of branches aren't trunks at all. They are prop roots that are all connected to the same root system underground. It's an impressive sight.

Back in the city, we ticked off another tourist 'must-do' with a visit to Flurys bakery and café on Park Street. A Swiss expatriate couple (you won't be surprised to read their names were Mr and Mrs Flurys) founded the legendary breakfast place in 1927. Its traditional European confections soon made the café a popular meeting place, and over the decades it has become an institution, part of the culture of Kolkata. A makeover in 2004 introduced a pink candy shop look inside its traditional exterior, and large French windows. I found the interior slightly disappointing if I'm honest; I think I was expecting a bit more of a traditional Viennese coffee house atmosphere... something with a nostalgic European feeling to show off its long heritage. I guess the owners are trying to appeal to a younger generation and I was just showing my age. A delightful Viennese coffee and slice of Baba Cake mitigated the disappointment and made me feel a lot better about life in general.

Our day's blast around the city tourist hotspots wouldn't have been complete without taking in one last church and graveyard, so we headed for St John's church, another oasis of calm in the sensory maelstrom that is downtown Kolkata. The East India Company constructed the former Anglican cathedral in 1787 to bring Christianity to the city and to remind the Indian people who was in charge and who they should be worshipping. On the way up the sweeping drive leading to the church, we admired the bravery and skills of the Indian painters, who were re-decorating the white pillars outside the pale-yellow building. They were clambering ten metres up and down bamboo scaffolding that swayed alarmingly as they moved. It looked like an accident waiting to happen, but maybe God was taking care of the glaring health and safety issues for them, instead of their work supervisor. Inside the church, the atmosphere was grand, as you might expect. There was plenty of elegant wood and masonry, and many fine paintings. Shafts of sunlight streamed through the large stained-glass windows and tinted the stone floor in a colourful, blurred mosaic. It was calm and peaceful, but then most buildings seemed like that when you get off the hot and bustling streets of Kolkata. We left the church and stopped off to look at the Black Hole Monument, which lies in the church grounds, built to honour the British prisoners who died in the tragedy.

The Black Hole of Calcutta relates to an incident I dimly remembered from my school history days, although I'm ashamed to admit I couldn't remember what it was all about. The horrific story goes back to 1756. Calcutta was one of several military strongholds in India held by the British East India Company. As in other parts of the country, the company's hold on power was tenuous and relied upon a series of uneasy truces with bordering princely states. When he heard of the British plans to re-enforce the fort in

Calcutta, the Nawab of Bengal took exception to the potential power shift. Getting his retaliation in first, he marched on Calcutta with 50,000 troops, fifty cannons, and 500 elephants. It must have been quite a sight. The British defence was short-lived. The garrison was short on numbers and their commander, Governor John Zephaniah Holwell, was more used to collecting taxes than defending forts. Vastly outnumbered, the British soon surrendered to the Indian troops. According to Howell's account of the incident, they herded the 146 surviving soldiers and civilian support staff into a humid prison cell measuring 5.5 by 4.3 metres. They left the prisoners overnight in temperatures of over forty degrees. By the time they opened the cell doors the next morning, there were twenty-three survivors and a mound of dead bodies. The incident inflamed public opinion back in Britain, but there have been questions raised by historians over the years about the accuracy of the report. It's difficult to judge: you can only go by what you read and hear, and that depends on who's doing the writing and telling. It has, however, left us with a well-known idiom (like the Black Hole of Calcutta) to describe a cramped space, which is glibly used without giving much thought to its derivation.

We headed back to our hotel. Nick and I left Ellen to get some peace and quiet. She was going to get some quality time with the feline occupants of the hotel while us lads headed for the airport for a brief foray into Bangladesh.

CHITTAGONG

Nick and I had one last fling left on our old boys' adventure before we had to return to our 'normal' lives back home. In keeping with the rushed timetable we'd followed for five weeks in India, our dash from Kolkata to Chittagong and back gave us a little over twenty-four hours in Bangladesh. It was a trip of indecent haste, but it would allow me to fulfil a lifelong ambition. By the time we got back to Kolkata, we would only have half a day left on the subcontinent before boarding our flight to Heathrow, via Delhi.

Nick and I set off for the airport by mid-afternoon after our unorthodox and cemetery-biased tour of Kolkata. We set off with trepidation because, according to our calculations, we could only satisfy one of four conditions necessary to be allowed onto the flight. Getting back into India might also be challenging. In our favour, we both had return tickets, but on the negative side we didn't have an invitation letter, we had no visa, and we were well short of the $500 cash required. With no justification, we were fairly relaxed about it. We'd bluffed our way through a few things, so international borders were just another challenge. That laddish bravado could easily have backfired on us, but good fortune (aka Ganesha) was still on our side.

Our transit through Kolkata airport, given the circumstances, was remarkably smooth. We had a pleasant chat with the security guy who checked our paperwork, and we soon established a friendly rapport with him. Discussing great Indian cricketing victories certainly helped. Our account of the recent game against Australia might have swung things our way, but Nick wearing his 'I love India' headband was a masterstroke. It showed his pedigree at international level blaggology. We asked about carrying liquids because we'd heard they were not permitted in traveller's luggage. We admitted that we had bottles of water, toothpaste, shampoo, and hand gel in our bags, but we were reassured that none of that was a problem. We had no visas, but that was 'absolutely fine.' There was no mention of the need for an invitation letter and no request to inspect our $500 cash. It was all too easy. I spent most of the forty-five-minute flight thinking that we'd be sent back to Kolkata as soon as we landed.

We were in luck in Bangladesh as well. Perhaps Ganesha was taking an awayday break with us, although I'm not sure what his position would be on post-partition borders – do half elephant deities acknowledge such man-made artificial constructs? Once again, we had a good chat with the guy on the immigration desk, who seemed very friendly and genuinely helpful. He was impressed when we told him how much we were looking forward to visiting his great country, how we enjoyed all the amazing dishes cooked by the Bangladeshi community in Britain (I gave the Cinnamon Bay, Hamble a mention), and how brilliant the Bangladesh cricket team was. We had to fill in a couple of forms (obviously; it used to be India), and we were sent off to find an ATM to get $50 in local currency. When we returned to the immigration desk, we were given our visas – once again, very easy.

Our return trip the following day was also filled with strikingly similar good fortune. Although Nick had applied for and received an eVisa to enable entry to India, he couldn't find the documentation when we came to leave Chittagong – even though his 'proper' visa had been stamped in his passport on arrival at immigration in Mumbai. I'm still not sure what happened, but we bumped into the same immigration official we'd met on the way into the country, and he recognised us. Some combination of the documents we had, some magic dust, and I suspect some leniency by our friend, and we were through. And it didn't stop there – while we were sitting in the lounge awaiting our flight back to India, our friendly official appeared again with two cartons of mango juice for us! I immediately wanted to give him twelve out of ten on the 'Would you recommend our service to others' customer survey form they didn't have.

But I'm getting ahead of myself again – let's go back to our arrival in Chittagong. By the time we landed, it was dark. We found a taxi and set off on the hour-long ride to our hotel. The journey took us through the centre of Chittagong and out to the south side of the city, as close as we could practically get to our objective – Patenga Beach.

Let's sort that Chittagong name out. We'd arrived in Chattogram according to its Bengali and official name. In my experience, most people in Bangladesh, and abroad, still use the old name of Chittagong, so I'll stick with that, while acknowledging it isn't the official version. The most widely accepted explanation for the name Chittagong is that it's just the way the British incomers pronounced the name because they couldn't get their tongues around the Bengali version. I prefer to think they were one jump ahead; they came up with a snappy alternative because they foresaw the potential confusion the name Chattogram might cause with future developers of social media apps.

I should mention a few of the wonderful things about Bangladesh that some readers won't know about. Most people will be unaware of its abundance of wildlife, nature, and heritage. The UNESCO-protected Sundarbans National Park, for example, on the Ganges delta, is a national park that contains the largest mangrove forest in the world. It's a complex network of tidal waterways, mudflats and small islands which is home to 260 bird species, crocodiles, pythons *and* the Royal Bengal tiger, being the home to the world's largest single population of tigers. Beach lovers can head for Cox's Bazar, where they will find the longest natural beach in the world. Those more interested in history and heritage could visit Paharpur, in the north-west of Bangladesh, which dates from the 18th century and was once the largest Buddhist monastery south of the Himalaya. Much as we would have loved to, Nick and I didn't see any of those (some more places to visit next time), given our time constraints. Our main goal was to visit *that* beach.

Along large stretches of our route through the centre of Chittagong city, the pavements were packed with hundreds of people on the move. Our taxi driver told us they were textile workers on their way to and from work. It was like an Asian version of a Lowry painting, illuminated by bright shop lights, with a brighter colour palette perhaps, but the overall impression was of hundreds of people, heads down and shuffling along. The 5,000 textile factories in Bangladesh churn out millions of ready-made garments every year for export around the world, and many of those factories are in Chittagong. H&M, Calvin Klein, Tommy Hilfiger, Hugo Boss, and Marks and Spencer are among the global brands that keep almost four million workers, mostly women, employed in the Bangladeshi textile industry. This makes it the second (to China) largest exporter of garments in the world. The sector accounts for 80 per cent of Bangladesh's total export earnings. The industry has grown at breakneck speed over the last two decades, boosted by low wage costs, a favourable business climate, and good transportation facilities.

In the early days, growth occurred with little regard for the working conditions of those involved. It was all about keeping costs low. Cheap foreign labour was in fashion. Demand from the West was huge, no doubt fuelled by the trend towards inexpensive, throwaway, and micro-trend items, that were invariably already out of fashion by the time they were taken home. Progress was interrupted by several high-profile factory disasters in 2012/13 that left over 1,200 workers dead. This put the spotlight on the atrocious working conditions conveniently overlooked by Western retailers, who were searching for ever cheaper fashions to fill the high street shops. Keen to sustain one of its key industries and its most valuable export, the Bangladeshi government, with support from foreign governments and image conscious retailers, introduced reforms to improve safety and working conditions. Conditions gradually improved, although it was from a pitifully low base. Since that low point, the minimum wage has doubled, and a range of safety standards has been agreed by factory owners. Hopefully, the improvements will continue alongside a more sustainable approach to clothes purchasing and more environmental and social awareness in the West... we'll see!

When we eventually arrived at our hotel, we found it was functional but not exactly spotless. Cleaning and maintenance weren't priorities for the management. We settled in and while I caught up with writing my daily blog, Nick went off in search of a pint. When we'd checked in, we had asked about an evening meal. No problem, but they told us it was impossible to be served alcohol with our meal in the dining room. Drinks could be obtained in the lounge, but not the dining room. After fifteen minutes of writing up the day's events, I wandered off to find Nick. I eventually discovered the lounge. It was a very smoky and dimly lit room with visibility so restricted that I had to go round from table to table, peering at the drinkers to identify my pal. I reckoned punters would have a maximum of half an hour in there before breathing difficulties would set in and an emergency resus' team would have to be sent in with oxygen. The room appeared to be set aside just for smokers and drinkers... basically a drinking den. We left, and by the time Nick's lungs were operating again, we'd found the dining room. We both had an amazing meal, with the added advantage of being able to breathe. Thanks to Nick's rigorous diary keeping, I can report that I had a chicken jalfrezi and Nick had a prawn bhuna. Halfway through the meal, one of the staff came over to demand payment for Nick's earlier drinks back in the den. Apparently, it was impossible to put the beer on the hotel bill. Hadn't they heard of the 'ice-cold coffee' trick in Bangladesh? We asked if we could have a couple of the ice creams that were listed on the menu but were told that would be impossible because it was winter. Well, of course; and suddenly, it felt like India.

Sleep during that hot and humid night was regularly interrupted by the unmistakable high-pitched, and terror-inducing whine of mosquitoes. They were hard to ignore and every now and again, one of us would jump up, flick the light on, and there would be a frenzied killing session. They kept coming back and by morning, most of the former mosquito population of Chittagong was distributed around our blood splattered bedroom and bathroom walls. With the killing fields scene from a horror movie as a backdrop, I frantically searched the Internet to discover how widespread malaria was in Bangladesh. I thought about the mosquito net I'd left at home, when I'd reassured myself that it wouldn't be needed anywhere we were going to visit.

I can't fault the food in that hotel even if the general standards of cleanliness weren't up to much. Like most places we'd visited, it's probably a good job we didn't see the kitchens. On that subject, I was told by an ex-pat Brit who had lived in India for many years, that visitors are more likely to get food poisoning in the big posh hotels, where the ice in your cocktails and the water used to wash salads can be dubious. In the less expensive cafés and restaurants frequented by the locals, they're more likely to cook on high heat and kill off any nasty bugs. That was the theory, anyway.

We had an excellent breakfast that included some unusual items labelled as chicken sausages. Don't tell anyone but they were really made of pork. After breakfast, we headed out to find the local Commonwealth War Graves cemetery. You can see the continuing theme here, can't you? If only we had had time to visit the local builder's merchant to see what they had to offer in the way of cement.

When we arrived at the cemetery, we found it was exceptionally well laid out and maintained. It had the very dignified feel it should have. Nick and I strolled around the 756 marked graves. It was poignant to see a separate area marked out for Japanese war dead. Despite the atrocities we were told about after the war, someone had provided their dead with a respectful burial. After an hour or so, we headed back to the hotel so we could link to their Internet to order an Uber taxi to take us to our main goal for this foray into Bangladesh – Patenga Beach.

Picture the scene. It's 1945 and all around the world people are at war. In India, with Britain in conflict with Japan, two young English people are in Chittagong, thousands of miles from home for the first time in their lives. She's a shy teenager, working as a nurse for the Red Cross. He's a little older and a dashing RAF officer, the skipper of an Air Sea Rescue boat. His job is rescuing downed aircrew from the Bay of Bengal and hers is patching them up and mending them in hospital. Somehow, the couple's paths cross. They meet up a few times and fall in love. In their rare moments of spare time, they'd throw a picnic, a wind-up gramophone and a few records into a military Jeep and drive off to the white sand dunes and swaying palm trees of nearby Patenga Beach. A young couple thrown together in adversity in a far off, but exotic, foreign land. Could it be more romantic? When the war was over, they returned to Britain and got married. They bought one of those old rescue boats the RAF no longer needed and converted it into their first home. They lived aboard it on the River Clyde and named it *Patenga* in memory of where they had fallen in love in those heady days, far from home. A few years later, I became their second son, and the rest is (my) history.

So, there I was, standing on Patenga Beach, seventy-five years after my mum and dad were there. I'd finally got there. Of course, the scene was not quite how it was in 1945 when my parents were there. I didn't think it would be. I'd been tipped off about what to expect by the Bangladeshi owners of our local Indian restaurant back home. The sun kissed white sands leading down to clear azure waters, and the palm trees lazily dipping their leaves into the ocean were no more. Nowadays you approach Patenga Beach along a dusty narrow road, across half a mile or so of flat and unremarkable scrubland. There's not much, or anyone, to see. On the landward side of the beach, there is a massive concrete breakwater. It runs for about a kilometre, forming a ten-metre-wide promenade that stops abruptly at either end. I imagine someone has big ideas for development in the future. Piles of concrete blocks on the seaward side of the breakwater tumble down to the beach – a long strip of litter-strewn, dirty sand. The sea defences hint at rougher seas than the calm waters we saw on the day of our visit. Out in the Bay of Bengal, there were scores of cargo ships and tankers moored up, stretching far into the distance out to sea, and to the left and right along the coast.

Patenga Beach

Some of those ships might have been awaiting their last voyage; an appointment with the grim re-cycler on the nearby Sitakunda coastal strip, a few kilometres north-west of Chittagong. It's one of the world's biggest shipping graveyards; the last resting place for over one in five of all large vessels scrapped worldwide. That's approximately 200 ships each year. To keep the world's clapped-out super tankers, cruise liners and bulk carriers coming to them, the local yards must outbid their competitors in India, Pakistan, China and Turkey. Dismantling ships on the Chittagong mudflats and recycling the materials doesn't require much investment in high-tech equipment; it involves a lot of cheap labour. The cheaper it is, the more competitive the shipyards can be. Once the ships are beached on the mudflats at high tide, they're sliced up and dismantled within a few months by labourers equipped with hand tools, blowtorches, and diesel-powered winches. For the equivalent of around £1.50 for a long day, men scramble up down precarious rope ladders over the beached ships in steamy tropical conditions. They're often dealing with oil, asbestos, and toxic chemicals, and dodging chunks of falling steel and other bits of scrap. The workforce endures appalling conditions, with hundreds dying each year and thousands being injured for life.

The Bangladesh economy benefits: the shipyards provide around half the country's raw steel supply. Developed countries benefit: they can claim some use is being made of their unwanted maritime leftovers. Exposure-shy multinational shipping firms benefit: they can dispose of their unwanted vessels to cash buyers, who are based offshore, where ownership details are kept on a need-to-know basis and no one needs to know. The yards, in what has become a powerful ship-breaking industry, benefit: there are plenty of ships to dismantle and labour is cheap. Do the labourers benefit? Well, if it's about being able to have a job with some security, a recognised wage structure, medical provision, days off, and reassuring health and safety provisions – forget it! The workers endure hardship to survive, to feed and clothe their families. For less than $200, you can even book yourself on the Chittagong ship-breaking yard tour.

As soon as Nick and I arrived on the beachside promenade, we were pestered by kids who wouldn't take no for an answer when they offered us peanuts for sale. Trying to have a logical discussion and hoping they would understand that we didn't want any peanuts didn't work. Issues like customer demand, economics and personal space hadn't been factored into their marketing strategy and pricing policy. As far as they were concerned, they had peanuts for sale, we could afford them and we should buy them. Nick and I made a deal; one bag each for their very best price if they'd just leave us alone. We have a lot to learn about negotiating and good business practice... but we could continue our walk in peace.

To our right, as we looked out to sea, the coast eventually led to the port of Chittagong and round to Sitakunda, although they were both out of sight from where we stood. To our left, the beach continued to a peninsular, bounded by the sea on one side and the Karnaphuli River on the other. We headed towards the point but were stopped in our tracks long before we reached it.

The Bangladesh Naval Academy, which is presumably the successor to the RAF station where my dad was based all those years ago, occupies the last part of that peninsular. The security fence surrounding the military compound ended at the top of the beach, so we could, in theory, carry on walking along the sand. We did. There were no barriers or signs to suggest the area was out of bounds. We continued our walk towards the point, initially ignoring the loud shouting and whistling coming from the uniformed security guards, who were thankfully some distance away. Watching from the corner of my eyes as we marched on regardless, I couldn't help but notice various items of weaponry being waved around as the shouts became more urgent. Such formalities rarely stop Nick and me, but the security guys sounded serious and there was no point in pushing our luck. Those words 'And don't go off doing silly things' drifted into my head once again, as they always do at such times, and we turned around. As the sound of a developing full-scale international incident faded behind us, a group of a dozen teenagers came to meet us. They were volunteers, spending the day clearing plastic and other rubbish off the beach. We stopped to chat, joined in for a while and posed for the inevitable selfies. My mind wasn't there: it was still thinking about Mum and Dad. Further along the beach, almost back where we'd started, we spotted a chap flying a spectacular kite, in the form of a bird of prey. The kite seemed easy to fly and spent most of the time flying by itself. Nick and I invested in one each and then decided it was time to head for the airport.

The following day, we'd be leaving India. I had a moment of reflection on what was our furthest point from home; we were about to head back after an unforgettable five weeks. By finding my way to my mum and dad's special beach, I felt in some small way that I had fulfilled a mission; it had been a personal pilgrimage. If it wasn't for that place all those years ago, I wouldn't be alive now – although, on the bright side, the world would have been spared this book. I thought about my wife, Jan, and wished I could have shared the moment with her – but I knew she would have been uncomfortable travelling on the subcontinent. I thought of my older brother back on the Isle of Wight, who would have loved to have been there with us. My three grown-up kids would have enjoyed the adventure for different reasons, although maybe not with the oldies. I was enormously privileged to have my best mate by my side. He lived with my mum and dad for over two years back in the 1970s and became part of the family. I gave him a manly hug and thanked him for coming up with the crazy idea for the trip, travelling with me on our amazing *Journey through India* and making it the incredible experience it had been.

Although we still had to get back to Kolkata and then home again, it felt in some ways that the journey was over. As we pulled away in the taxi, I took one last look back at the beach. There might have been a speck of sand in my eye as I thought about my parents again, in their prime, their heads dizzy with romance... wherever you are now, Mum and Dad, I hope you're still dancing on the sand.

REFLECTIONS

My senses were assaulted, battered, totally mangled, and spat out.

One sense that normally doesn't get such a dramatic and comprehensive overseas holiday is taste. Sights and sounds – obviously – but in India your taste gets a better workout than on most foreign trips. My mouth salivates at the thought of those subtle aromatic spices dancing seductively across my tongue – oh stop it, Mark! People talk about an addiction to curry, like other kinds of natural high addictions, like gambling, shopping, or social media. I think in my case, that includes a compulsion to travel to India again... I feel the urge, and as I mentioned before, I hope I can. India certainly lived up to my expectations. It's difficult to sum up succinctly or adequately, but if I'm calling this chapter 'Reflections' I'd better get something written down.

It was just amazing. I mean, really amazing. Nick and I mostly trod a well-worn tourist path that linked many of the popular visitor sites, and so our impressions of the country are skewed. There are so many parts we didn't get to see, especially the south, the northeast and the more remote and rural regions. India could provide a lifetime of journeys and experiences, so our brief dash only scratched the surface. I've already identified a rough outline for a *Journey through India; Part II* that takes in the southern half of the country. I should tell Nick one of these days.

The memories that will stick from our five-week traverse are of spectacular sites, exquisite dishes, special moments, and many unpleasant smells. The Golden Temple in Amritsar, the Taj Mahal, Jodhpur's Mehrangarh Fort, and the Lake Palace Hotel in Udaipur always spring to mind. But so does sleeping under the stars in the desert, sharing an early morning roadside chai warmed by a log fire, eating home cooked food with a family in Shimla, being given tickets for the International ODI match, running the Kolkata 10 kilometres with thousands of happy people, and standing thoughtfully on the sands of Patenga Beach.

Images of cows, dogs, litter, squalor, monkeys, temples, smiling faces, especially those of children, soon come flooding back. Our first impressions in Mumbai, of so many people frantically going places, remained throughout the five weeks. I imagine they're all still in a hurry right now. Anyone coming from the West can't help but notice the blatant disregard for health and safety in all walks of life, and the total lack of road discipline. Apart from a few notable exceptions, it seems the construction of many of India's buildings is a work in progress – maybe that's why we had so many encounters with bricks and cement.

The Indian people deserve a special mention, just as much, if not more, than their world-famous sights. My endearing image is of happy, smiling people with unshakeable cheerfulness. Many seemed to have little to be upbeat about. They appeared to have an acceptance of the hand they've been dealt; maybe it's a Hindu thing. We met so many lovely people. We were treated as celebrities and/or objects of fascination by most people we met, and we are responsible for several gigabytes of Indian smartphone images. Being in the tourist areas, we also met quite a few beggars and scammers. We're now quite familiar with the various opening gambits to engage us in conversation. I admit that I found this confusing – you need to be on your guard, but at the same time you will meet so many kind and generous people and you don't want to suspect everyone. We felt humbled by the hospitality shown to us.

I'm pleased to say that, justified or not, Nick and I always felt safe in India. That was helped by the stream of wonderful people we met. More than anywhere else I've visited, so many seemed to consider our wellbeing as a matter of their personal responsibility. How comforting is that?

There's a joke in India: 'We don't drive on the left of the road, we drive on what's left of the road.' We found one stretch of good road from Agra to Lucknow, but it stood out as the exception. After a while, your incredulity at Indian driving fades into stunned acceptance. I'm grateful to Ganesha or any other deity that might have been involved, for seeing us safely through so many near-death road experiences. Seriously, that is something to be aware of if you want to travel long distances by road in India – it's not going to be relaxing and it's not without risk.

What to expect – more than anywhere else I've travelled, India is endlessly unpredictable. The very unusual is going to happen. Wonder at it, embrace it while you can, and enjoy it. Debbie, my travelling companion on the flight out to Mumbai, summed it up nicely when she said, 'Crazy shit will happen.' Maybe it's not the most evidence-based or scientifically justified summary, but I struggle to find anything that sums up travel in India better. This is perhaps more relevant if you are travelling independently; there will be constant changes to plans, timetables and paperwork –

that's how it is. People on a package tour are less likely to have those problems. Indian people will do things their way. Don't expect it to be like home and don't expect to change anything. And anyway, if it was like home, there would be no point going. Keep an open mind; you are travelling in someone else's country, and they have their way of doing things. Accept it. Even the driving.

I've already mentioned that anyone going to India for the first time needs to be prepared for the poverty. What can you do? Well, not a lot. You, as an individual, will not solve the problem of world poverty. Each handful of rupees you give to a beggar may leave you internally tormented that you didn't give the same amount to the next one... and the next one. And you didn't give them enough. But you can never give them enough, and there will always be someone else around the corner. Does that mean you turn your back? You can do some small thing to help someone – they will be affected by it, and you will have made a difference to them, even if you can't do the same for everyone.

In terms of regrets, I try not to go there, but I must admit, I've had a few. One big one is not taking the time to eat with the Sikh faithful at the Golden Temple in Amritsar. Nick and I thought we were doing the right thing by turning down the opportunity because we didn't need the food and it would deprive someone else. We totally missed the point, however. It was the best way possible of showing our respect and appreciation – to eat and talk with our fellow visitors. My regret is so deep that I want to go back and put it right. I wish we had stayed longer just about everywhere we went. Spending the appropriate amount of time in each place is something everyone must work out for themselves, but I rarely feel I get it right. I can't think of anywhere where I could say 'Great we've done that; let's move on.'

An overwhelming emotion I feel is gratitude, and there

should always be room for that. Having somehow missed India for sixty-five years, I've finally had the experience of visiting the country, seeing its sights, and meeting its people – now I realise what I was missing. Being born where and when I was, is another stroke of good fortune for which I am continually thankful – it's something the poverty in India has made me remember. And it's quite good for me to bear it in mind when my team loses at football, my Wi-Fi signal is interrupted, or a traffic hold-up makes me half an hour late – it's helps me keep things in perspective.

For those of you wondering if you can do your own journey through India – of course you can (global pandemics allowing). You've just read how a couple of old duffers managed it. I don't want to diminish the personal problems some people have, and we all have our own set of circumstances to deal with, but I'd love to think that someone reading this book will say: 'I could do that.' In fact, I'd love to think there's someone out there reading this book.

My memories from the adventure are held as a series of images in my mind – hundreds of snapshots held somewhere in my head as single images frozen in time, or brief little cameo flashbacks lasting a few seconds – all in techno-colour and with a backing soundtrack that usually involves a sitar and/or a Bollywood beat. Like all good memories they get better, and fonder, each time I recall them. Writing this book has forced me to fill in many gaps and remember more details.

Luckily, I have a few thousand photo images on my laptop for when the neural ones begin to fade. And I'm sure in years to come, when Nick and I recall the adventure, the curries will be tastier, the escapes narrower and our deeds more daring. I hope anyone reading the book will get some sense of the sheer wonder that Nick and I felt as we travelled through India – I hope I've managed to convey some of our incredulity and appreciation of the country and its lovely people.

Each time I go into my study at home, I see all the mementos I've brought back from my various foreign adventures. One that always catches my eye is the brightly coloured 'I love India' headband that I wore for the India v Australia ODI match in Bengaluru. It always makes me smile. Well, I think I do, and I can't wait to go back if I can.

Thank you for reading *Journey through India*. If you have enjoyed it, I would be very grateful if you could give the book a review. If you didn't like it – don't worry, the next one will be much better. You can find out more, and register for updates at: https://mgprobert.com

ACKNOWLEDGMENTS

I'm indebted to so many people for enabling me to complete my *Journey through India*, and for helping me to turn my account of the adventure into my second published book. It wasn't just *my* journey, of course, because I shared every step, biriani and special iced coffee along the way with my great pal, Nick Lindsay. Without wishing to embarrass him (I probably did enough of that in the main text of the book), I have to shower him with praise for coming up with the idea for the adventure and for being such a bloody good mate. Everyone should have a pal like Nick.

The two of us owe a huge thanks to all the owners and managers of the hotels, hostels, homestays, B&Bs, and various forms of public transport in which we stayed overnight. So many lovely Indian people befriended us on our travels, and we could still be there now sharing their kind hospitality and posing for selfies. We still have several phone numbers of complete strangers who wanted us to know we could call them at any time if we got into difficulties. I might have to get back in touch if Southampton Football Club fail to reach thirty-five points by the end of April. To the all those tuk-tuk, taxi and bus drivers to whom we entrusted our lives – well, somehow you did it; thanks for depositing us safely at the end of each journey. I didn't mean what I said about your driving; I was only joking. Whether he exists or not, Nick and I both feel that Ganesha should get a mention; he had some say in our wellbeing and the success of the adventure.

I am hugely indebted to Kirstie Edwards again for her editing and proofreading expertise. Once again, her professionalism, and a small pinch of magic dust, has turned my 84,000 words into something readable. Tom Probert at www.tomprobert.design is the creative genius behind the fantastic book cover and map, while Bill, Greg, Sarah and Nick provided crucial beta reader feedback and support. Special thanks also to Curtis Batterbee for his insightful feedback on several key sections of the book. My Indian former work colleague, Naina, provided valuable comments before and after the trip. Congratulations on your new baby, and I hope the Siberian gulls will fly south at their normal time this year. The envelope is in the normal place.

I continue to be inspired by other writers in the self-publishing community. The websites and podcasts of Joanna Penn, Orna Ross, Dave Chesson, Bryan Cohen, David Gaughran and Mark Dawson provide an ongoing stream of information, new ideas and encouragement. I'd also like to mention Mariellen Ward, a writer, blogger and traveller who's award winning travel website https://breathedreamgo.com has provided me with much inspiration and practical information – thanks!

Last, but always top of the list – the biggest thanks go to Jan, who somehow continues to put up with a wandering husband, who goes off and does silly things.

MARK PROBERT

Mark Probert has spent most of his life as a mapmaker. His early career with Ordnance Survey (OS), the national mapping agency, allowed him to travel widely in Britain. He set up his own company in 2003 and over the following sixteen years, he travelled extensively overseas, working on four continents. Now retired, and living in rural Dorset, he spends his time writing, walking, cycling and motorcycling. Mark and Jan have a daughter, two sons and a granddaughter.

Mark published his first book in 2020. In *Another Journey through Britain,* he uses gentle humour, to describe a two-week motorcycle ride through the back lanes of Britain. Along the way, Mark compares what he comes across with the Britain of fifty years ago, as described in the book *Journey through Britain*, written by John Hillaby.

NICK LINDSAY

Born in Cardiff in 1957, proud Welshman Nick Lindsay began his working life with OS, the national mapping agency. He left in 1980 to continue his education with a degree, followed by a PhD in geology at the University of Liverpool. Employment as a geologist gave him the chance to travel extensively. Now retired and living in the Highlands, he spends his time as chairman of Clyne Heritage Society, running, writing, and walking in his beloved Scottish mountains. Nick is married to Ellen, and they share their house with four cats.

Nick published his first book in 2010, *Cape Wrath to Brora: A walking adventure across Sutherland*. His second book, *Clyne, Loth & Golspie place names,* was published in 2016 and his third, a biography of a larger-than-life character from Doll: *We had nothing, but we had everything: George MacBeath's memories of growing up on a croft, at Doll, Brora*, was published in 2020.

बैठने / सोने
TO SEAT

'Take everything you like seriously, except yourselves.'
— Rudyard Kipling